The
DOLLS' HOUSE GARDENER

The DOLLS' HOUSE GARDENER

FEATURING 8 GARDEN PLANS IN ¹/₁₂ SCALE

Lionel Barnard & Michael Hinchcliffe

David & Charles

An artist's creations are influenced by intuition and vision but they are far from perfect. The creation of a simple flower is beyond man's capability. To an artist the flower symbolises beauty and colour which he can only copy. I therefore dedicate this book to the flowers and plants which grow for us to marvel at and admire.

To my friend Lionel, without whose help this book would not have been possible, and to my daughters Kim and Zoë who in years to come will remember what a grumpy old sod I was while working on this book.

Michael Hinchcliffe

To Ann and Sean for their constant understanding, support and encouragement.

Lionel Barnard

Frontispiece   *A scene from the Edwardian Summer House Garden*

A DAVID & CHARLES BOOK

First published in the UK in 1999

Designs and Illustrations Copyright © Michael Hinchcliffe 1999
Text Copyright © Lionel Barnard & Michael Hinchcliffe 1999
Photography and layout Copyright © David & Charles 1999

A catalogue record for this book is available from the British Library.

ISBN 0 7153 0779 7

Photography by Jeremy Thomas
Book design by Maggie Aldred
Printed in Hong Kong by Imago Publishing Ltd
for David & Charles
Brunel House   Newton Abbot   Devon

Contents

Introduction

In the real and full-sized world gardening has become one of the most popular pastimes ever. Hundreds of gardening books are published every year, gardeners become TV stars overnight, specialist magazines are found in every newsagent and you can even take residential courses in garden design. The Royal Horticultural Society and many stately homes have opened their gardens to the public and professional gardeners and nurserymen produce outstanding designs at the Chelsea Flower Show every year. So is it any wonder then that so many dolls' house enthusiasts are showing interest in building and maintaining miniature gardens?

Gardens in miniature were made for pleasure as long ago as 2000BC but are to be found more recently in antique dolls' houses, sometimes called baby houses. The garden would often be contained within a decorated room or courtyard, the walls would have been painted with outdoor scenery, the floor paved and the whole scene set off with a decorative fountain and plants in pots. All this in a space less than twelve inches square.

When dolls' houses first became really popular in Britain there were few owners possessing a miniature garden too, although Queen Mary owned a dolls' house that had a superb garden created by Edwin Lutyens and Getrude Jekyll. Complete with lawns, plants, hedges and trees, the whole garden was contained within a drawer set under the house. Cleverly, the larger trees and gates were

separately hinged to fold down across the flower beds as the drawer closed.

In the last few years the dolls' house and miniature scene has been gripped by gardening fever and whilst gardens have traditionally formed part of the dolls' house they are now being built as stand-alone projects, complete in themselves. Unlike a dolls' house, which should conform to certain architectural and historical considerations, a separate garden can show much more of the owner's personality, although there are certain constraints which should be followed if only for the sake of authenticity. So much character can be introduced into your own miniature garden: it can be untidy, formal, historical or contemporary.

We will show you how to make a garden to fit your dolls' house or as a separate structure. We begin with advice on how to design a garden so that the elements are in balance and pleasing to the eye. We go on to give instructions for making many garden features and accessories such as paving, fencing, flower beds, lawns and seating, and how to combine all or some of these with other features, like water and lighting displays. We have incorporated many commercial items as there are now quite splendid planters, garden tools, ornamental pots, flowers, plants, seating and conservatories available from specialist doll's shops and fairs.

The size of your garden is not important, and although throughout the book we have maintained

a scale of one inch to one foot (¹/12th), we suggest that an area of less than three square feet will provide a good start. You will see that we have used imperial measurements as we feel that most miniaturists are comfortable with this. Where we find that suppliers will only quote metric sizes (as with thickness of some timbers) we have given them for guidance.

We have provided eight comprehensive and distinctive garden plans, but bear in mind that no garden, real or miniature, stands still – it grows and evolves. Treat your miniature garden the same way you do your real one and be open to changes. Just as you set out Christmas decorations in your dolls' house, move elements in your garden around and plant fresh for the coming season. Use

the Making the Elements section as a resource to dip into time and time again.

Both of us have been involved in the dolls' house business for a number of years, myself as a maker of dolls' houses, miniature furniture and as a writer, Michael as a designer, miniaturist and maker of gardens in ¹/12th scale. Throughout the book we have borne in mind the needs of both the beginner and the accomplished miniaturist when describing the various procedures and techniques in making and assembling all the many garden elements. We are both keen to share our professional skills so that you too can achieve results that will be both pleasing and highly competent. After reading this book we feel sure you will agree that miniature gardening is definitely here to stay. 7

Principles of
Garden Design

Good design is the key to all successful gardens – be they full size or miniature. The following section is full of ideas and the practical information you need to create a miniature garden of your own design. We look at the importance of siting, scale and size, consider how a garden may be styled using period detail, and finally show you how to draw up a garden plan and site eye-catching features and plants.

SCALE, SITE AND SIZE

THE IMPORTANCE OF $1/12$TH SCALE

Scale is a way of relating a large object, such as a real house, with a smaller one, a dolls' house. A common example is a road map, which might have a scale of 1in on the map to 25 miles in reality – a convenient way of fitting a lot of information onto a small surface.

An antique dolls' house would have been made to a scaled measurement calculated by the maker, perhaps the estate carpenter. But there were no set rules to follow and any furniture or accessories purchased later could well have been made to a totally different scale, which is why so many of the older houses sometimes appear clumsy and over full.

In the first half of this century many companies, such as Triang, were making children's houses, furniture and accessories to the scale of $1/16$in to 1 foot. Dolls' house plans drawn up by woodworking and hobby magazines throughout the post-war years continued to use this scale, which is also referred to as $3/4$in to 1 foot.

Dolls' houses these days are usually made to the scale of $1/12$th, or 1 inch to 1 foot. For every foot of the real house one inch is used for the model, and this scale is carried on throughout all the furniture and accessories. So popular is this scale now that almost every maker and enthusiast uses it. A few collectors have adopted a new scale of $1/24$th or $1/2$in to 1 foot, but we think this is unlikely to surpass $1/12$th. Every garden project in this book has been made using the scale of $1/12$th, so you should have no difficulty in finding accessories from makers anywhere in the world.

Throughout the book we have used imperial measurements and good workshop practice proves that metric and imperial measurements do not mix. Some manufacturers routinely use only metric sizes, as in timber yards, and these have been quoted for guidance only where there is no alternative.

SITING A GARDEN

It cannot have escaped your notice that dolls' houses are constructed differently to real houses, both in terms of scale and layout. Most full-sized houses have rooms at the back and the front, whereas dolls' houses are almost always one room deep. This alteration of a very basic architectural feature changes our perception of the location of various elements in and around a building and we have therefore to accept some limitations in the size and scale of our gardens too.

If we refer again to the real world, the location of the main garden is, generally speaking, behind the house. This is not always the case as the approach to some country houses is to the rear, in which case the house faces the garden and allows the occupants to look out onto private grounds.

Country cottages in the Tudor style might have had a small flower garden to the front whilst the rear of the property would have vegetables and perhaps animals. Georgian town houses, built into relatively small

Opposite: *Using a selection of miniature garden tools will bring authenticity to your garden*

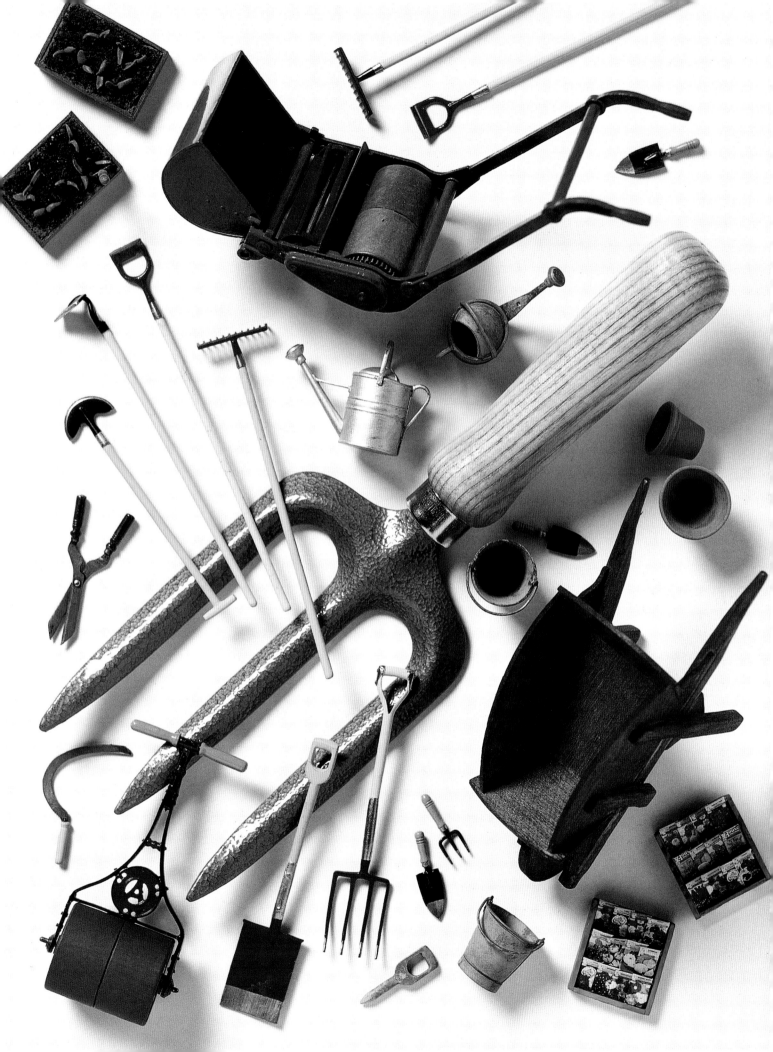

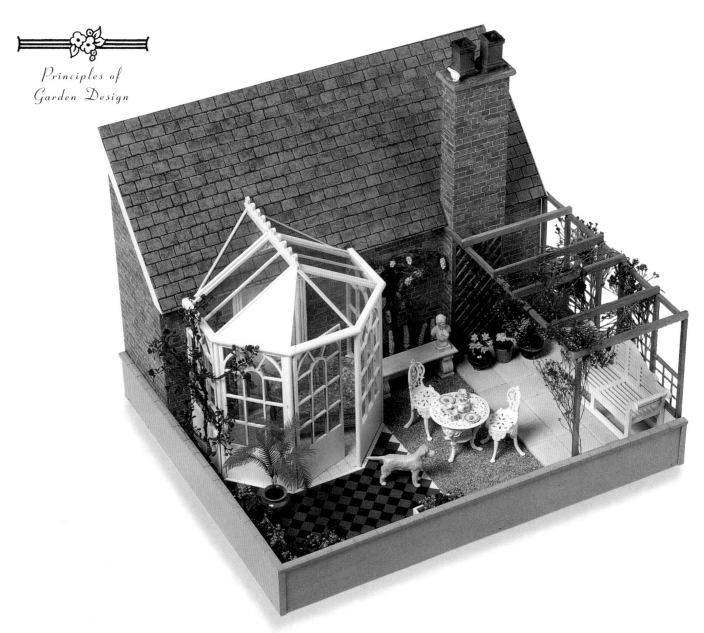

Gardens don't have to be at ground level. Consider making use of the valuable flat area on a roof – ideal for a cosy roof garden

spaces, would have had small courtyards front and rear and as the public would see only the front garden this was the one which would have received the most attention. Victorian and Edwardian properties, particularly those built in the ever-expanding suburbs, had long narrow plots to the rear and were often designed to be miniature versions of the countryside they had in fact helped to change so dramatically.

Deciding on the best place to site your dolls' house garden will depend on a number of factors such as how big is your dolls' house? what sort of garden do you want? how much space do you have available? Houses that hinge open at the front, as most made in the United Kingdom do, pose a problem for the dolls' house

gardener as the doors may not even open without destroying most in their path. If you are not prepared to move the garden each time you open up the house, consider building it at a lower level by raising the house up onto a platform – in effect treating the garden as a basement.

Many dolls' houses in the Georgian and early Victorian styles are made with flat roofs and this can prove to be a wonderful place to site a conservatory or roof garden. Ideally some way should be provided for the occupants to reach the roof from the inside of the house, a small roof hatch or a set of stairs with a covered exit, so that reality is not suspended too far.

You could place the Formal Georgian garden in a drawer. Using this simple but

innovative idea you can have the best of both worlds – a garden only when you are in the mood! You can also situate your garden on one side of the house and conservatories can look particularly striking in this location. Unless you have a lot of free space to give to your dolls' house we do not recommend placing the garden at the rear of the property: in our experience placing the garden to the front of the house will give the best results.

We hope that you will also consider making a garden as a stand-alone project without placing it against a dolls' house. With a self-contained garden scene you can let your imagination come into play and create for yourself a garden you might have always wished for. Your dolls' house, if you have one, might be a Georgian mansion but a stand-alone garden could be from the Tudor period, or a cottage garden with herbs and vegetables growing profusely and with chickens running around. You could design an elegant Victorian conservatory with ladies taking tea or if you feel adventurous you could use some of the water features we show you later to create a river bank scene. Even with a stand-alone garden, a representation of the house is a good idea as it will give the garden some feeling of reality and just a wall or half a building will be quite sufficient.

GARDEN SIZE

The size of a dolls' house garden, particularly the width, is so dependent on the type of house it accompanies that there are only a few rules. Obviously gardens that are not attached to a house may be any size you wish.

As a general rule, the width of a dolls' house garden should match the width of the house and a court-yard garden nearly always looks best when placed to the front. A garden for a country mansion though could easily extend beyond the boundaries of the house. Several small features, such as a walled herb

garden and a pond, can be incorporated into one large garden but such gardens must still follow design principles and not look over-crowded. A conservatory can look very attractive when placed to one side of a house as it will reveal its profile but this is such a versatile feature that it can be placed almost anywhere or used as part of the garden, as we have done with the Victorian Roof Garden with Conservatory on page 141.

The depth of the garden is governed mainly by the overall design. You will see from the gardens shown later in the book that the features have to balance and it simply isn't good enough to add six inches of lawn to a garden in order to make it larger when this may upset the overall design.

We suggest that if you make the width of your garden match that of the house it will, in most cases, result in a width of between 23in and 30in. The depth should be in a ratio of about half, say between 10in and 15in. Free-standing gardens work best at

Siting the garden at the back of the house may be the logical choice for some dolls' houses. This backyard has been designed with the house style firmly in mind and also conforms to the limitations of site use and size, particularly the narrowness of the plot

TIP

*Avoid a piecemeal
approach to designing a
garden, simply putting
bits and pieces around.
Instead treat each ele-
ment as part of a single
design, bearing in mind
colour, shape, texture
and function.*

24in x 12in, but the design may dictate otherwise and the depth of your plot will, in most cases, be regulated by the space available in your home. Real gardens can be as much as 100ft deep, which translates in 1/12th scale to 100in or 8 feet 4 inches – far more than most of us can manage. Remember, keep it simple.

DESIGNING AND STYLING

We have supplied eight complete garden designs in this book which, with a little adjustment, can be incorporated with any existing dolls' house. However, we understand that there will those amongst you who want to make your own gardens and to enable you to do this we give below essential tips and hints on the principles of garden design and styling.

Good garden design is based on geometry and balance – the placing together of basic shapes and elements, each balancing the other to produce a harmonious plan. Think about a garden that has already been designed and envisage in your mind all the various elements. Apply basic rules of design, trying to avoid obvious mistakes such as placing all the features at one end or into one corner. Remember that areas covered with grass or gravel are as important as other, more 'busy' areas, and if bright colours are used do so sparingly or consider balancing them with physical objects, such as a rockery.

Bear in mind that paths and flower beds are usually long oblong shapes or sinuous curves; trees, shrubs and ponds are often round and paving is usually square – all simple shapes to look at and use. Aim to use the shapes to produce a plan that has balance. Remember that straight lines that converge give an appearance of leading somewhere and they can make a small site look longer. Serpentine or sinuous curves must be used with care – too large and they will overpower a garden, too small and they may look lost. Strong colours, such as on a

*Using symmetry is very
effective in garden design, in
particular balancing pairs
of objects on either side of a
more dominant feature such
as this elegant iron gate.
The patterns formed here,
including the cross-shaped
path, are regular and
balanced and so are*

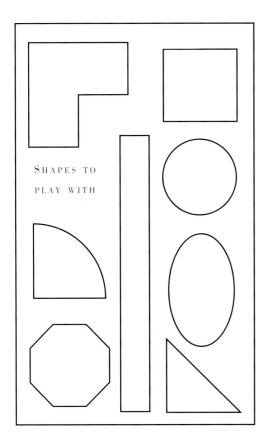

SHAPES TO
PLAY WITH

*When designing a garden, think
of shapes and patterns. Try drawing
shapes, colouring them, then
cutting them out and arranging
them into a harmonious and
interesting whole*

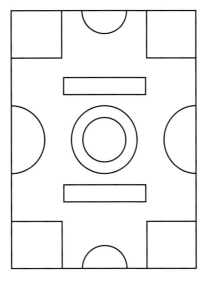

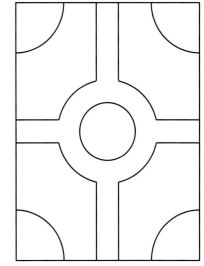

terrace wall, will bring it closer to the eye and may make it overpowering. Whilst many people regard gardens as places of rest and quiet this need not be so in yours, it could be a busy area which excites the mind.

When designing a garden it is very important to think about the period in which your garden is to be set. Formal gardens demand formal lines whilst cottage gardens will look better if they ramble. Colonial houses had large gardens but they were kept simple; Victorian and Edwardian gardens were often walled and would frequently contain new and exotic plants. See Period Garden Styles overleaf.

As you can see there are many things which affect the way in which you design a garden, and careful research is essential before you start planning. A visit to your local library for garden design books and a trip to garden events will provide a fund of good ideas that can be incorporated into your plans. The Chelsea Flower Show held in London each May is a wonderful source of small garden design and there are courses available on garden design, and although

these are for full-sized gardening the broad principles remain the same.

One of the exciting aspects of design is flexibility. If you refer to the photographs accompanying each of the garden projects you will see that subtle changes have been made to the way in which they have been finished for each photograph. This has been done to show how, with a little imagination and very little work, you can change the appearance of a garden, altering it to suit your individual requirements. Some plants have been shown together in flower contrary to the natural seasons. This is to show how a design may be changed to achieve a good balance of colour and interest. Michael and I also plead that we are miniaturists, not proper gardeners!

DRAWING UP A
GARDEN PLAN

The most important rule when planning a garden is to think first and act second. However eager you are to start, in order to build a good garden you must make a plan before starting any cutting and gluing. The plan must take into account certain basic

TIP

Make the most of your garden space. When considering the design, think of it as an outside room, give it atmosphere, planning it for, say, entertainment and fun or perhaps peace and solitude.

TIP

The best foundation for any garden is good design and all good design starts with a plan.

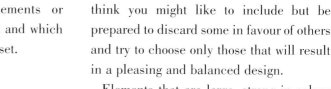

TIP
*Using graph paper,
draw and cut out shapes
to help design your
garden site.*

*Consider continuity of
styling when designing your
own garden. In this scene
the dovecote, woodshed and
tree swing have been chosen
to balance each other and
reflect an overall rustic style.
A modern metal-framed
swing would have detracted
from the country look*

points such as location, elements or features that are to be included and which period style the garden is to be set.

Location

Decide first of all on the location of your garden and if it is going to be free-standing or placed against your dolls' house. Remember that conservatories attached to houses ideally need to stand against a blank wall with no windows, although a door is permissible. The design and planning for free-standing gardens is just as important as for those placed against a house, perhaps more so. There will be no natural boundary to a free-standing garden and it may be necessary to consider a line of railings or shrubs to hold the design together.

Garden elements

Garden elements are those features that make a garden something other than a plot of ground, such as trees, shrubs, flower beds, streams, paving, terraces, sheds and pots. Make a list of all the elements you

think you might like to include but be prepared to discard some in favour of others and try to choose only those that will result in a pleasing and balanced design.

Elements that are large, strong in colour or which occupy large proportions of your garden become dominant and will almost certainly dictate how the remainder of the garden evolves. A stream running from one end to another for instance, a fountain, a broken-down shed, trees or a plot given over to entirely to vegetables, will all determine how the remainder of the garden evolves. Conservatories are often gardens in themselves and may easily overpower anything and everything around them. Generally speaking it is not a good idea to introduce more than one dominant feature into a small garden or it will swamp the design. Conversely it may be necessary to introduce a second dominant feature into a larger garden in order to balance the first and so avoid a lopsided look.

The inclusion of some garden elements will make demands on the way you plan your garden. For instance, water features such as streams run from one point to another and always to a lower level, whereas ponds are static and need a level surface. Pools look best when planned as geometric shapes – squares, oblongs or circles. Space permitting, streams should follow a slightly irregular line, becoming wider towards the finishing point. Above all your garden design should make sense. For example, steps should lead up or down to a definite place in the garden and will look unrealistic if they appear out of nowhere or end against a blank wall.

Period garden styles

If you are building a garden to accompany an existing dolls' house then you will need to match the period styles, and this aspect of planning and design is just as important when building a stand-alone garden too, although you will have more scope for choice.

*This tumbledown rural
cottage is a dominant
feature determining how the
rest of the garden should
look. The style of the fencing
and plants needs to be
casual, a little ramshackle,
in order to balance and
continue the theme*

COUNTRY TUDOR GARDEN

The English Tudor house is something of an artist's dream, often pictured at the end of a country lane and surrounded by roses and wild flowers. In reality it might be a farm worker's or smallholder's cottage without modern amenities. Victorian artists managed to depict the scene very well and a careful look at birthday cards and National Trust booklets will provide much useful visual information.

To reproduce a garden of this period, the overall impression should be natural with rough surfaces for walls made from local materials. Paths should be of stamped earth, rubble or brick and fencing should be roughly lapped or woven, although there may be a hedge surrounding the plot and a wooden picket gate.

Useful items such as beehives, water pumps and watering cans can be included and, if the garden is large enough, you could add a privy at one end. Terracotta clay pots and simple garden tools, such as besom brooms, scythes and hoes will give evidence of hand cultivation. Use rambling roses and herbaceous perennials for decoration and a small vegetable plot for practicality and do not forget that some domestic animals, rabbits and chicken may be included too. The water feature will most likely be either a well or a pond used for keeping ducks.

FORMAL GARDEN

To reproduce a garden in this late Tudor/early Georgian style, the first impression should be one of a large garden with sweeping views and plenty of space. The contents of these gardens should, similarly, be large. Statuary of Grecian and Roman influence with classical poses should be mounted on plinths and pots and urns should be of stone and lead. Formal walks

---

TIP

*The small country
garden will need lots of
flowers to make it look
real. Make sure those
you use are correct for
the period.*

along gravel paths and under rose arbours lead to clipped topiary hedges and perhaps a maze. Terraces and balconies have stone balustrades paved in York stone. If the plot has different levels the water feature should be a stream or a fountain. Follies and small temples in the Greek style can be included if there is sufficient space although they would make good garden projects in themselves. Larger houses were usually self-sufficient and often had separate walled vegetable and flower gardens – again something that could be produced as separate project.

GEORGIAN TOWN HOUSE GARDEN

To reproduce a garden of this period you need to include more formal elements and a greater sense of overall design. Moulded terracotta pots, cast stone balustrades and small garden statuary will be typical, as are small, manageable water features. Flowers should be in pots and small beds with larger, shaped shrubs in wooden Versailles pots. Formal motifs in the Chinese Chippendale style could appear in the form of seats and fencing. Paving should be crisp and very geometric, with the use of gravel on neat pathways a strong point. Strictly speaking, 5ft high brick or flint walls should mark the boundaries of the garden when it is situated at the rear, although this may not be practical in miniature. Walls built just 3in high will still convey the impression of seclusion and front courtyard walls may be lower still. Water features should be small and decorative and may contain fish.

VICTORIAN AND EDWARDIAN GARDENS

The Victorian age saw the introduction of much of today's garden machinery and the steam engine enabled great works to be carried out without the use of manual labour. This mechanisation means that suburban gardens reproduced in this style should include such items as lawn-mowers – before this, grass was cut with a scythe. Also at this time just about everything for the garden became available from specialist mail order catalogues – from terracotta lawn edgings to garden swings and chairs. Decoratively wrought wire arches and borders complement the cast iron fences and ornamental gates. Smaller town gardens should be walled, often with rough flints and mortar, and paving and paths should feature gravel and slabs. Country and Edwardian houses should have wooden fencing and gates but the use of hedges and shrubs could mark some boundaries. Water features were not so common in this period although a large garden may have a formal fish pond close to the house.

AMERICAN COLONIAL GARDEN

To reproduce this style of garden you will need to create their simplicity and sense of space. Expansive lawns reflect the space available in America and large trees should be included, grown in real gardens to create shade. The taste for wooden gingerbread decoration should be continued onto the porch where stoop and wicker furniture and swing seats will also be kept. Formal paths should be laid with gravel although the paths to any outbuildings may be paved in brick. Boundaries look good with white picket fences and gates. The water feature should be natural, perhaps in the form of a running stream.

PRACTICAL STEPS IN PLANNING

To draw up your garden plan you will need some plain white drawing paper for producing roughs and a pad of squared tracing paper for final drawings. Use an HB pencil for most work and a good quality eraser. Any accurate ruler will do but we find that one made of clear plastic with imperial and

metric divisions is best. A small compass and a couple of clear plastic triangles should provide all the curves and lines you require. Plastic templates for drawing circles and 'French curves' are quite inexpensive but very useful additions to a drawing kit.

Measuring up

Start by measuring up the site on which your garden will stand – height, width and depth. Using tracing graph paper, prepare one master drawing of your basic garden site in plan view, marking the front clearly, or overhead as if you are looking down from above. If it is going to be a complicated garden with several levels a second, third, or even fourth view, from the front and sides might be useful later. Confident illustrators will find that dividing the drawing of the garden into slices will help greatly in the planning of multilevel sites. If possible, draw your garden plan the same size as you want the finished garden to be but if this is not possible decide how many squares on your paper plan will equal one inch in the actual garden.

Drawing structural features

On all the plans, draw in place any fixed structural items such as walls, steps, terraces and fences. The next step is to add in the dominant features you wish to use, such as pergolas, small buildings or ponds. It is a good idea to draw all the various garden elements on good quality paper in $1/12$th scale, cutting out these shapes and labelling them, tree, shrub, pot and so on. Colouring them with felt-tip pens will make your designing easier. Position each of the cut-outs onto the overhead site plan, moving them around until you feel that you have the beginnings of a balanced garden design. It is important that you allow yourself to think freely, adding and subtracting elements until you reach a pleasing result – that way the garden will evolve the way you want it to.

Making a mock up

Before committing yourself to the final garden design it is a good idea to produce a three-dimensional representation by building a cardboard mock up. This can be especially useful when a design has a number of levels or a high terrace. Transfer the measurements from your plan onto a plain sheet of card and make up basic shapes to represent the larger objects such as sheds and terraces. Draw in the main paths and flower beds and lightly glue the large objects into place. You can now add all the smaller objects and move them around until it looks just right, adjusting your master plan accordingly.

Your garden plan may take considerable thought and some time to draw but it is a crucial part of the garden-making process and well worth the effort. Once you are happy with your plan, you can begin the construction of the actual garden.

Structural features such as these steps need to be carefully planned, with accurate measuring and thoughtful siting within a garden

Basic Tools and Materials

Most experienced miniaturists will already have a number of useful tools and be familiar with the various glues and modelling compounds. None of the tools mentioned here are expensive but buying those of good quality will always pay. When using new materials, always try to experiment with a small quantity before committing yourself.

TOOLS

The tools used throughout this book are those which can be found in most tool collections, although any collection will be improved by the addition of some small drills and drill bits. We strongly recommend that squares be checked for accuracy before use and that any tool with a blade, such as a chisel or craft knife, is as sharp as possible – surprisingly, blunt tools injure far more people than sharp ones. Generally speaking it is worth paying a few pence extra for a good quality tool that will prove both accurate and long lasting.

Saws

Tenon saw With its fine set teeth, a tenon saw is ideal for cutting smaller pieces of timber sheet and will give a far more accurate cut than a rip-saw which is only used for cutting large sheets. Smaller versions of these saws, known as gent's saws, can also prove useful for cutting small

Tenon saw

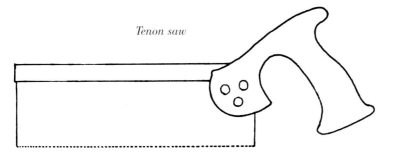

pieces of wood. All tenon saws are easily identified by the supporting bar along the top of the blade.

Razor saw This is a miniature version of a tenon saw. Its teeth can number as many as fifty per inch and both the thickness of the blade and the set is very fine indeed, making it very sharp and extremely useful for cutting small pieces of jelutong and obeche woods accurately.

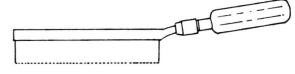

Razor saw

Fretsaw This is ideal for cutting out apertures and intricate shapes and is best used with a bench pin, which supports the wood, enabling accurate cutting. The blades for these saws are available in several grades and are easily changed should they break. Vibrating and scroll saws are mechanical versions of fretsaws.

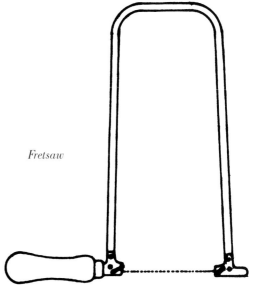

Fretsaw

Power saw A powered bench or table saw will prove invaluable in the accurate cutting of all woods, particularly when many pieces of the same size have to be produced. Powered table saws for full-sized woodwork, 8in diameter blades and over, are best fitted with tungsten carbide-tipped blades that

give superior results particularly in the finishing cut. Powered table saws are also available as attachments to lathes and drills. Hobby table saw blades are usually 4in or less in diameter and the set of the teeth is rather fine, which limits the thickness of wood that can be cut, and saw blades of less than 3in in diameter often have difficulty in cutting wood more than 1/4in thick. However useful they may be though, they are not obligatory for making any of the gardens in this book.

Mitre box

A mitre box is not in fact a box at all but an open U-shaped channel used for the accurate mitring of narrow pieces of wood. Each of the two upright sides of the box have pre-cut 45- and 90-degree slots. The wood is laid into the bottom of the 'U' and the saw drawn across the appropriate slot. These boxes are available in many sizes and miniaturist versions are usually made of wood, plastic or aluminium. Used with a razor saw the aluminium table-top version will prove best for miniature work.

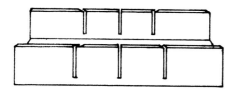

Mitre box

Plane

A small hand plane is useful for cleaning up the edges of plywood and MDF timber. The best size for this work is one that will fit easily into the palm of your hand and the blade should be kept accurately ground and sharpened for good results.

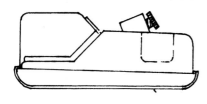

Hand plane

Knives

A sharp craft knife with renewable blades is a good investment for any miniaturist and those made by the company Stanley have very useful, strong blades that can be used for almost any craft work. We also find that a No.3 scalpel is invaluable for fine work. Change the blades as soon as they become blunt and discard worn blades safely.

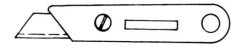

Stanley knife

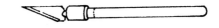

Craft knife

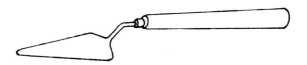

Palette knife

Ruler and set square

A good quality metal ruler giving inches and metric equivalents is essential. Choose one 12 inches in length for most jobs and a second 6in long for measuring in small areas. 1in to 1ft rulers are available from specialist 1/12th craft suppliers and may prove useful when working out a site.

An accurate set or try-square is a valuable

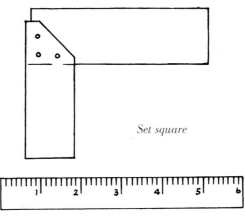

Set square

Ruler

TIP

Use a small surgical scalpel, No 3a, to cut fine lines into timbers or for making paper flowers. The blades are very sharp so great care must be taken when renewing the blades.

TIP

Use goggles when cutting materials liable to shatter and wear a face mask if dust is given off. Users of resin products may find rubber gloves useful.

tool to have in your tool box as it will make all the difference to the miniaturists' work. The all-metal versions, also known as engineers' squares, are definitely the best.

Drills

Any hand-held drill with a small chuck capable of holding a drill bit as small as $^1/_{32}$in (1mm) will be useful when making miniature gardens. 12 volt electric drills are also useful and readily available from specialist shops. Miniaturists will also find that the small hand-held pin drills and Archimedes drills are good for any close miniature work. A selection of small drill bits ranging from $^1/_{32}$in (0.8mm) to $^1/_8$in (3mm) will prove useful for all the jobs in this book. Drill bits are almost always sold in metric sizes but imperial equivalents may be quoted on the packaging.

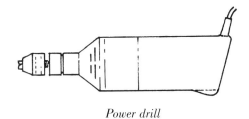

Hand drill

TIP
When drilling into hard materials such as MDF, white metal and resins, it is a good idea to make a small indentation with a sharp awl or nail as a location for the drill tip. Use a small amount of fine grade oil as lubrication when drilling through metal.

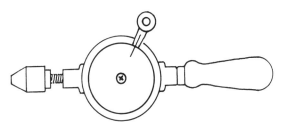

Power drill

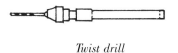

Twist drill

Other tools
You will almost certainly need a hammer (the smaller the better), a pair of pliers and an awl (for making starter holes for drilling in blockboard and MDF).

A pair of tweezers is a very useful tool for picking up and placing small parts and plants accurately. G-clamps are also a useful addition to the tool box. They are obtainable in a variety of sizes and are most useful for applying firm and constant pressure when jointing wooden structures with adhesives.

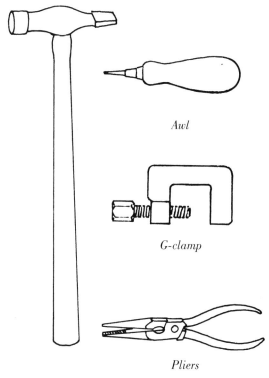

Awl

G-clamp

Pliers

Small hammer

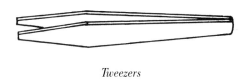

Tweezers

Abrasive papers
Glass paper, or sandpaper, can be purchased in several grades and used accordingly. In later chapters we refer to fine grade abrasive paper but any grade of garnet paper or cabinet paper will prove a useful alternative for delicate work. Using these papers in conjunction with a cork sanding block will give superior results to flat surfaces.

Sanding block

Goggles, gloves and masks

Protective wear is an important part of your tool kit. Goggles should always be worn when using powered machines such as drills or circular saws. Face masks are strongly recommended when spraying adhesives and spirit-based paints and when cutting or drilling MDF with power tools. Gloves will provide protection against splinters when cutting large sheets of plywood or blockboards.

MATERIALS

As you might expect there is a wide selection of materials available today for miniaturist work, and what follows is brief descriptions of those we used in the gardens made for this book.

Timbers

Although the projects in this book have been designed using imperial measurements (feet and inches), timber and hardware merchants supply their goods almost exclusively in metric. We have therefore given metric measurements followed by the imperial sizes for plywoods and MDF boards.

MDF The initials MDF represent 'Medium Density Fibreboard' a man-made board. This is an excellent alternative to plywood as it is unlikely to warp and is easy to cut. It can be purchased from most timber merchants and large DIY stores in various handy sheet sizes. Common thicknesses are 2mm, 6mm and 9mm.

There has been some publicity given to the risks associated with the dust and formaldehyde given off by MDF when subject to machine finishing, such as sawing or drilling. The Health & Safety Executive apparently consider the risk to be very low especially as British manufacturers are reported to be using low levels of formaldehyde, however, we recommend that when cutting MDF (or any other wood-based material) with electric saws, routers

or drills that you wear a protective mask and ensure good ventilation or dust extraction.

Plywood The best quality plywood is usually faced with birch wood and is resistant to water. It is produced in large 8ft x 4ft (2400mm x 1200mm) sheets and thicknesses commonly available are 6mm (1/4in), 9mm (3/8in) and 12mm (1/2in). Offcuts can usually be obtained from a timber merchant and some DIY stores stock small sheets.

Blockboard This is made up with a scrap pine core and a thin wood veneer facing. It is generally available in the same sizes as plywood. Purchase boards without knot holes or obvious defects and avoid imported boards that have a coarse grain.

When painting, varnishing or papering any 'sheet' wood such as plywood or MDF it is recommended that both sides are treated equally to avoid warping, particularly on materials of less than 9mm thickness. These sheets have good finishes on both surfaces and can be reversed without problems.

Hardboard This is a useful man-made board usually available in a 4mm thickness and identified by a smooth upper surface and a patterned back. Thin sheets can be bent, with care.

Very thin plywood This is 1/32in (1mm) thick and is used in aero and boat modelling. It is a very strong and flexible material that is ideal for bending around sharp curves and can be purchased in small sheets approximately 1ft square.

Jelutong and obeche Jelutong is a straw-coloured timber that is the most easily worked wood used in modelling and miniature furniture making as it has a tight grain and will shape and carve easily. Unfortunately it is not always easily available and we recommend obeche as a

> **TIP**
> *Cheap far-eastern plywood sheets are often coarse-grained and liable to leave ragged edges when cut across the grain.*

21

> **TIP**
>
> *Always follow the*
> *manufacturer's instruc-*
> *tions when using*
> *adhesives and resins.*

Opposite: *There is a great*
selection of building
materials to choose from,
some ready prepared and
others you can make
yourself, to make a whole
range of structures, includ-
ing walls, paving, floors,
steps and rockeries

22

good alternative. The grain in obeche wood is similar to that of mahogany and it may deflect thin craft knives making the cutting of straight lines difficult. However, it is light in colour, takes stain and paint quite easily and can be undetectable from jelutong in most circumstances. Both are obtainable in pre-planed and sanded sheets, usually 3in or 4in wide x 36in and in a wide variety of thicknesses, the common ones being 1/16in (1mm), 3/32in (2mm) and 1/8in (3mm). Although not directly equivalent, both metric and imperial measurements are usually printed on the sheets. A number of specialist suppliers also stock a number of square and moulded sections that can save a great deal of cutting and sanding. The thinner sheets and sections of jelutong or obeche woods are best cut with a razor saw as this tool leaves a very small 'rag' or rough edge.

We do not recommend the use of spruce as this has a strong and often 'wild' grain making working with anything other than powered tools difficult and we do not recommend balsa wood under any circumstances except aero-modelling, as it is too soft and easily crushed.

Plasticard

Plastic styrene sheet is available in two colours, black and white, from most model shops in a variety of thicknesses, usually quoted in millimetres. Most sheets are approximately 10in square and are easily cut with a sharp knife but care must be taken to stop the sheet moving whilst being cut as it is very soft and pliable under pressure. A variety of mouldings, usually square or round tubes and beam extrusions are also available. Use plastic weld adhesive, applied with a small brush, to glue parts together (see adhesives below).

Panel pins and nails

Standard sizes found in ironmongers are in metric and 12mm (1/2in) long pins will prove to be the most used in your garden projects. Longer veneer pins and stronger nails may be useful for some projects.

Adhesives

PVA type adhesives   There are a variety of PVA adhesives available but not all of them are suitable for wood; some do not provide permanent results and others are specifically designed for use with paper and card. PVA tacky glue will stick a number of materials together and provides a quick grab facility, useful in some situations. Where instructions simply say glue, we have used a white PVA formulated for use on wood. Elmers glue is a PVA adhesive manufactured in America but sometimes available in the UK.

Epoxy adhesives   Materials such as plastics and metals are difficult to glue together and the so-called 'five minute' rapid-set epoxy glues are especially useful for these jobs. Parts should be cleaned with a de-natured alcohol (methylated spirit) first and clamped together when possible.

Spirit-based adhesives   These adhesives, such as UHU, are very useful and provide a permanent hard joint for all manner of materials. Spread it over the two surfaces to be joined and allow to dry until tacky, it will then act as a fast-grab adhesive and provide an instant bond.

Other adhesives   There are a variety of adhesives available for specific gluing tasks, as follows: Scatter Grip is a proprietary brand of adhesive designed to be used with 'scatter' materials such as grasses and fine gravel. Copydex (rubber cement) has a thick consistency that makes it ideal for fixing gravel to pathways. Plastic weld is an adhesive specially developed for making two plastic surfaces adhere. It does this by partially dissolving the surfaces and should therefore be used with care. Photo mount or display mount adhesive supplied in aerosol cans are adhesives generally used by artists

> **TIP**
> *Wood and plaster fillers are also available pre-mixed in handy tubes although you may find that these products dry out very quickly.*

> **TIP**
> *When using casting powders, modelling compounds and resins for the first time, it is a good idea to test small batches of the materials until you are familiar with their properties. Measure casting powders with kitchen scales or measuring spoons and keep a note of the quantities used to achieve different effects. That way you can reproduce paving slabs and bricks at a later time. Resins need special handling so always follow the manufacturer's instructions and keep tools and containers clean.*

and designers, and we found them very good for fixing 'earth' to flower beds and some of the brick sheets to walls. If you want to reposition materials then spray mount adhesive is a good choice but it may not prove to be a permanent gluing solution, especially if the surfaces are uneven.

Generally we have avoided the use of any of the so-called 'super glues', as traditional adhesives have proved best for us. Miniaturists should take care when using any adhesives, especially 'super glues' and we recommend that all labels be read first and suitable precautions taken. Avoid smoking and naked flames when using any spirit-based adhesives.

Perspex (plexiglass) and other clear plastics

This is an optically pure plastic that looks like glass. Used extensively for water features, the ideal thickness of 1/16in (or 2mm) can be cut, drilled and sanded. Best cut with a saw, it can be scored with a sharp knife and snapped into sections, although this material is rather brittle and may shatter if care is not taken, so always wear goggles when snapping plastics. The thicknesses of Perspex varies but 1/16in is used in most of our projects.

Acetate is a thinner transparent material similar to Perspex but can be easily cut and shaped with a knife and can be used for glazing conservatories and other structures such as sheds. As it is much thinner it is therefore more flexible and also has the advantage of being slightly impure thus giving a more realistic appearance to water.

Plastic sheeting

We use cling film (or Siran food wrap) to protect boards and prevent adhesion when casting paving stones.

Specialist materials

None of the following materials are particularly difficult to find but they are not in every miniaturist's workshop and some are almost certainly particular to miniature gardening.

Clear resin This material is used to simulate water and is ideal for small areas such as fountains or rock pools. The clear resin is mixed with a chemical hardener and is then poured into a mould or shaped area (see also page 49).

Resin colouring agent Specialist coloured dyes can be added to resins before pouring to create water effects.

Stonecast casting powder This is used in casting of paving stones and bricks. Follow the manufacturer's instructions.

Colouring agents These are coloured powders that are mixed with the casting powders to achieve different paving and walling effects.

Modelling rock A plaster-impregnated bandage (brand name Mod-Roc) used for forming mounds and high ground.

Celluclay This is a papier mâché type material used for forming mounds and slopes.

Releasing agent Using a releasing agent prevents casting resin and powder materials adhering to the sides of moulds, ensuring a clean casting.

Plasticine This is a versatile children's play material used here to make up moulds for brick walls.

Building blocks (Lego) These are ideal for building semi-permanent moulds using Plasticine.

Oasis (florist's foam) This is used as the basis of flower beds and topiary and can be cut and shaped using a craft knife or hacksaw.

Expanded polystyrene This is very useful as a bulk filler or as the basis for hedging and can be found used as a packing material or insulation board.

Tea leaves Taken from tea bags, these are used to simulate earth.

Powdered plaster and wood fillers (eg, Polyfilla and Tetrion) Used with the addition of a little fine sand, these materials are excellent for casting stones and slabs, filling gaps and for the building of rockeries.

Self-hardening air-drying clay (DAS) This is ideal for building up rockeries and producing rough-looking stones.

Polymer clay Fimo, Sculpey and Formello are the trade names of coloured clays that can be worked, moulded and hardened in an oven. Used to make a variety of items, clay is especially useful for making flowers, vegetables, plants and fish.

Lichen, mosses and dried flowers These are used to simulate real flowers, small trees and shrubs.

Slate and stones Chipped into small pieces these are useful for building up rockeries and paths. Silver sand and the very small grade of gravel, normally used in fish tanks make ideal materials for paths.

Paints and stains

Vinyl emulsion paints These are extremely versatile modern materials for the miniaturist in two basic types, matt and silk. Matt colours tend to retain dirt and finger marks whereas the silk finishes, having a slight surface sheen, can be washed over. Being water based, different colours can be mixed with ease and they will usually mix with other water-based paints. Available in standard 1 litre containers, emulsions can also be found in tiny trial pots, although this may be restricted to matt finish only. All emulsions can be applied directly to bare wood, although the first coat should be thinned with 10 percent clean water.

Artist's acrylics and gouaches These are water based and may be mixed to produce any colour or shade. These paints result in a matt finish on drying and are best applied with a small brush. An acrylic glaze or scumble can be added to give a glaze. Both may be applied to bare wood and acrylics can used on metal.

Poster paints Water-based paints made in many colours to give a matt finish. Like acrylics and gouaches, they can be mixed to provide an infinite variety of shades. Application can be made to new wood but is not recommended for metal.

Enamel paints These are oil based and cannot be mixed with water-based paints. Humbrol is a reliable trade name but there are others. The range of colours is vast and they may all be mixed together for subtle shading. Paint-brushes should be cleaned with white spirit or enamel thinners. Bare wood should be primed first with a varnish or sealer, and although a water-based acrylic can be used in some circumstances, we recommend that you test first on an oddment. Enamels are ideal for painting metal and give a high gloss finish but matt finishes are available too.

Wood stains A range of spirit wood stains will prove very useful for colouring garden furniture, sheds and fences and can be lightened by dilution with white spirit, or darkened by mixing with a deeper shade. Stain will not penetrate through wood that has been previously painted or covered with glue, so to avoid 'white' spots on assemblies stain all the parts before gluing. Do not smoke or have naked flames when using spirit-based stains or enamel paints and thinners as they have very low flash points.

Basic Tools and Materials

> **TIP**
>
> *Most water-based paints can be mixed together to produce unusual and interesting shades. Acrylics can be applied to metal as well as wood.*

Making the Elements

Many of the elements or features in a miniature garden may be purchased but it can be far more fun to make your own and throughout this resource chapter we show how you can make just about everything – from bricks to flower beds, fences to ponds. There are basic instructions and many mini projects that will help you choose the best materials and successfully make all the main elements for the projects shown later in the book, or when creating your own garden design.

The materials described here can all be easily obtained and there are no requirements for specialist tools. There are many references throughout this chapter and the projects to jelutong wood. This is one of the best modelling timbers, however, you could use obeche wood instead as it is very similar (see Basic Tools and Materials on page 18).

PAVING AND PATHS

Paving should be used carefully in any garden design and it should be borne in mind that several different types may be combined to produce interesting effects. Bricks used as paving appear warm, cobbles give texture, straight paving is functional, mixed shapes and colours provide an energetic feel, whilst tones of grey combined with still water will give a peaceful feel to an area. Varying the patterns used in laying paving materials, especially bricks, can also introduce a different atmosphere to a garden.

The paving found in real gardens can be anything from York paving, a natural stone, to cast concrete slabs. Many of the latter are designed to mimic real stone, with patterned surfaces but some are just simple blocks. The art in using any garden paving is to make it blend in with the surroundings.

It should fit neatly, with no untidy edges and be chosen to complement the other garden elements.

PAVING SLABS

Full size paving comes in a selection of sizes, the most common ones being 9in square, 12in square or 24in x 12in. You can choose to scale these sizes down to suit your miniature garden or make paving any size you wish. Uncommon sizes are often multiples of those already given, such as, 18in x 24in and 18in x 18in. There are also a number of special shapes available such as circles and interlocking blocks, some of which are discussed later. You can, of course make dolls' house paving any size you wish but remember to always follow the $1/12$th scale or 1 inch to 1 foot and make your slabs correspond to full size.

The paving stones around the edges of a real garden usually have to be cut to fit and you can achieve this in miniature by cutting with a sharp razor saw, although a better method is to cast special sizes to fit the planned area. Realistic paving can also be made from thin 2mm or 3mm sheet MDF (described on page 21).

Measuring up

The first task is to measure the area to be covered with paving and see if it will divide equally into squares. In your calculations remember to allow for the tiny gap between each slab – ideally not more than $1/32$in all round. If the area will not divide equally you will need to deal with the outer edges using a number of smaller slabs. Paving should always be laid from a centre mark outwards so that the outer edges have stones of equal sizes, but you may find it easier to start from one corner. Place whole paving slabs where they can be easily seen and any odd or cut paving can then be hidden in a corner or at the back. An irregularly shaped plan will result in unequal stones at the edges but calculations should still start from the centre.

MAKING PAVING SLABS

Dolls' house garden paving stones or slabs also look best when they exactly fit the area to be covered and, as it is unlikely that ready-made miniature paving will fit the area to be covered perfectly, the best solution is to make your own.

MATERIALS

- *¹/₂in thick blockboard pieces about 12in square (or any sheet board, such as plywood, with a smooth, flat surface)*
- *¹/₈in x ³/₁₆in strips of jelutong or obeche wood for spacers*
- *Panel pins*
- *Cling film (Siran wrap) or transparent thin polythene sheeting*
- *Casting materials and colouring*
- *Small trowel or spatula*

Prepare the base, using a small plane, so that at least two adjoining edges are dead square. Mark these for future reference and use them as a starting point whenever drawing or measuring. Using a set square, draw a line along one side of the base about 1in in from the edge. Now draw another line parallel to this, the exact width of your paving slab away from the first line. Lay a piece of the spacer strip along this second line. Hold the strip in place with the wider side against the board, and draw the next line. Draw another line the width of a paving slab away from this line, and continue in this way across the blockboard. You should now have a series of straight lines up the blockboard showing, alternately, the width of the slab and the width of the spacers.

Turn the board round and draw another

It is possible to create a wide range of paving surfaces. Those shown here include bricks (top left), paving slabs in various shapes (centre and bottom left), slate (top right), crazy paving (centre right) and sand (centre)

TIP

Make up a small cutting jig to ensure that all cross spacers are exactly the same size by placing a clamp in a miniaturist's mitre box at the required distance from the cutting slot and make cuts with a razor saw.

set of lines at right angles to the first set. The blockboard should now be divided up into a number of slab-sized squares separated by spacing strip with panels. If the area being covered requires some odd-sized paving around the edges, mark these on another piece of blockboard.

Cover the prepared blockboard with transparent polythene sheeting or cling film (Siran wrap), pinning it tautly in place along the outer edges. Cut spacer strips to match the longest side of the blockboard and carefully pin these onto the board following the lines. Now cut shorter 'cross' spacers to fit between these and pin into place on the board (see fig 1).

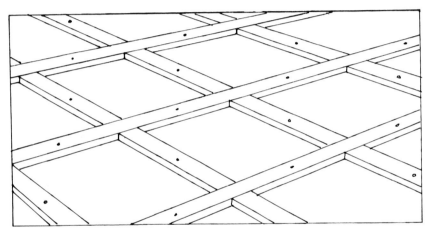

Fig 1 Making the paving stone moulds

Fig 2 Pouring the paving stone mixture into moulds

Mix up the casting material following the manufacturer's instructions and add any colouring. Lay the prepared paving stone blockboard onto a flat surface and pour, or trowel out, the mixture into the moulds (see fig 2). Fill all the mould spaces to the height of the spacers, or a little above. Smooth the surfaces using a trowel or by dragging a straight piece of wood across the

spacers. Carefully pick up the board, without tipping it, and tap the underside to allow the mixture to settle and disperse any trapped air. Check again that the surface is smooth and allow to dry thoroughly (up to twenty-four hours). Once dry the top surface of the slabs can be rubbed down to a smooth finish with a fine grade abrasive paper wrapped around a flat cork sanding block.

CASTING LARGE AREAS

An alternative to casting individual paving stones is to cast one slab to cover the entire area, making it appear as if single pavers have been laid. However, as it is difficult to maintain an even thickness over the whole surface, it is not recommended for really large areas.

Draw out the shape of the area to be covered on a piece of blockboard and cover with cling film (Siran wrap). Cut and pin $1/8$in x $3/16$in spacer strips all around the edges. Pour in the casting mixture and smooth off the surface, tapping the underside of the board to remove any trapped air.

Allow the mixture to set until the surface is firm, but still soft enough to mark. Place a straight edge on the surface and using a sharp point carefully score the spaces between each slab. Use a soft brush to remove any debris and leave until set hard.

When the slab is hard, carefully remove it from the base and transfer it to the garden site. A little PVA glue placed under the slab in places will keep it secure.

Casting on site

It can prove very difficult to transfer large areas of casting from the board to the site without breakage. A useful alternative is to cast large slabs in the final position. Mark out the area to be covered as before but do not use the cling film (Siran wrap). Place the spacers around the edge, as above, pour in the mixture and finish off. Use fine grade abrasive paper to flatten if necessary and brush away any debris after marking out.

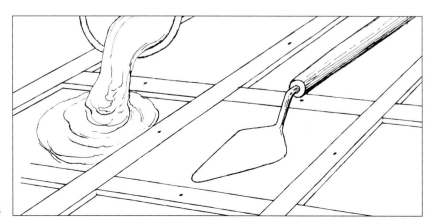

Special effects on slabs

In real life paving becomes worn where there is a lot of use and frost and rain leave chips and marks on steps and paving edges. By introducing this sort of character any garden scene will appear far more realistic.

Using a very fine grade abrasive paper wrapped around one finger press down, with a slight side-ways movement, into the centre of a slab until a slight indentation is formed. Brush away any dust and residue as you proceed and continue until the required effect is achieved, being careful not to over-do it. Chipping the edges of some slabs with a scalpel will mimic frost damage and inserting the odd broken slab will add realism.

Miniature slabs will be the same colour all the way through because they have been cast using a uniform mixture. However, you can mimic the pale, worn areas on real slabs by mixing up some of the colour used for casting and, adding a little white acrylic paint, apply sparingly.

CRAZY PAVING

Crazy paving is a type of surface where paving oddments are used, laid randomly with no discernible pattern. Whilst there are no rules regarding sizes you should avoid placing very large pieces around the edges and try at all times to make the paving look balanced. There a number of ways the miniaturist can make crazy paving, perhaps the easiest being to make a casting for the whole area as one piece.

Follow the basic instructions for the casting of a large area as before and leave until it has a firm surface but has not set hard. Lightly pencil in the paving shapes or follow your paper pattern if you've drawn one. Now take a sharp instrument and following the lines, scribe in the joints between the stones (see fig 3). Finally, brush away any dust and residue.

Making crazy paving out of real stone or slate, which can look quite striking, is worth considering as an alternative and the

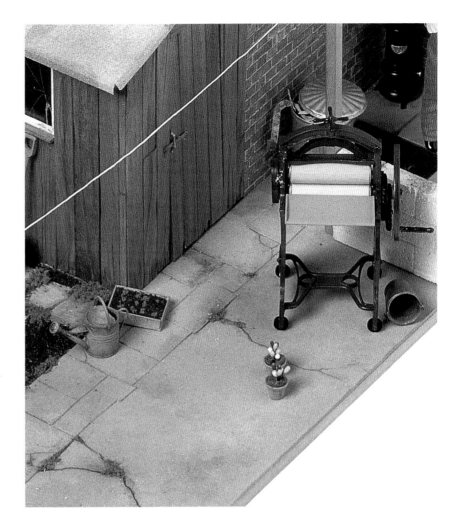

best thickness to use is ¹/₁₆in. A garden centre is a good source and small pieces of slate can often be obtained in various colours. Use ceramic tile cutters or a pair of pliers to snip pieces off until workable shapes are obtained. (You must wear protective goggles when breaking or snipping slate.) Assemble all the pieces and start laying them across the area, building up a pattern as you go. Using UHU, glue them into place one at a time and when set hard, grout between them using a proprietary wall

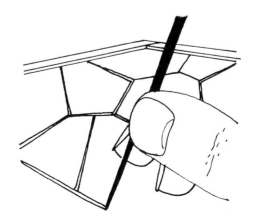

Paving cast as one slab, marked to look cracked and worn and with the addition of some weeds looks very effective. Old 'concrete' can be made this way, as in the Terrace House Backyard on page 113

TIP

Plan out the crazy paving area on a piece of tracing paper until the sizes look about right for the space to be covered.

Fig 3 Scribing the joints in still damp crazy paving

tile filler. Finally, clean off the whole area using an old soft toothbrush and a paper towel.

UNUSUAL PAVING SHAPES AND MOULDS

Producing unusual shapes to fit specific areas or to build up patterns requires special moulds. There are several ways a mould can be made and a number of every-day items can be used provided you can remove the stone mixture once it has set. It is best to use a release agent before casting difficult shapes.

Round paving can be made using one of those small plastic caps found on the top of a film canister. As they are so readily available you can cast several stones at once using the same colour mix and discard them when you have finished the job. Any similar plastic bottle top can be used provided that it is not too deep and does not have screw threads around the sides. Lightly coat the inside with a releasing agent, pour in the stone mix, tap the bottom to release trapped air bubbles and drop out the round paving when it has set.

Small, square paving can be produced using one of the casting methods described previously but for really small slabs of say 1/2in square or less, cutting the spacers accurately can become a long and tedious job. A good alternative is to cut them from larger stones using a razor saw.

Plastic tile spacers, produced in small neatly divided blocks, make ideal moulds for small paving, and breaking out one of the spacers results in a doubling of the slab size. To use, secure the spacers to a baseboard covered in food wrap (Siran wrap) and spray lightly with releasing agent, pour in the mixture, tap to release trapped bubbles and allow to set. Release the paving slabs carefully and save any damaged ones for later jobs.

An unusual type of crazy paving can also be made using a mould, although in this case the same pattern will be repeated on each slab. First prepare a small mould from a suitable plastic container, about 3in square and 1/2in deep. Line the bottom of the mould with Plasticine and brush on a little talcum powder or French chalk. Take a 2in square paving slab, made using one of the methods described previously, and score a pattern of breaks across the surface, the depth of which will be reproduced on all subsequent slabs produced from this mould. Gently press the face of the paving slab into the Plasticine to create the mould. Carefully remove the slab, pour in the stone mixture and allow to set. Repeat as often as necessary.

PAVING FROM MDF

To make this sort of paving, first determine the area to be covered and cut and shape a piece of 2mm thick MDF to fit. With a sharp pencil, mark out the irregular paving stones. When you are happy with the design make a series of V-shaped cuts with a sharp scalpel or craft knife along all of the joints and remove the waste. Alternatively make two cuts, each 1/16in apart and 1/32in deep. Remove this waste and leave the bottom of the joint slightly rough to mimic a mortared finish.

Paint the MDF paving using khaki and grey spray paints to obtain a stone effect and when the surface is dry paint in the joints and cracks with a streaky dark brown or black acrylic paint. Finish off by gluing on a few weeds and lichen using a PVA adhesive, and then glue your completed paving down into place.

GRAVEL AND COBBLED PATHS

Various grades of gravel and sheets of fibreglass moulded gravel can be purchased from model shops in several grades and you should choose those which will suit your garden best. Prepare the site and cut a piece of stiff card to fit and then coat with a layer of adhesive – PVA glue will be suitable for fine gravels but use Copydex

---

TIP

Slate can also be laid directly onto tile cement.

TIP

Broken miniature paving can be reassembled into a random pattern and has the advantage of being of uniform thickness.

TIP

Make some of the joints slightly deeper than others and sand off some of the MDF edges between the paving stones to give a worn appearance, but try not to overdo this effect.

(rubber cement) adhesive for anything larger. Allow the surface of the adhesive to become tacky before sprinkling the surface with the gravel. After the card has dried, tap lightly to remove any surplus.

Sheets of ready-prepared fibre-glass moulded gravel are very useful and easy to use. Once cut to a template they can be glued directly into your garden site (see Suppliers for the garden projects page 173).

Cobbles can look quite good in some areas, particularly in courtyard scenes or as rough infill to walls. Cobblestones can be simulated by using split lentils; in fact a whole variety of small seeds and grains can be used, depending on the effect you wish to achieve. Prepare a piece of stiff card as the base and glue the lentils on with the raised, half-round surface uppermost. Spray or paint the surface with matt varnish to seal off.

BRICKS, WALLS AND ROOFS

Real bricks are made from clay mixed with water and fired in a kiln. The clay type and mixture and the firing temperature will affect the final colour, so a wall built in the south of the country may appear different to one built in the north. The pattern in which bricks are laid, called a bond, will also alter the appearance of a wall. The longest face of a brick is called the stretcher and the shortest is the header, and it is the pattern in which the stretchers and headers are laid that determine the name of the bond. Most modern walls are laid in a plain 'stretcher bond' in which only the stretchers show (see fig 4).

Walls are built of layers of bricks arranged so that each brick covers the joints between the two bricks below. Ideally the outer edges of a brick course, or layer, should start and finish with a whole brick, with alternating rows having a half brick. It is a good idea to build miniature walls with these principles in mind.

Another variable in walls is the mortar used to hold the bricks together, and before

A low brick wall in familiar stretcher bond can be made of individual bricks or covered with brick-patterned paper, adding interest, height and realism to a miniature garden

---

TIP

Ensure that any grains or seeds are dried off in a warm oven before use, as using damp materials may result in mould growth.

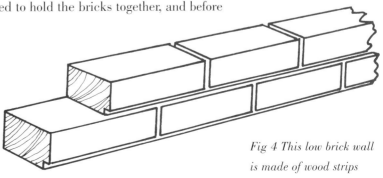

Fig 4 This low brick wall is made of wood strips

31

the advent of modern cements most of this was lime based. This material was more friable than its modern counterpart but it had the advantage of allowing buildings to move and breathe without breaking the very bricks it was meant to secure. Lime mortars are much whiter than modern mixes, which tend to be more of a sand colour.

In the United Kingdom bricks are currently made to a standard size, 215mm x 102.5mm x 65mm (8^1/$_2$in x 4in x 2^1/$_2$in). Victorian bricks were slightly larger (9in x 4^1/$_4$in x 2^1/$_2$in), although other sizes can be found and special bricks were cast for unusual architectural effects. Reducing brick measurements to ^{1}/$_{12}$th scale produces odd imperial fractions that may prove difficult to reproduce accurately when making moulds or setting saws. To avoid confusion we recommend using the standard measurements of ^{3}/$_4$in x ^{3}/$_8$in x ^{1}/$_4$in for stock bricks. Occasionally projects call for special brick sizes and they can be made up as the job demands using the methods below.

Ready-made bricks, slips, moulded fibreglass sheets and printed papers are also available from specialists for creating wall effects, along with other building materials such as mortars (see Suppliers page 173).

MAKING WOODEN BRICKS

Wooden bricks made from strip jelutong or obeche wood can look very effective, particularly for a neat, contemporary look.

MATERIALS
___

- *^{1}/$_4$in x ^{3}/$_8$in strips of jelutong wood*
- *Fine grade abrasive paper*

Lay the strips down with the side measuring ^{1}/$_4$in uppermost (this is the face) and use a set square to draw a series of lines ^{3}/$_4$in apart. This will produce stretchers only; drawing the lines ^{3}/$_8$in apart will create only headers. Specific bonds with alternating headers and stretchers can be worked with a little planning.

Lay each strip in your mitre box and use a fine saw to make a shallow cut across each line to simulate the mortar joint between each brick. Take a piece of fine grade abrasive paper wrapped around a cork block and carefully chamfer along one edge of each strip to enhance the appearance of a lateral join when the bricks are assembled to form a wall (see figs 4 and 5).

If you have a bench saw or router capable of making a very fine cut you can incorporate the mortar joint into the strips. Prepare the strips in the usual way but increase the size to ^{1}/$_4$in x ^{7}/$_{16}$in and machine away a strip ^{1}/$_{16}$in wide x ^{1}/$_{32}$in deep along the ^{7}/$_{16}$in side to produce the mortar joint, leaving a ^{3}/$_8$in brick (see figs 4 and 5). (See page 36 for painting bricks and walls.)

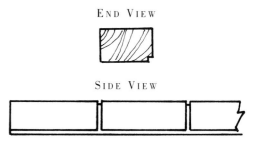

END VIEW

SIDE VIEW

Fig 5 Making wooden bricks

CASTING BRICKS

The basic method for making stock bricks is very similar to the one used when casting paving stones and slabs but first a very accurate mould has to be made (see figs 6, 7 and 8).

MATERIALS
___

- *Blockboard or MDF baseboard 12in x 12in*
- *Two jelutong formers ^{3}/$_8$in x 1in, approximately 12in long*
- *Wooden or plastic spacer strips ^{1}/$_{16}$in x ^{3}/$_8$in*
- *Cling film (Siran wrap)*
- *Releasing agent*

Mark out the baseboard with two lines down the centre exactly ^{3}/$_4$in apart and cover

TIP

Go and look at a real wall, built in the correct period before making up bricks.

TIP

When measuring heights of walls and calculating the number of courses remember to allow for mortar in the joints.

TIP

These wooden strips are best prepared on a bench saw but they can be purchased ready sawn and sanded from specialist suppliers.

tightly with Cling film (Siran wrap) or thin polythene. Prepare the jelutong formers by drilling them with ¹/₁₆in-diameter pilot holes at each end of the 1in side to take panel pins, and turn them over ready for marking up. Using a small set square, draw the first line 1in in from one end and continue marking at exactly ¹/₄in intervals. Use a tenon saw to make a ¹/₁₆in deep cut, ¹/₁₆in wide at each of the ¹/₄in marks.

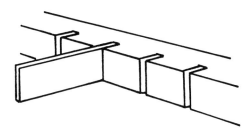

Fig 6 Making the mould for casting bricks

Assemble the formers onto the baseboard along each of the previously drawn lines and lightly fix in place using panel pins through the pre-drilled holes (see fig 7). When fixing the second former into place ensure that the two sets of slots are exactly aligned or the bricks will not cast square. Cut a sufficient number of the ¹/₁₆in x ³/₈in strips exactly ⁷/₈in long to fill all the slots.

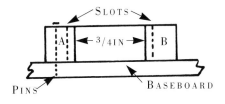

Fig 7 Making the mould for casting bricks

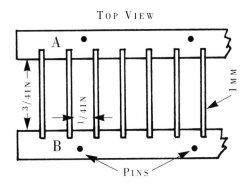

Fig 8 Making the mould for casting the bricks

Insert, but do not glue the spacer strips into all the slots and give the mould a final check for accuracy with a set square then lightly spray all the inner surfaces with releasing agent to prevent the stone mixture sticking. Prepare the stone mix using the method described for making paving stones on page 28 and add any desired colouring. Pour the mixture into the brick mould, tap the bottom of the baseboard to remove any trapped air and smooth off the top surfaces.

After the mixture has been allowed to set thoroughly, carefully release the two outer formers and you should be able remove each of the spacer strips to release the bricks. Chipped or broken bricks can be trimmed using a razor saw to produce halves that can be used at the ends of walls or in building other bonds.

CASTING BRICK WALL SECTIONS

Whole walls can be cast in one piece, although there are some limitations on size and very large walls would probably need to be made up from several smaller castings. This is a good method for casting any unusual sections and for patterns that might be difficult to produce any other way.

MATERIALS

- *Lego bricks*
- *Lego baseboard*
- *Plasticine*
- *Cocktail sticks*
- *Casting powder*
- *Talcum powder*
- *Releasing agent*

Roll out the Plasticine until it is about ¹/₈in thick and lay this onto the base leaving a border around the edge one Lego brick wide. Make sure the Plasticine is flat and add the border bricks all round to form your mould. To make a stretcher bond casting prepare twelve separate wooden bricks ³/₄in wide x ³/₈in x ¹/₄in using the method described

---

TIP

Place both formers in a vice and cut slots in each at the same time to ensure that they will all line up when assembled.

TIP

The accuracy of these strips is important to the success of making bricks and we recommend that you use both a razor saw and a mitre box with a stop to achieve this.

TIP

It is not necessary to use Lego materials to build up a mould: we found them particularly useful, but any sturdy plastic box or tin will do.

previously and drill a ¹/₁₆in-diameter hole about ¹/₈in of an inch deep, on the long or stretcher side of each brick. Cut the sharp ends off the cocktail sticks and glue one into each brick.

Lightly cover the surface of the Plasticine with talcum powder, removing any surplus. Gently press one brick into the top left-hand corner of your mould. Press a second brick into place leaving a small gap for the mortar joint between them and continue like this across the mould. Leave the first row of bricks in place to prevent the second from distorting the mould and start a second row, again leaving a small gap between impressions for the mortar gap. Remember to stagger the joins, starting with a half brick on the second row. When the second row is complete you can remove the first row and continue down the mould. When all the impressions have been made, remove any remaining bricks, allow the mould to relax and then place it into a refrigerator to harden off the Plasticine.

When you're ready to do the casting, spray the mould with releasing agent, then mix sufficient casting powder and colouring in a clean container and pour into the mould to a depth of approximately ¹/₄in. Tap the base to remove any air bubbles and when set remove the casting and clean up any rough edges.

This method can be adapted for making any brick pattern or bond and it is very useful for modelling panels of rough-cast, flint or herringbone bricks to be placed into an otherwise flat wall.

COVERING WALLS

Walls can be covered in different materials to mimic stone and brick and you will find good examples of this throughout the eight gardens featured in the book. Ready-moulded and coloured paper sheets of bricks and wall finishes can be obtained in several bonds from specialist suppliers (see page 173). The thin sheets can be applied directly to an already prepared MDF board

and have the advantage of producing instant results. The fibre-glass versions are three-dimensional and have variable colours which look far more realistic than the paper. Care must be taken to show the correct bond pattern at the end and tops of any wall covered in these materials.

Ready-made brick slips to ¹/₁₂th scale can be readily purchased. These are small tiles that can be glued directly onto a MDF wall, and any bond can be achieved with a little imagination (see Suppliers page 173).

BUILDING WALLS

Mark out the site for the wall and calculate how many stretcher bricks are needed for the base, remembering to include the mortar joints in any calculations. If possible adjust the length of the wall to give whole or half bricks at each end, especially when building walls that abut others to produce 'L' shapes, as this will avoid cutting lots of odd sized bricks and give neater edges. Using old bond patterns will enhance period garden walls and we suggest you use English Garden wall bond whenever possible, as this was designed for free-standing walls and has a complete course of headers after every three or five courses of stretchers to give it strength. Stretcher bond is the most easily recognised and probably the easiest to reproduce, however it is mostly used for modern cavity walls and 'English' or 'Flemish' bonds tend to look best on period buildings.

The simplest wall to build is one that uses a printed or moulded sheet glued onto a piece of MDF or plywood. For a free-standing wall ensure that it is the correct thickness and that the brick pattern matches at each end with whole or half bricks. Adjust the sheet by cutting out bricks from the centre or five bricks in from each end.

Walls built up from wooden bricks should always start at the base and with the mortared edge at the bottom. Start by gluing the bottom row into place and then add layers until you reach the required height,

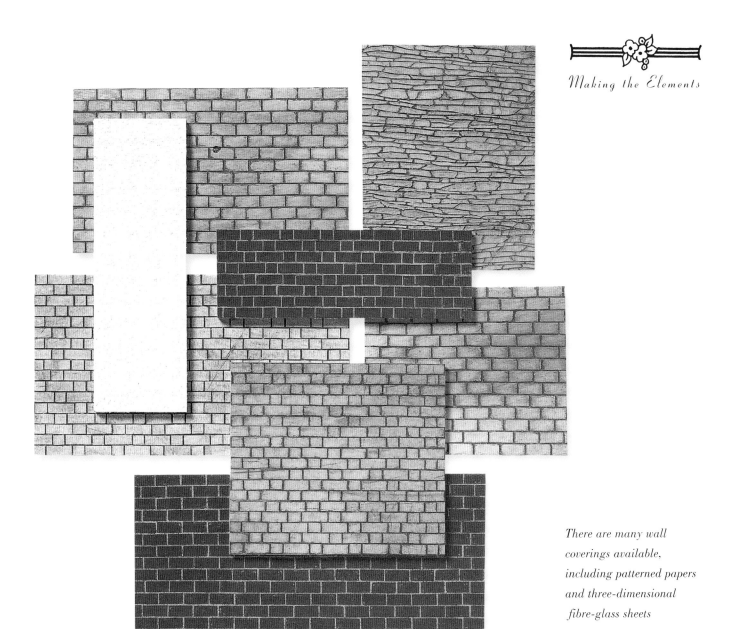

There are many wall coverings available, including patterned papers and three-dimensional fibre-glass sheets

topping off with an appropriate pattern.

Building a wall from loose bricks will produce the best results and patterned bonds are much easier to control. Assemble the bottom row first and carefully add rows as soon as the one below is firm enough to build on. PVA glue mixed with a little plaster filler and some grey acrylic paint makes an ideal 'mortar' for all wall building.

Walls sections built up from castings look very effective provided that the joins between the cast panels are carefully disguised. Camouflage these by removing random bricks from the edges to produce a 'tooth' pattern and cut matching gaps in the adjoining panel.

Brick slips can be glued onto a prepared MDF wall and look very effective if care is taken to ensure that brick lines are straight. First of all wash over the entire wall with a mortar-coloured acrylic paint. Start at the top of the wall and use a set square to draw the first guide line one brick wide. Draw a second line $1/32$in below this for the mortar joint and another, the width of one brick, below that and proceed in this manner until you reach the bottom of the wall. By starting at the top any trimmed and odd bricks are placed at the bottom, out of the way. The mortar lines can be left as they are, or the gap can be filled with a proprietary filler following the maker's instructions.

TIP

You may find it easier to assemble walls on a flat piece of MDF laid on a level surface, erecting the whole wall once completed. Complicated shapes will prove easier to assemble around former blocks especially made for the purpose.

35

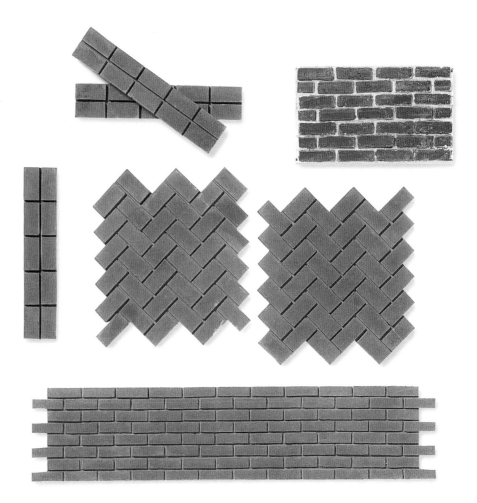

The distinctive appearance of brick walls can be achieved in various ways – with patterned paper, fibre-glass and resin sheets. Resin castings (centre) are useful for decorative paving and flooring

---

TIP

Art card comes in many colours and if you can purchase a basic red-coloured sheet for tiles or grey for slates, as this will help in the final colouring.

PAINTING BRICKS AND WALLS

Walls made from wooden bricks will require several coats of acrylic colour, starting with the mortar joints. Use a water-based colour wash and brush over the entire surface until you are satisfied all the joints are covered. The bricks must now be coloured separately using a small artist's brush. As well as the basic brick tone keep a little white and black acrylic paint on the corner of your palette and add one or both from time to time to produce variations in the colours. Self-coloured cast bricks can give a very flat appearance to a wall and the addition of a little extra random colouring as described above can bring a welcome improvement.

Brick panels (such as the wall sections made on page 33) are best cast in natural plain white powder and painted later by washing over the entire surface of the finished casting with a pale mortar-coloured paint then finishing off patches of several bricks with colour variations as described above.

ROOFS

There are various roofs in this book, for example the Terrace House Backyard house extension has a roof made of plasticard cut and painted grey to look like slate. The Rustic Garden features a tumbledown cottage with a roof covered in fired clay tiles from a specialist supplier.

There are times when you want a roof to look delicate and in this case wooden shingles are too large and a moulded fibre-glass sheet will not do. A good workable alternative is to make the roof slates, or tiles, from card, which has the benefit of being flexible and easily cut and shaped. It will require painting but a surprising number of effects can be achieved and it will look very close to $\frac{1}{12}$th scale.

The best material is art board, from art shops. It is available in many different colours and a variety of thicknesses. We find that two-sheet card is the best but up to four-sheet is acceptable. Start by using an HB pencil to mark up a sheet of card into $\frac{3}{4}$in wide strips. Turn the card round and

draw the tile divisions at right angles to the first set of lines, again at $^3/4$in intervals.

Cut the card into long strips using a scalpel and a steel rule, being careful to keep the lines straight. Take the strip(s) and cut up each of the marked divisions no more than $^5/8$in, leaving each tile attached to the strip by an $^1/8$in piece (see fig 9). Keep one or two strips uncut for use on the roof edge. To introduce character into the roof and give it a run-down appearance, trim the ends of some tiles to indicate breakage and weathering, just as you would see on a real roof, but be careful not to overdo this effect or make it appear too uniform. Prepare sufficient strips in this way to cover the roof, remembering that each row overlaps the one below.

Use a fast acting clear, spirit-based adhesive such as UHU and glue an uncut strip along the front edge of the roof and trim off at each end to lift the bottom row very slightly upward and throw off the 'rain'. Follow this by gluing a strip of tiles on top of the first but overlapping the front edge by $^1/8$in (see fig 9a). Prepare the third row, remembering to stagger the joints. If you have done this correctly the two outer tiles will be half the normal width. Glue this row over the one below, overlapping by $^1/8$in. Repeat with alternating rows until you reach the ridge, or top of the roof. Pencil lines can be made for guidance along the roof line before gluing down tile strips and to keep the rows evenly spaced.

Trim a piece of uncut card strip down to $^3/8$in wide and use a sharp pencil to score

lines at 1in intervals to use as ridge tiles. Glue this along the top ridge to finish off the roof.

Mix up some red and black acrylic paint into a streaky mixture and apply this all over the roof. Ensure that all the cracks are covered by paint and finish off by adding small splashes of white for bird lime. The roof can now be placed into position and glued down if required.

ROCKERY

A rockery, as the name implies, is an assembly of rocks planted with small plants such as alpines and succulents. The Victorians often made very large rockeries using an artificial stone mixture poured over smaller stones and rubble. Miniature rockeries tend to look best when located in a corner, balancing another feature (see the rockery in the Edwardian Summer House Garden).

Various materials can be used but nothing is better than the real thing, even in miniature, and a trip to your local garden centre will almost certainly produce a bag of suitably coloured stone chips. None need be much larger than a walnut although larger pieces can be broken down using a suitable hammer (use goggles to protect eyes from flying chips).

A useful alternative to stone is rough natural cork, often found in florists' displays. Break off and shape enough pieces to complete your rockery and crush any oddments to use as filler between larger pieces.

> **TIP**
>
> *When tiling a roof, expert tilers can introduce a tile of 1$^1/2$ widths on alternate rows. To do this a separate piece of card will need to be marked up and cut.*

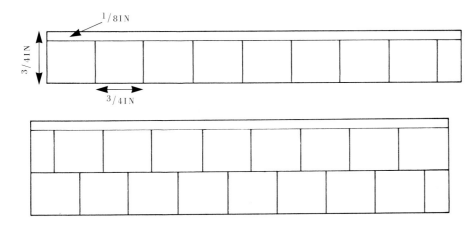

Fig 9 Making the roof tiles

Fig 9a Positioning the roof tiles

A block of self-hardening clay can also be used to produced rough looking stones. Simply break pieces off the block and allow to dry, but remember that wet hands will leave giant fingerprints in 1/12th scale, so smooth away marks with a damp brush or cloth. When dry the blocks can be cut and sanded into any shape you want.

If you only have a limited quantity of stone or if the rockery is to be built around another feature, such as the steps in the Edwardian Summer House garden, you can build up the base using scrap polystyrene blocks which have been roughly shaped with a craft knife.

MATERIALS

- *2mm MDF or hardboard for base*
- *Rock pieces or chippings (or other 'rock' material such as self-hardening clay or cork)*
- *Self-hardening clay*
- *Tea bags*
- *Polystyrene packing for bulk filler*
- *Plaster filler*
- *Very fine gravel*
- *Plants, lichens and mosses*

Decide on the location for your rockery and prepare a base from 2mm hardboard or MDF. Select a batch of rocks of various sizes and start by placing the largest pieces at the bottom, reducing the sizes as you progress. Three layers are generally sufficient for a miniature garden but you can add more if necessary. Make a note of which rock goes where and place them to one side ready for assembly.

Prepare a base pad of self-hardening clay and press the bottom rocks into it so that they are securely held and then leave to dry. Once the clay has dried out remove the rocks and using a clear (UHU) glue, stick them back into their positions. Repeat this for the second and third layers and finally fill any gaps between the rocks with fresh clay and allow to dry.

Stones made from cork material should be glued together using a clear adhesive such as UHU. The crumbs can be mixed with PVA glue and added to the gaps as the rockery is assembled.

To finish the rockery, paint over the surface of the clay or filler (not the rocks), with PVA glue and whilst this is still wet sprinkle the surface with fine gravel. Allow this to dry and repeat, this time using tea from tea bags to simulate earth. Allow to set and brush off any loose dust.

Drill small holes into the clay for plant stems and add a selection of plants, gluing small pieces of lichen or moss into some of the blank spaces.

FENCES, TRELLIS AND GATES

A fence has traditionally been used to mark the boundary of a property or estate, and a gate was simply a means of access through it. Fencing has also been used to prevent domesticated animals from straying and for keeping out predators: Tudor cottage gardens were often fenced for this reason alone.

The earliest fences were probably woven chestnut hurdles but later examples are post and rail and picket. Modern fencing tends to be lapped or woven so that it forms a solid barrier, more against neighbours than animals. Decorative fences, called trellises, can be used as dividers within larger gardens. Fencing in real gardens rarely exceeds six feet in height and therefore 1/12th scale miniature fencing should not exceed 6 inches.

Wooden fencing is not the only material used to enclose spaces, lengths of metal railing and metal gates are quite commonly found around properties and there are miniaturists who specialise in this type of work. Short lengths of these can be seen on page 44 together with wooden and metal gates. It is not proposed to show here how to make metalwork gates and railings but there

Opposite: *Fences, gates and trelliswork are common features in a garden and if chosen carefully can add greatly to its character. Note, fencing shown is from more than one maker and includes post and rail (top, centre), featherboard with trellis top (top, centre), interwoven (centre, right), featherboard (centre, right), picket (centre) and trellis (bottom, right)*

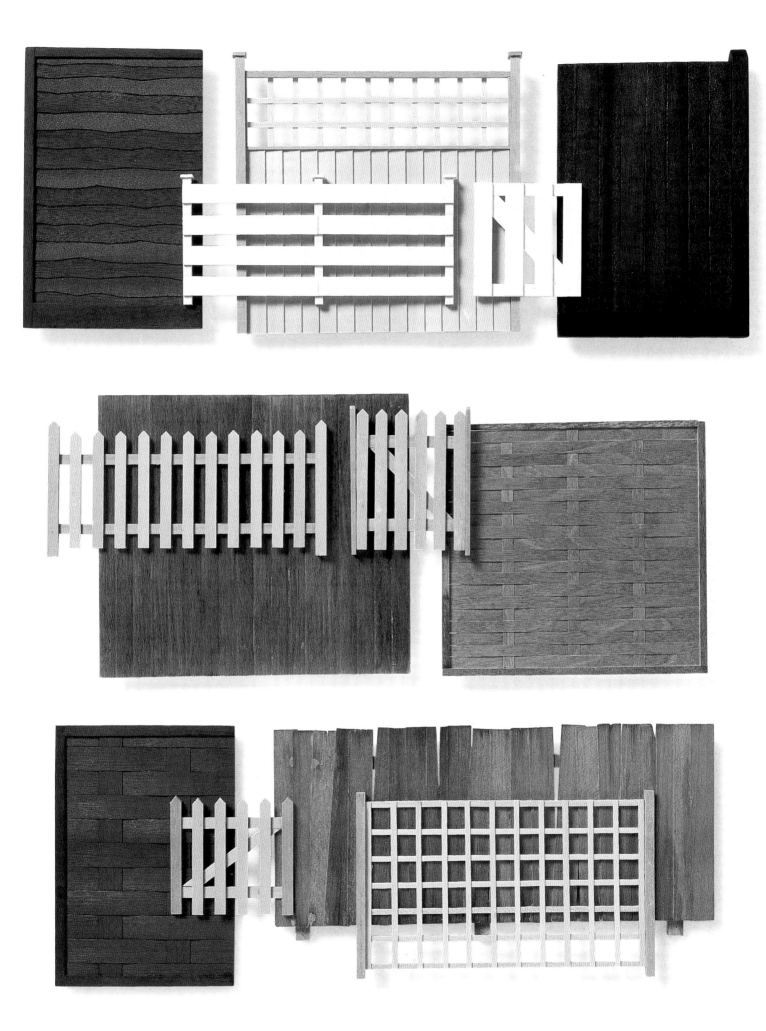

is no reason why miniaturists should not paint wooden turnings or some of the plastic moulded decorative fencing to resemble ironwork. Traditionally we think of ironwork as being black, but other colours can be used to good effect. Blue was a very expensive colour during the Georgian period due to the cost of the raw materials and painting any ironwork this colour would indicate the wealth of the owner. Dark green can be a useful alternative. However nice fresh timber may look, the colour will change as soon as it is exposed to the weather and the application of a little light wood stain will mimic this effect.

The fencing described in this section has all been made in nominal 6in lengths, but you can make longer or shorter lengths following the same principles.

SIMPLE TRELLIS

Trellis can be made to any length or height and can be placed on top of or against walls, on top of fences or left free standing with climbing plants (see the Victorian Roof Garden with Conservatory on page 149).

To make trellis look good it is necessary to make sure that all the parts are cut to the same length and that the spaces between the strips are all the same as nothing looks

worse than uneven work. To achieve this we suggest that you first make a drawing of the panel and work out all the spacing on paper. Pin the paper to a flat piece of board and lightly oil the surface to stop the glue sticking parts to it. Use dressmaking pins to secure the thin strips in place until the glue has set. Do not push pins through the thin strip or they will split but place two or three pins on either side to secure.

MATERIALS
_____

- *Jelutong $^3/_{16}$in x $^3/_{16}$in x 8in*
- *Strip jelutong $^1/_8$in x $^1/_{32}$in x 90in*

To make up a 6½in long section cut two 4in posts from $^3/_{16}$in x $^3/_{16}$in jelutong. Using $^1/_8$in wide x $^1/_{32}$in thick strip jelutong, cut seven horizontal strips 6¼in long and twelve strips 3⅝in long. Pin the two posts to the drawing so that the outer edges are 6½in apart and cut the seven strips so that they will fit neatly inside the posts, touching but not overlapping. Lay the first strip onto the drawing ¼in above the bottom and position the remainder so that they have a $^7/_{16}$in gap between them. Lay and glue the twelve shorter strips starting from the left, with the first flush to the post, but do not

Trellis work as shown here can form a decorative feature on a wall or act as an attractive boundary to a garden

glue this to the post at this stage. Proceed across the trellis, again maintaining a gap of ⁷/₁₆in between each strip, finishing with one against the right hand post. Place a weight over the trellis work to keep it flat while the adhesive sets.

Carefully remove the trellis from the drawing and glue the posts onto each end, adding posts caps if required. Stain as desired.

Trellis work can also be made using fine chicken or garden wire with a ¹/₂in square mesh. Use tin snips or cutters to cut a strip matching the length of your fencing, with the mesh dead straight or on the diagonal and keeping the mesh strip flat. Paint it with brown acrylic or enamel paint (you may find it necessary to prime the surfaces first).

INTERWOVEN FENCE

This type of fence is not often available full size and was probably not made until the 1950s. It can look very decorative and though it is reasonably fragile, it does look very good in miniature. The panel shown in the photograph on page 39 measures 6in wide x 5¹/₂in high and the slats are built up on a simple jelutong framework.

MATERIALS
***

- *Strip jelutong ³/₁₆in x ³/₃₂in thick x 24in*
- *Plywood ¹/₆₄in thick x ¹/₄in x 1³/₈in approximately*

Make up the framework from ³/₁₆in x ³/₃₂in thick strip jelutong, cutting two uprights 5¹/₄in long, a bottom horizontal bar 6in long and a top bar 5⁵/₈in long. Lay the parts onto a flat surface and assemble into a framework, making sure that the corners are dead square. Apply glue sparingly, support the assembly and leave the adhesive to dry.

The interwoven slats are made from the ¹/₆₄in thick plywood, as used in model making. Cut twenty slats 6in long and three uprights 5¹/₁₆in. Lay the frame onto a flat

surface and use a fast grab clear adhesive such as UHU to fix the slats onto the left-hand side of the framework, laying the first one above, not on, the lower bar of the frame. Keep all the slats as close together as possible and do not proceed until the glue has really set.

Working from the right, slide one of the uprights behind and in front of each alternate horizontal slat, starting behind the bottom one. Position this 1¹/₄in from the left and add a small spot of glue to the top and bottom joints to hold it in place. Work in the second vertical, again through alternates, but this time start with it in front of the bottom slat, positioning it dead centre and gluing as before. Continue with the third vertical as for the first, ¹/₄in away from the right-hand side. Finish off by gluing all the horizontal slats to the right-hand side of the frame, weighing it down until the adhesive has set. Stain the assembly as desired.

FEATHERBOARD FENCE WITH TRELLIS TOP

Featherboard, perhaps better known as weather-boarding or ship-lap, is a very useful material and is primarily used on the sides of houses, sheds and greenhouses with the boards laying horizontally. Each division on the section we used was approximately ³/₈in wide, which is ideal for fencing when the boards are reversed through 90 degrees so that they appear to lie in an upright position. This material is flat on the back surface and this permits the additions of rails if required (see page 39).

MATERIALS
***

- *Two pieces of featherboard (clapboard) each 4in x 3in*
- *Jelutong: lengths of strip ¹/₈in x ¹/₈in x 6in; ¹/₈in x ¹/₁₆in x 9in and ¹/₈in x ¹/₃₂in x 30in*
- *Two posts ³/₁₆in x ³/₁₆in x 6in*
- *Two post caps ¹/₁₆in x ⁵/₁₆ x ⁵/₁₆in*
- *Back support ¹/₈in x ¹/₄in x 6in*

(see page 39)

TIP

Spray painting wire mesh for trellis will give an even and professional finish. Use a protective mask and do not smoke or spray near naked flames.

TIP

Don't forget you can stain all trellis parts before gluing.

41

TIP

*You can keep the
divisions in trellis work
even by cutting and
using a template spacer.*

TIP

*Add the appearance of
nail heads to alternate
boards at the same level
as the rails on the back
of a fence with the point
of a sharp HB pencil.*

To make the fence panel, lay the two pieces of featherboard on a flat working surface with the boards all laying in the same direction and use a PVA wood adhesive to glue them together down the 4in height. Lightly clamp together until the glue has set, ensuring that the bottom edges are level with each other.

Keeping the panel on the flat surface glue the posts on either side and when this assembly is set turn it over and glue the back support to the bottom of the panel and across the two posts. Turn the fence panel over so that it is face up and lay it onto a flat surface. Cut the 6in strip of ^{1}/8in wide x ^{1}/16in thick jelutong strip to fit neatly on top of the featherboarding and glue into place, flush with the back. Cut two more pieces from the same material, each 1^1/2in long, and glue these onto the inside of each post to build up the sides of the trellis framework. The sides should not lie flush with the back, but be inset ^{1}/32in to allow the trellis work to lie flush. Cut and glue the ^{1}/8in x ^{1}/8in strip across the top, laying it onto the side pieces but flush with the back. This completes the frame.

Turn the fence over, face down, so that you can glue the trellis work directly onto the back of the frame. Using a razor saw and a jig or mitre box with a fixed stop, cut ten pieces of the ^{1}/8in x ^{1}/32in strip x 1^5/8in long and two pieces 6in long. Trim the 6in pieces to fit the framework so they rest on the side frames inside the posts. Glue on, equally spaced, approximately ^{7}/16in apart. Check that they are both level across the frame and allow the adhesive to set.

Mark the top and bottom rails with eleven evenly spaced divisions and glue on the ten pieces of ^{1}/8in x ^{1}/32in x 1^5/8in strip to complete the framework.

Finish off by gluing on the two post caps. When the adhesive has set the fence can be coloured and weathered with an oak spirit wood stain, diluted 50/50 with white spirit (although better results may be achieved by staining all the parts before gluing).

Longer and taller sections of featherboard fence can be made up to suit your project, with or without supporting posts. Simply join longer lengths as required and support the assembly with ^{1}/4in x ^{1}/16in wooden rails along the back surfaces which are machined flat.

POST AND RAIL FENCE

Post and rail fences are a basic way of enclosing an area. They are simple in structure, give little protection or privacy and traditionally are used to stop livestock getting out rather than intruders getting in. Made up in sections no higher than 3ft in real life (or 3in in miniature), post and rail fencing has recently become popular as it conforms to open plan ideals on modern housing estates.

The white fence shown in the photograph on page 39 is made entirely from white styrene plastic sheet and mouldings, but could just as easily be made up in wood. The example shows how two shorter lengths may be joined or a longer fence made from several pieces. Joins should always be made with a butt joint over a post.

MATERIALS

- *Following pieces of white styrene plastic sheet:*
  rails ^{1}/16in x ^{3}/8in x 24in
  three posts ^{3}/16in x ^{3}/16in x 2^3/4in
  three post caps ^{1}/16in x ^{1}/4in x ^{1}/4in
- *Plastic weld adhesive*

Begin with the 24in length of white styrene, cutting the rails into four 6in lengths and laying them onto a flat surface ^{1}/4in apart. Place a weight at one end to keep them in place and lay one of the posts flush with the other but ^{1}/4in below the bottom rail. Apply plastic weld adhesive and press down onto the post all the time as it sets, keeping it vertical. Glue the second post dead centre and the third at the other end. As a final touch glue on the post caps and leave to set.

PICKET FENCE

A ¹/₁₂th scale picket fence is usually about 2¹/₂in high and is easily recognised by the fact that it has pointed upright rails and is more often than not painted white. The rails are supported by horizontal pieces called arris rails, attached to upright posts, the tops of which are cut at 45 degrees in two directions. The uprights are laid onto the arris rails and separated by a measurement equal to the width of one upright. Fences can be assembled easily by using a spare upright as a spacer. A picket fence is featured in the Rustic Garden on page 96 and the method of construction for the length illustrated here is given below.

MATERIALS

- *Two jelutong arris rails 5⁷/₈in x ¹/₄in x ¹/₁₆in*
- *Two jelutong posts ¹/₄in x ¹/₄in x 2⁷/₈in*
- *Eleven jelutong rails 2¹/₂in x ¹/₄in x ¹/₁₆in*

Using a small jig or mitre box and a razor saw, shape the tops of all the rails with two 45 degree cuts to give an inverted 'V' shape.

To position and locate the arris rails, lay the two posts down onto a flat surface and place them together so that the ends match exactly. Measure and mark across both posts, at ¹/₂in and again at ³/₄in from the bottom. Repeat these two marks from the top end to give two ¹/₄in wide divisions on each post. Find the centre of this division and use a small ¹/₄in rebate in which to place the ends of an arris rail. Repeat to produce four slots on the inner surfaces of the posts.

Lay the two posts onto a flat surface so that the slots face each other, to the centre. Place a small spot of PVA adhesive to the end of each arris rail and glue them into the slots. Press together firmly, checking that all is square and leave the adhesive to set. The centre portion should be 5³/₄in.

Place one upright rail onto the two parallel arris rails and against the left-hand post as a spacer (do not glue this one) and glue a second into place level with the bottom of the posts and against the spacer, to the right. When the glue has set, use the first

TIP

Use a drill stand to set the depth and drill a series of ¹/₁₆in-diameter holes to make the post slots, finishing off with a sharp scalpel.

43

A selection of 'metal' gates and fencing, showing the wonderfully decorative effects that can be achieved with materials such as plastic mouldings and wire

rail as a spacer again and then glue a second into place, repeating this process until all the rails are glued onto the fence.

Paint the fence with a white emulsion or acrylic with a soft sheen or use a wood stain of a suitable colour for your project.

GATES

A gateway is, for most gardens, approximately the same width as a doorway, 2ft 6in or 2½in in ¹/₁₂th scale. In many cases the gate itself will be made of the same materials as the fence but this is not always so, as a quick look around your neighbourhood will show. Wooden fences may be coupled with metal gates and vice versa. An iron gate and wooden gate are shown below and on page 39 respectively. The latter is a simple picket fence type and is made in exactly the same way as for the fence above but with the addition of a 45 degree brace at the back for support. A method for making a white   picket gate is also given in the Rustic Garden project.

The Terrace House Backyard shows how to make a wooden-panelled, non-working gate. The Formal Georgian Garden features a gate made of plasticard and wire (see page 82), made to look like metal, complete with decorative finials.

HEDGES AND TOPIARY

Real hedges vary a great deal according to location and season and it is said that you can tell the age of one from the number of established plants growing within it. Not all hedges are neat or of uniform density and model gardeners must be prepared to adapt hedges to their surroundings; basic rules to follow are, neat hedges for formal gardens, untidy for wild ones, low for suburban and high for country gardens. Very few hedges grow right down to ground level so stems can usually be seen. Free-standing hedges will need to show some sort of base but you need show only tops above fences or walls.

SIMPLE HEDGE

The best materials to create a simple hedge are Oasis (floral foam) or fine grade polystyrene, often be found as packing . (avoid coarse types as they may prove difficult to shape).

MATERIALS

- *Oasis (floral foam) or polystyrene*
- *Green florist's wire*
- *Card*
- *Jelutong ¹/₄in x 1¹/₂in (for base)*
- *Double-sided adhesive tape*
- *Tea bag*
- *Sawdust*

Cut the Oasis or polystyrene to shape and size and, depending on whether the hedge style is formal or not, round off the corners. Many hedges are uneven at the top, unless they have just been cut, and leaving yours slightly unfinished will add to its realism.

If the base of the hedge will be hidden, pin on a card base and strengthen the joint with a little PVA glue. The amount of stems that should be left showing will vary from hedge to hedge but about ¹/₂in will generally suffice. To make the stems cut green florist's wire into two 2in lengths and two 3in lengths and twist them together using a

pair of pliers for about the first inch. Fan out the remainder of the wires bending the ends upward and insert into the bottom of the hedge after painting. Add further stems as often as necessary, according to the length of hedge.

Prepare a suitable length of wooden base from $\frac{1}{4}$in x $1\frac{1}{2}$in jelutong and bevel off all the edges so that the base resembles a very slight mound. Lay the hedge against this length-wise, marking where the stems will be positioned, and drill a series of holes about $\frac{1}{8}$in in diameter to take them. Turn the base over and cover with double-sided adhesive tape.

Paint the entire surface of the hedge and the top surface of the base with a medium brown acrylic, ensuring that all the crevices are covered and no base colour shows through. Spray the surface of the wooden base with display mount adhesive and cover liberally with the contents of a tea bag. Card bases can be left unfinished.

Spray the hedge with display mount adhesive and cover with loose sawdust. Repeat this until it is completely covered and remove any surplus by brushing or shaking. Finally, paint with a suitable green acrylic paint or spray, adding odd spots of darker and lighter greens for realism.

Further instructions on making simple hedges are also given in the Formal Georgian Garden on page 79 and the Knot Garden below.

TOPIARY

Topiary, the clipping of trees and hedges into imitative and imaginative shapes, is created by carving and shaping blocks of Oasis (floral foam) or polystyrene packaging. To create complex shapes, assemble the pieces together using fine wire or cocktail sticks and then spray the surfaces with artist's display mount adhesive and sprinkle with scenic foam or tea leaves. Mount topiary on top of hedges or in decorative containers for best effect (see the Formal Georgian Garden).

This informal hedge in a country garden forms part of the garden boundary and is softened further by casual planting

KNOT GARDEN

Knot gardens were popular in Elizabethan times, reflecting their love of symmetry and pattern and in some ways representing the addition of another room to a grand house. They were made of low clipped shrubs or herbs, of different hues, worked into interlacing threads with the spaces in between filled with sand or gravel. A book published in 1613 contains the line 'it shall appear like a knot made of divers coloured ribbons. . .'.

The knot garden shown on page 47 has been added to the Formal Georgian Garden and uses some of its low hedges – an example of how you can adapt a design from this book and make it your own. Although the knots appear to be made up from several pieces, they are in fact one piece, made from $\frac{1}{2}$in thick fine-grained polystyrene: the effect of 'cross-overs' is created by slightly carving the profiles.

MATERIALS

- *Polystyrene $\frac{1}{2}$in thick x 12in x 9in*
- *Carbon paper*
- *Dark and light green scenic powder*
- *Stiff card*
- *Coarse glass paper*

TIP

Polystyrene may be dissolved by some spirit glues and spray paints. Always use a test piece before proceeding and use in conjunction with a protective mask. Never use sprays near naked flames.

Trace off the knot pattern from fig 10 and use a photocopier to enlarge it to the size you wish. Lay your finished pattern onto the sheet of styrene and use a piece of carbon paper under the pattern to carefully transfer the design.

Use an X-Acto No.15, or similar, keyhole saw blade to carefully remove all the waste materials and trim up with a very sharp craft knife. You will notice from the drawing that the middle part of the knot (B) is diamond shaped and that parts of this appear to go under the outer pattern (A), whilst others go over. Mark all the cross-over points with a fine felt-tipped pen and use a scalpel or sharp craft knife to pare off a fine strip about 1/8in wide x 1/16in deep from those sections that go under, leaving the uppermost piece standing proud. Use the scalpel to round off the edges of the strips so that they do not appear too square. Finish off all the sections by gently rounding off the inner and outer edges with a scalpel or some fine abrasive paper.

Transfer the design and cut two semicircular pieces from the 1/2in thick polystyrene to match parts (C) on the plan and round off the outer edges as for the main pattern. The centre section is made up from a block of polystyrene or Oasis (floral foam), carved and shaped into a half ball shape 2 1/2in high.

Lay all the parts onto a sheet of newspaper and paint with green emulsion paint to seal the surface and to give a dark background to the finishing coat. In order to differentiate between the two parts of the pattern, sections A and C are covered with a lighter coloured green scenic powder than B and D. Spray all the surfaces with artist's display mount adhesive and apply the lighter scenic powder first, carefully shielding or masking section B. When this is complete sprinkle the darker powder over

---

TIP

If you cannot obtain a large piece of polystyrene for the centre section, glue several layers together until the correct height is reached.

Fig 10 The topiary design for the knot garden

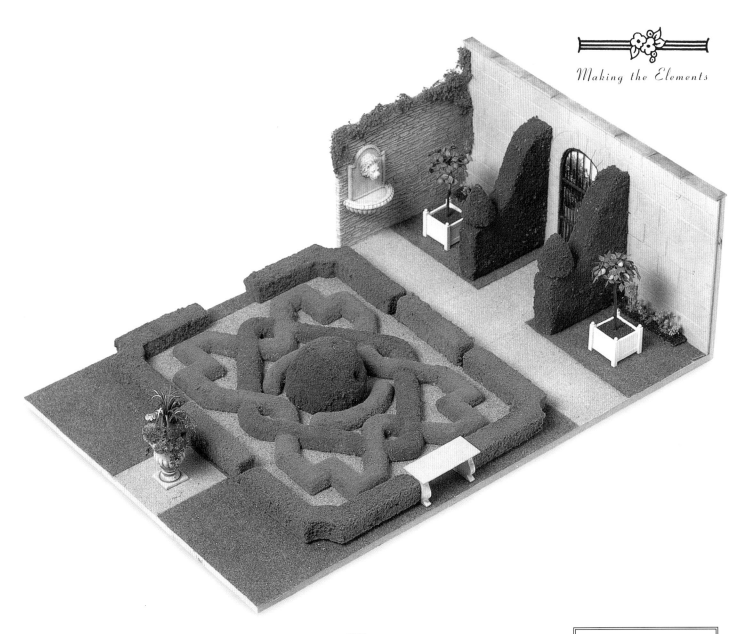

section B and the centre bush, D. Finish off all the covered surfaces with spray mount adhesive to seal in the powder.

The areas between and around a knot garden are usually dead or inert ground. We have used gravel but you could imitate chipped bark, coal-dust or sand if you wished. Cut a piece of stiff art card or 2mm MDF 13½in x 10½in and cover with coarse grade glass paper of suitable colour to mimic gravel. Alternatively use spray paint of the correct colour over the surface and allow to dry. Glue the finished knot garden onto the gravel sheet and assemble the centrepieces into place. Position the knot garden into the centre of the Formal Georgian Garden project or create your own garden surroundings for it.

WATER FEATURES

Water lends a special dimension to a garden and a small water feature will enhance any garden design. The size and shape of the water feature will depend to a large extent on its surroundings and it will have to be incorporated into the design at an early stage (see Principles of Garden Design).

Still water, such as you might find in pools and ponds, is usually quite shallow and will have a level surface. Plants tend to grow upwards to the light and tall ones may reach out of the water and lay on the surface. Plants are usually grown in containers on the bottom of the pool. Formal pools are often geometric in shape and edged with hard bricks or paving slabs. Ponds are

47

generally round with softer, less defined edges of grass or earth and plants tend to be rooted into the bottom.

Streams flow to the lowest point possible and most plants bend in the direction of the flow. The faster the speed of the water the more they bend, although strong rushes may stand straight up above the surface.

The two principal methods for making an artificial water feature, moving or still, are given below. Using real water is not recommended as it is difficult to maintain and tends to attract dust and dirt, however if you want to use one of the working miniature fountains then real water will have to be used.

STILL POOL

A still pool is an elegant addition to a garden. The one described below is for a $1/2$in deep, flat-bottomed pool in $1/12$th scale.

MATERIALS

- *Stiff card*
- *Jelutong $1/8$in thick x $1/2$in*
- *Jelutong $1/8$in x $1/8$in*
- *Perspex (plexiglass) or acrylic sheet $1/6$in thick*
- *Plaster filler*
- *Sand*

Pools look best when they lie flush with the surrounding garden, and to achieve this the height of all the other features must be raised. Begin by transferring the shape of your pool to a stiff card base and cut out using a sharp craft knife and a steel rule. Cut four pieces of $1/8$in x $1/2$in jelutong as edge boards and glue these around the base. If you want the bottom of your pool to shelve at one end, glue a $1/8$in x $1/8$in jelutong former on the inside of one edge board and bend up the card to rest on it.

Cut and fix $1/8$in x $1/8$in jelutong formers around the inner edges to support the Perspex (plexiglass) or acrylic sheet about $1/8$in from the top.

Take a piece of card and cut a template

for the Perspex so that it will rest on these formers. Transfer the pattern onto the protective paper layer of the Perspex and cut out. Drill $1/16$in-diameter holes through the Perspex for any tall reed plants appearing above the surface of the water. If you intend to use clear casting resin to simulate the water, discard the use of the formers and the Perspex (see page 49 for using resin). To simulate a slightly murky appearance, apply a little colour wash to the underside of the Perspex and set to one side.

Mix up plaster filler and apply to the corners, around the edges and over the base to give a natural and slightly uneven appearance. Apply PVA glue to the inner surface of the base and cover with a thin layer of sand. Finish off by painting the bottom and sides of the pool with acrylics in a mixture of light browns and dark greens, adding plants when this is dry.

POND

A pond is a more natural looking feature than a pool and it is best to plan it so that it lies below the surrounding earth so you can disguise the hard edges.

MATERIALS

- *Lengths of jelutong $1/8$in x $1/8$in and $1/8$in x $1/2$in*
- *Perspex (plexiglass) sheet $1/16$in thick*
- *Plaster filler*
- *Thick card (200gsm)*
- *Fine sand or gravel*
- *Mod-Roc plaster bandage or Celluclay*

Prepare the base and edge boards in exactly the same way as if you were building a flat-bottomed pool, adding in the formers to take the Perspex (plexiglass). Add lots of filler around the edges in order to create a shelving effect towards the centre and when this is dry coat with PVA glue and fine sand. Allow the base covering to dry and paint with a mixture of dark brown and green acrylics.

TIP

Be aware that complicated shapes in Perspex are difficult to cut out with a craft knife as the plastic may shatter.

TIP

When using Perspex or acetate for water features, disguise the edges by spreading a thin layer of PVA glue $1/8$in wide and scatter on sand or earth for authentic stream banks, or use brick or paving for pools.

Fix the pond to the base of the garden and add Mod-Roc (or Celluclay) and filler around the edges allowing some to overflow into the pond. Smooth off until the edges look natural and finish with earth or grass. Add plants, rocks and ornaments as desired.

STREAM

Although a stream in a miniature garden will more often than not be on the level a slight drop of even a ¼in will look more natural and this can be achieved by placing a wedge at one end of the base before fixing. The surrounding earth will need to be built up with Mod-Roc plaster bandage and filler once the base is fixed into place.

Make up the base as for the still pool on page 48 but alter the shape so that the stream is long and narrow. Add a few small rocks into the centre of the stream bed before painting.

FILLING AND FINISHING

Realistic looking 'water' and a well-placed selection of aquatic plants will make all the difference to your water feature.

Using Perspex for water

Perspex (plexiglass) is an ideal material to mimic water, usually being supported on formers glued around the edges of the water feature. Once cut to the correct shape (use a template if necessary) it can be placed or glued onto the formers. Drill ¹⁄₁₆in-diameter holes through the surface to take any long-stemmed plants that will be anchored through this into the base. Finish off by inserting reeds and gluing on any surface flowers such as water lilies.

Placing rocks onto the bottom that break through the surface of the Perspex will need some careful cutting of your plastic sheet and this is best achieved by making a template first. Finally glue on the border paving or grasses around the edges.

Using clear resin for water

Resin is best poured in several thin layers rather than one thick one and this process will allow you to place plants and objects into the 'water' as the layers are built up. It also helps to give the water a deep rather than a surface sheen as colouring can be added to layers as you progress.

After preparing the base as described above, put in place the first of the plants and bend over as many of them as required to indicate flow. Mix the clear resin with the catalyst according to the manufacturer's instructions and pour in the first layer. Ensure that any plants, rocks or ornaments are in their correct position before the resin sets. Continue to add plants and resin until you have built up the surface to the correct level, keeping the face of any rocks that appear above the surface of the water clear of the resin. Drill small holes in the set resin to take any plants sitting on the surface and glue these into place.

Water plants

Plants for a water feature are of three main types – those growing in and below the surface of the water, those growing above and on the water and marginal plants happy growing at the side in moist soil. You will need to drill pilot holes through the base filler to take the stems of plants that will remain below the surface and glue them into place. Where you are trying to create the impression of a flow of water, plants will need to be bent over in the direction of flow, facing the same way.

> **TIP**
> *Shaping the tops of the stream's edging boards will help to create a more natural surface once the filler has been built up.*

Aquatic and marginal plants will bring a water feature to life, blending it in with the other flower beds. Try reeds and irises around the edges, water lilies on the surface and oxygenating plants in the water

The feature pond and seat

FEATURE POND WITH SEAT

This small, moveable feature may be sited within any suitable garden design.

MATERIALS

- *Bricks strips in stretcher bond, 120in*
- *6mm MDF 2in x 5^1/$_4$in for back wall*
- *2mm MDF ^{7}/$_{16}$in wide x 20in for coping stones*
- *Perspex (plexiglass) or acetate sheet, ^{1}/$_{16}$in thick x 5^1/$_4$in x 3in*
- *Stiff card 5^1/$_4$in x 3in for base*
- *Jelutong, four off ^{1}/$_4$in x ^{1}/$_{16}$in x 2^1/$_4$in long, and two off ^{1}/$_8$in x ^{1}/$_{16}$in x 1in*
- *Jelutong formers, ^{1}/$_8$in square offcuts*

Build up the right-hand side wall first remembering that it will interlock with the one at the front (see fig 11 right and Tip box, left). Start by laying down a row of four whole bricks onto a flat surface. Add the second row, this time with a half brick to the rear and a whole one to the front (which should overlap the brick below by half a brick). Repeat this until you have laid eight courses, finishing with a whole brick at the front. The height of this wall should be 2in and it should appear even at the back and 'toothed' at the front. Repeat this process for the left-hand wall, in reverse. Use a PVA wood adhesive to glue these two walls at right angles to the piece of 6mm MDF which forms the back.

Build up the right-hand front wall, starting with two whole bricks and interlocking with the side. The second row must be 2^1/$_2$ bricks, and so on until eight courses have been assembled (see fig 11a). Repeat for the left front keeping both walls at right angles to the sides.

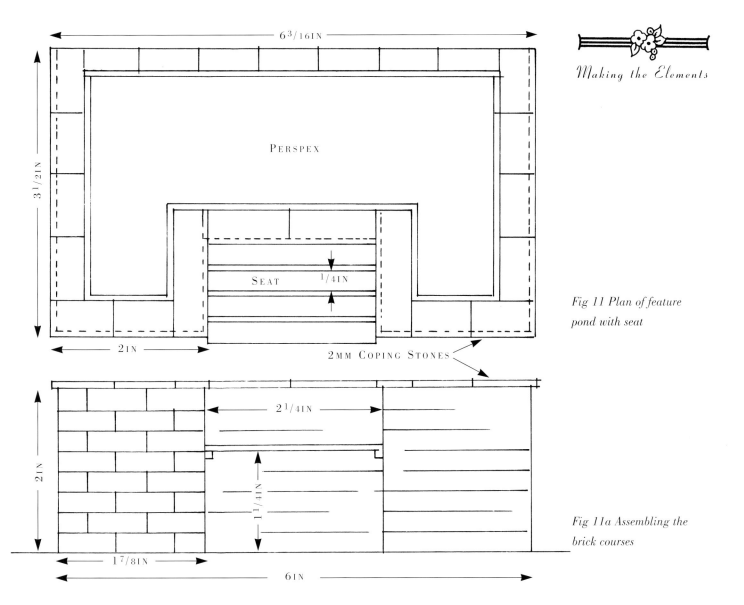

*Fig 11 Plan of feature
pond with seat*

*Fig 11a Assembling the
brick courses*

The two inner walls may now be assembled in the same fashion: two whole bricks in length on the first course; a half, a whole and a half brick on the second course. Whilst there is no need to finish the back ends of these walls with interlocking bricks you might like to do it.

To build up the centre section, proceed as before if interlocking, if not build up eight rows commencing with three bricks, followed by two and two halves and so on.

Paint the walls (and joints) by mixing some sand and mortar-coloured acrylic paint together. Leave to dry and then mix up a suitable red brick colour paint and finish off the bricks making sure that none of this colour reaches the mortar joints. Darken a little of this colour and add to some bricks to break up the surface colour.

When dry, turn the assembly over and trace the shape of the inside onto a piece of card to use as a base and as a template for the Perspex (plexiglass) 'water'.

Glue ¹/₈in x ¹/₈in jelutong offcuts around the inside of the walls as formers, ³/₈in from the top onto which the Perspex (plexiglass) will sit. Repeat with another set of formers ³/₄in from the bottom, on which the base will be glued (see fig 11b). Turn the assembly over and paint the inner surfaces of all the walls with a dark green acrylic paint, mixed with a little light green or yellow.

Cut two pieces of ¹/₈in x ¹/₁₆in jelutong for the seat formers and glue into place 1in above the bottom, making sure they are level. Cut four strips of ¹/₄in x ¹/₁₆in jelutong, each 2¹/₄in long and glue onto the formers leaving a ¹/₃₂in gap between each strip.

TIP

*Don't forget when
cutting wooden brick
sections to leave the
mortar joint attached to
the brick, that way it
will look natural when
interlocking takes place.*

*A formal pool makes an
elegant water feature*

*Fig 11b Formers supporting
the Perspex and base*

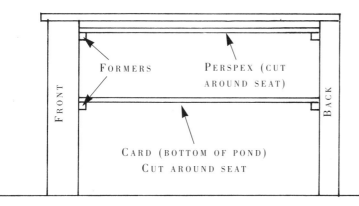

FORMERS

PERSPEX (CUT
AROUND SEAT)

FRONT

BACK

CARD (BOTTOM OF POND)
CUT AROUND SEAT

Using acrylic paints, paint the card base a dark muddy green colour and add a few streaks of brown or yellow. When this is dry glue on some lichen, foliage and a goldfish or two. Turn the assembly over and glue the base into place on the formers.

Using the card base as a template mark out the piece of Perspex (plexiglass) and cut out the 'C' shape of the pond using a sharp razor saw. Drop the Perspex 'water' into place and glue on water lilies to finish off.

For the coping stones, cut lengths of the $7/16$in wide 2mm MDF, cutting V-shaped grooves for joints at $1^3/8$in intervals. Paint the surfaces with a mixture of grey and brown acrylic paints, emphasising the joints with a little brown. Assemble the coping stones around all the walls and the back, overlapping at the outer edges, and gluing into place (see fig 11).

FORMAL POOL

This elegant, symmetrical water feature (see above) is suitable for the centre of a large garden and is based on a simple rectangle.

- *9mm MDF, two off 8in x 1^1/$_8$in (framework plinths) and two off 7^3/$_4$in x ^{3}/$_4$in (framework sides)*
- *6mm MDF 10in x 8in (top) and 4in x 1in square blocks (supports)*
- *2mm MDF 10in x 8in (base)*
- *2mm MDF (edging) ^{1}/$_2$in wide x 10in, eight off ^{11}/$_{16}$in square and semicircular ends cut from two pieces 2in x 5^1/$_2$in*
- *Perspex (plexiglass) or acetate 5^1/$_2$in x 7^3/$_4$in*
- *Grass sheet 10in x 8in*

Begin by finding the centre of the top piece of 6mm MDF and mark with a pencil. From this point measure off a rectangle across the width, 5in x 4in. Draw a line down the centre of the board, mark at 1^1/$_2$in outside the long sides of the rectangle and use a compass to draw a semicircle with a 1^1/$_4$in radius that touches the two marks (see fig 12). Drill a ^{1}/$_{16}$in-diameter hole inside the shape of the pond and use a fretsaw to remove the waste. Clean up the edges as necessary using fine abrasive paper.

Use a PVA adhesive to glue the four plinths to the underside of the top. Clamp the assembly and allow the adhesive to set. Once set, paint the inner edges of the pond with a dark green acrylic paint.

Lay the sheet of grass face down onto a flat working surface and place the pond assembly face down on top. Use a felt-tip pen to draw around the shape of the pond, remove the top and use a straight edge to enlarge this shape by ^{1}/$_8$in. Use a scalpel and a steel rule to accurately cut out the shape. Spread PVA glue or artist's display mount spray adhesive over the top and carefully lay on the grass sheet, checking that it lays properly around the pond. Allow to dry before trimming off any waste.

Turn the finished top over, face down, and lay the Perspex (plexiglass) sheet into position. When it is square lock this into position by gluing in four 6mm thick x 1in square

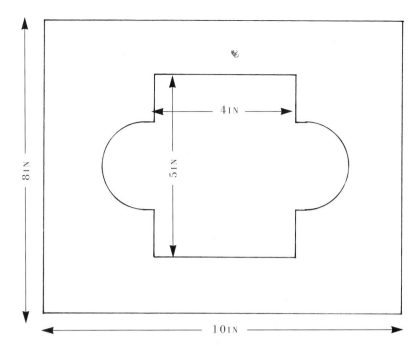

Fig 12 Basic shape of the formal pool

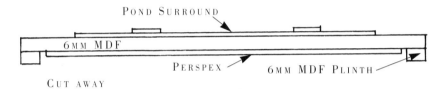

Fig 12a Positioning the Perspex

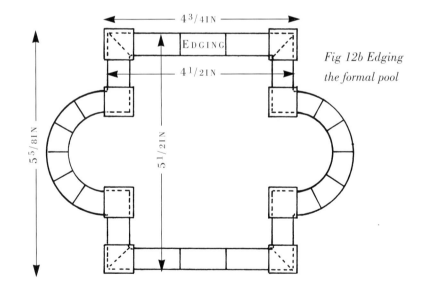

Fig 12b Edging the formal pool

blocks at the corners of the rectangle.

The pond edging is made up from small strips of ^{1}/$_2$in wide 2mm thick MDF that is incised with razor saw cuts to resemble separate stones, with the addition of eight 1^1/$_{16}$in squares that cover the joints and add decoration (see fig 12b). When assembled, the overall shape mimics the shape of the

---

TIP

Before attaching the Perspex (plexiglass) use the top as a template to produce the rounded ends to the surround in 2mm MDF.

pond but is slightly smaller, so giving an overhang. Use the top as a template for the rounded ends and then reduce the radius of the shape by 1/8in, keeping the width at 1/2in. There a number of ways to produce the shape and we suggest that you make them from straight pieces where possible, checking the shape until it overlaps the pond by 1/8in all round. Glue together and add the blocks to cover any joints after first cutting the joints.

Paint the whole assembly with a medium grey acrylic paint. The MDF base is painted with a muddy dark green and when this is dry glue on some lichens or other plants. A few goldfish will add character (ours were made from polymer clay). Use a PVA adhesive to glue the top assembly onto the base and clamp until set.

WATER SCENE

This scene (shown on page 55) could be a small stand-alone project or part of a larger garden.

MATERIALS

- *From 6mm MDF cut:*
  base 9in x 7³/4in
  back 9¹/2in x 3in
  side, two off 8in x 3in
  front 1in x 9in
  former A 7³/4in x ³/4in
  former B 7³/4in x ³/4in
  former C 6¹/2in x ³/4in

- *From 2mm MDF cut:*
  right bank 2¹/4in x 8in
  left bank 2in x 8in
  bed 9¹/2in x 7³/4in
  edge strip 6mm wide x 9in

- *Perspex (plexiglass) 8in x 6in*
- *Rocks, pebbles, sand*
- *Fibre-glass sheet for walling*
- *Mod-Roc plaster bandage*
- *Polystyrene blocks or packaging*
- *Artificial grass or tea leaves*
- *Plaster filler*

Start by gluing and pinning the back wall against the base and then add the two side walls and the low front to complete the basic assembly as an open box. Trim the former heights to match the inside of the front wall.

Glue former A against the right-hand wall running from front to back, inside the garden. Add a second former B, 1³/4in away from the first. Glue former C against the left-hand wall as support for the banks.

Lay the 2mm MDF piece (9¹/2in x 7³/4in) onto a flat surface and use a sharp craft knife with a steel rule to score a line 2³/4in from the right-hand edge about halfway through the sheet, leaving 6³/4in to form the sloping bed. Lay the short end of the bed onto the two formers and gently press down so that the cut opens up to form the slope (see fig 13). Glue into place, using panel pins if necessary. Glue the 6mm wide edge

TIP

An offcut of walling can be used to cover the front wall of the water scene when everything else is finished.

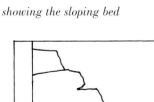

Fig 13 Plan of the water scene showing the sloping bed

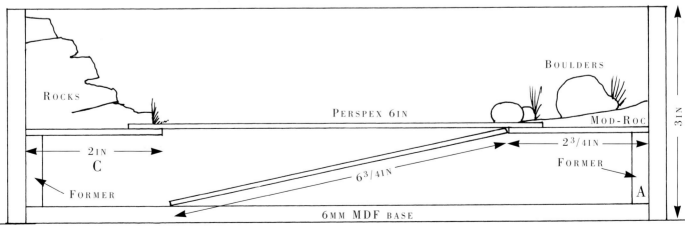

strip onto the front wall to bring the height up to match the bed and then glue on the 2¼in wide bank on the right and the 2in bank on the left.

Measure off the fibre-glass rough stone walling sheet to fit all the inside walls (approximately 1¾in) and apply using artist's display mount spray adhesive or PVA modelling glue.

Paint down the slope of the water bed using a dark green acrylic, adding brown and a little yellow to give a mottled appearance. Spread PVA glue or rubber cement adhesive (Copydex) over the top edge of the slope, about 1in will do, in a random pattern and sprinkle a little fine sand over it. Let this dry and add more if required before gluing on any lichen, plants and fish to finish off the bed.

Glue the Perspex (plexiglass) top into place so that it butts against the bank and add more glue and sand where the edge of the Perspex meets the bank, the front and the back walls, as this will disguise any joins.

The banks

Build up the right-hand bank by tearing up small pieces of damp tissue, fixing them into place with masking tape. Add dampened Mod-Roc plaster bandage to give an uneven appearance. Before the plaster is dry press into place one or two large stones, gluing these into place once the surface is dry. Finish off by covering the bank with PVA glue and sprinkling the surface with artificial grass or tea leaves, shielding the wall covering and any fixed stones. Add a few smaller stones in a random pattern to complete this part of the scene.

Build up the left-hand bank with rocks cut from polystyrene packaging material, over which has been spread damp plaster filler, such as Polyfilla. For the best effect start the bottom section about 2½in wide and gradually reduce the width of the blocks as they get nearer the wall. Paint these with a mixture of grey and brown acrylics with a little black added. Glue on small pieces of dried lichen around the area and your water scene is complete.

You could make a simple water scene such as this as a stand-alone project or include the scheme as part of a larger garden design

Grass is a highly versatile garden surface which can be adapted to suit many styles of garden, such as this rough and uneven area of a country garden

TIP

Small areas of grass can be made by copying the method for making earth described below, using tea dust and spray painting it green.

A smooth, green lawn is a common feature of many period gardens and when edged with flower beds is also very typical of a contemporary scene

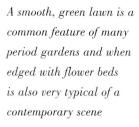

GRASS

A smooth grass lawn is a wonderful foil to lush flower beds and trees. Basically there are two materials to use – grass sheet and grass powder. They can both be obtained from specialist shops – grass sheet can be laid directly onto the garden, while grass powder is sprinkled on a layer of glue.

GRASS LAWN

Grass is best designed as a flat area but where you want to include unusual slopes and uneven areas of grass, these must first be built up by adding a base filler material and covering this with plaster and then grass. Start with torn, damp newspaper, moulding this into the shape you require and making sure that it will not move around while you work on it. Lay Mod-Roc plaster bandage over the site (alternatively you could use Celluclay), smooth it into place and allow it to harden. Sand down any rough areas before covering with a thin coat of PVA adhesive and sprinkling on an even layer of grass powder. Brush off any surplus and fill any bare patches. If you prefer, a proprietary brand of adhesive, 'Scatter Grip', is available for these materials.

EARTH BEDS AND BORDERS

Earth is visible in almost every garden – in containers, flower beds, borders and vegetable plots. It is rarely absolutely flat and often contains small plants, weeds and stones. It is rarely a constant granular size, and even in $1/12$th scale there should be differences in various parts of the garden.

For instance, the earth where large vegetables are grown could be coarse whilst that in flowers beds, regularly tilled for weeds, would be fine.

Beds and borders will vary too in type and composition according to where they are within your garden project. Generally speaking, borders define a boundary and are found along the edges of walls and fences and should be in proportion to the size of the garden. Raised borders are rarely more than one foot high (1in in $^1/_{12}$th scale) and are usually supported by a row or two of bricks. Special designs may incorporate shaped beds at ground level and a fine layer of earth would be expected here. Although raised flower beds are not common in a garden, apart from a rockery, in real life they are popular with gardeners who are disabled, and can look very attractive.

Fine earth

To create an area of very fine soil, mark out the area and cut a sheet of stiff card as a base. Coat this with PVA glue or spray with display mount adhesive, and empty the contents of one or more tea bags over the surface. Brush off any surplus and repeat if necessary.

Medium earth

To create an area of medium-grade soil, prepare the card base as above and coat the area with two layers of PVA glue or Copydex

rubber cement. Cover the surface with a suitable grade of sawdust and repeat this process until the base is covered. Spray this with an earthy brown paint and when dry stipple on a little light brown paint. Finish off with just a few specks of white paint to represent chalk and stones but be careful not to overdo this effect.

Coarse earth

To create an area of rough soil, cut a piece of Oasis (floral foam) or polystyrene board as the base and shave off the edges to produce a raised bed. Abrade the surface to roughen and spray paint a suitable colour as for the medium-grade earth effect above.

MAKING PLANTS AND PLANTERS

Plants and trees will bring your garden to life – without them it will just be a patch of ground. Specialist makers have supplied the plants shown in our projects but there is no reason why you should not make some of the simple plants and planters yourself; the materials are readily available and the making up simply requires a little time.

FINDING PLANT MATERIALS

If you plan to make the plants in your garden you will need as large a selection of materials as possible: some of the following suggestions should prove useful.

TIP

To create the appearance of vegetable beds, cut grooves in one direction along the surface of Oasis (floral foam).

TIP

Use natural materials for soil, not coffee and other types of food granules as they will absorb moisture and break down.

Vegetable beds tend to have coarser soil than flower beds, with the vegetables often 'earthed up' in neat, weed-free rows

Making the Elements

TIP

Bear in mind that, as in a full-size garden, not all the plants and flowers in a miniature garden are fresh and perfect: leaves wither and dry out according to the seasons, flowers fade. Just ensure that the seasons are not mixed and make some of your flowers and foliage a little less than perfect – it will add to the realism.

Your local craft and model shop may have a reasonable selection of trees and bushes; they should also have bags of lichen and moss. Pet shops usually keep a range of artificial plants for aquariums, which, if chosen and placed with care in the garden setting, can look realistic. Florists keep a wide selection of dried flowers and you should look for those with small flowerheads. You should also be able to find dried greenery which makes good leaves and branches. Shops which sell cake decorations are also useful sources – you should be able to find a selection of artificial flowers and different coloured stamens for flower making. Get into the habit of collecting oddments, such as beads suitable for flowerheads and real twigs and sticks for branches.

Trees are very difficult to reproduce in $1/12$th scale – even a small example will be over a foot high and English hardwoods might need to be three or four feet to still be in scale. We have not attempted to make any therefore, but there are specialists making trees for small gardens, you should be able to find them at dolls' house fairs.

LEAVES

A glance into any plant book will provide you with a variety of leaf shapes to copy. One basic shape is that of the aspidistra, a very popular indoor plant for the Victorians.

MATERIALS

- *Green florist's tape*
- *Green-covered florist's wire*
- *Spray varnish*
- *Paper punch*
- *Fine thread*

Transfer the leaf shape you want onto a strip of florist's tape using tracing paper or a photocopier and cut two of each. Using PVA glue, place a 2in piece of florist's wire down the centre of one leaf, not quite to the tip, and attach the second side, sandwiching the wire between the pieces of tape. Many leaves on real plants have vein markings and you can simulate these by gently marking the surfaces with the end of a toothpick. Using acrylics, add any colour required and allow the paint to dry.

Several leaves made in this way can be assembled together to form a plant by binding the stems together with masking tape or fine thread. Stagger leaves along the length of the stem by adding one leaf at a time onto a central stem of green-covered wire. Soak a length of fine cotton thread in white PVA glue and bind the first leaf at the top of the stem. Continue down in this fashion, adding one leaf at a time, until you have built up a sufficient length. Cut off any surplus wire and place the plant into a suitable container. Alternatively, individual stems can be put directly into a pot filled with clay. Arrange the leaves to form an attractive plant and spray with matt varnish to give a little sheen to the surfaces and body to the leaves.

Very small leaves can be made without using the centre wire stem and these can be attached with clear glue directly to the plant.

FLOWER PETALS

Various petals and flowerheads can be made simply with coloured paper and florist's wire.

MATERIALS

- *Coloured paper*
- *Green-covered florist's wire*
- *^{1}/$_8$in wooden dowel*

You can make up the fine petals found on plants such as marigolds using the small round pieces of paper produced by a paper punch. Using a bright yellow paper and a punch take ten circles for each stem. Mark the centre of each with a pencil and draw a faint circular line ^{1}/$_8$in from this. Using a scalpel make a series of cuts from this mark to the outer edge of each circle, the more cuts the finer the petals. Pierce the centre of one circle with a sharp needle and glue this onto a 1^1/$_2$in long wire stem, ^{3}/$_{16}$in from one end. Use the glue sparingly and only in the centre portion of the petal section.

Making the Elements

> **TIP**
>
> *You can use masking tape instead of florist's tape when making leaves and flowers, painting it with acrylics.*

> **TIP**
>
> *The length of wire required for a leaf's centre stem will vary according to the plant: if in doubt use too much and cut off the surplus.*

Making the Elements

When this first one is set in place add the other nine, making sure that they are tightly placed against each other. Arrange the petal sections so that the inner ones are nice and tight and the outer ones flare slightly.

Chrysanthemum and many other flowers can be made from paper strip. Cut a 2in strip of suitably coloured paper 5/32in wide and slightly coarsen one edge. Using a sharp craft knife, cut a series of 1/8in cuts 1/32in apart along the entire length. Shape each of the petals into a fine point. Cut a 1 1/2in piece of florist's wire for a stem. Roll the strip up tightly and allow it to relax. Place a line of PVA glue along the inner uncut side and form the strip into a tight roll again, this time with the wire in the centre. Gently splay the petals outwards from the centre and allow to dry.

For daffodil trumpets prepare the paper strip as above, roughen one edge and cut the petals approximately 1/8in deep. Wrap the strip around a small piece of 1/16in diameter dowel and glue as soon as it over-laps, pinching the bottom end to a point. Mount onto a 1 1/2in piece of thick florist's wire, then cut out four diamond-shaped petals from the same colour paper used for the trumpet and glue around the base of the trumpet. Repeat for each flowerhead.

Plants may also be made using polymer clays and the techniques for these are given in one or more of the specialist publications listed in the bibliography.

FLOWER TROUGH

The instructions for this small trough will allow you to make one of any size – simply increase the dimensions. It is made almost entirely from 1/32in thick jelutong that has been finished with white paint and filled with Oasis (floral foam), planted out with a selection of dried flowers and seed heads.

MATERIALS

- *From jelutong 1/32in thick cut the following:*
  base 2 5/8in x 3/4in
  back 2 15/16in x 3/4in
  front 2 15/16in x 3/4in
  front and side strips, seventeen off 1/4in x 3/4in
  top and bottom edge 1/8in x 9in
  feet, two off 1/8in x 1/8in x 7/8in

- *Oasis (floral foam)*
- *Tea bag*
- *Dried flowers*

Pots, troughs and planters come in many shapes and sizes

Lay the base onto a flat surface and glue the back, sides and front together to form a small, open box. Glue on the eleven front strips working from left to right, continuing on with three on each side. Glue on the top and bottom edge to the sides and front. Lastly glue the feet on at a 45 degree angle to the front, and glue onto the base 5/8in in from the outer edge.

Seal the surface with matt varnish and paint with a white silk finish paint. Finish off by cutting Oasis (floral foam) to fit inside. Remove and spray the top surface with a spray display mount adhesive followed by a dusting of loose tea from a tea bag, then plant out as desired.

TREE BOX OR VERSAILLES PLANTER

This neat, decorative planter is ideal for a traditional-style or formal garden. It has been made almost entirely of 2mm (1/16in) thick white plasticard sheet and styrene tubing, glued together using plastic weld adhesive.

MATERIALS

- White plasticard sheet 1mm and 2mm thick
- Styrene tubing 3/16in diameter, 6in approximately
- Plastic weld adhesive
- Four glass-headed dressmaking pins
- Oasis (floral foam) 1 1/4in x 1in
- Tea bag

Cut the base 1 1/4in square, followed by four sides each 1 1/4in long x 1in high. Use a sharp razor saw to cut four vertical grooves on the face of each of the sides and glue these onto the base (they should not meet at the corners).

Cut four legs from 3/16in square tubing each 1 1/4in long and fill these with offcuts of 1/8in square wood. If these are not a good fit glue the infills in with a little clear adhesive. Glue the legs onto the box, joining each side, with a 1/8in gap at the bottom and the top. Cut eight strips of plasticard 1mm x 3/16in wide x 1 1/4in and glue these

Some plants, particularly standards, are ideal for pots, and Versailles planters bring a touch of elegance to many plants

along the top and bottom of each side piece.

Insert four glass-headed dressmaking pins into the top of the wooden core of each leg and paint them white to match the plasticard. Cut a piece of Oasis (floral foam) 1¼in square x 1in deep for the inside of the planter. Spray with artist's display mount adhesive and sprinkle on loose tea from a tea bag. Plant up with a short, decorative tree or bush.

Other planters

There are many other types of planter that miniaturists can make – some looking like cast metal and some made of wood.

A neat planter can be made up from a miniature porcelain sink, however it can look a little pristine for the garden without some adaptation. Paint the surface with an acrylic or PVA glue to give a key and on top of this spread a thin layer of plaster filler

mixed with water and 10 percent PVA glue. Allow this to dry thoroughly and create a weathered effect with grey and brown acrylic paint. Cut a piece of Oasis (floral foam) to fit inside the sink, spray with display mount adhesive and cover with loose tea. Insert the foam and plant up as required.

Small turned tubs can be purchased from a number of specialist suppliers and these too can make attractive planters in the same way as the sinks. Alternatively you could turn the tub into a mini pond by painting the inside a dull green and adding a little lichen. Cut a round piece of Perspex (plexiglass) to represent water and glue this about ¼in below the top of the tub.

You should be able to find many planters to choose from, either hand-made or commercially produced, in a wide range of styles, sizes and colours to enhance any garden design

GARDEN FURNITURE AND ACCESSORIES

You will see that the gardens in this book owe much of their authenticity and period detail to the furniture, tools and accessories used within them. Seats, planters and objects for wildlife such as beehives and bird tables, bring a garden to life, and although there are many items available commercially (see Suppliers for the accessories used in the main Gardens page 173), a range of useful objects are described here for you to make yourself.

Making the Elements

Seating is not only functional but adds character to a garden. Instructions follow for making this bench seat, deck chair and picnic seat cum table

63

DECK-CHAIR

Although traditionally thought of as beach furniture the deck-chair is to be found in most gardens, although it may have been locked away in the shed in favour of something more modern.

- *Lengths of jelutong ³/₃₂in x ³/₁₆in:*
  frame A, two off 2in x 1³/₄in;
  frame B, two off 2in x 4¹/₈in
  and frame C, two off 2in x 3¹/₄in
- *¹/₁₆in diameter dowel x 2¹/₈in plus ¹/₄in*
  for hinges (or use fine wire)
- *Fine, striped fabric 5in x 1¹/₂in*

The framework of our deck-chair is made from ³/₃₂in x ³/₁₆in jelutong to which are added ¹/₁₆in diameter dowels for the adjustable back rests. Fine wire is used for the hinging but ¹/₁₆in dowel could be used for a more professional finish.

Cut the six pieces of the frame (a pair each of A, B and C) following the diagrams in figs 14, 14a and 14b. Use fine abrasive paper and a sanding block to gently round off all the corners. Place the two frames for part C together with the ³/₃₂in side uppermost and mark off the positions of the three rest slots at ¹/₄in intervals. Cut out a small V-shaped slot above each of the marks and using a ¹/₁₆in-diameter file gently round them off. Drill through a suitable size hole for the fine wire or dowelling hinges by laying each pair of frames exactly together, to ensure that they line up after assembly.

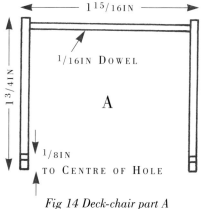

Fig 14 Deck-chair part A

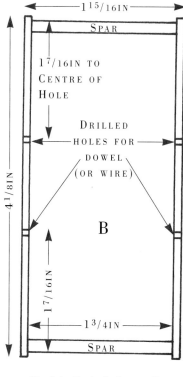

Fig 14a Deck-chair part B

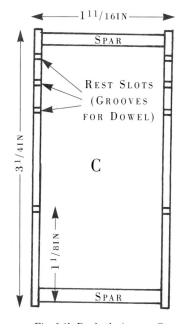

Fig 14b Deck-chair part C

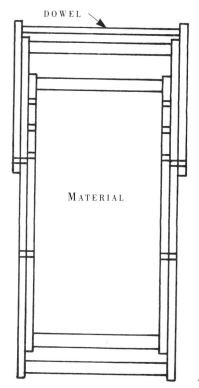

Fig 14c Complete framework
of deck-chair

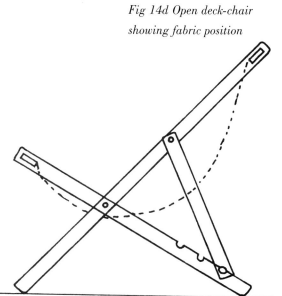

Fig 14d Open deck-chair
showing fabric position

Cut the four end spars and glue them into each of two larger frames 3/32in from the ends, checking carefully that they lie in line with the frame and that everything is square.

The striped fabric needs to be fine or it will not drop under its own weight to give that pleasing hammock appearance. Cut a piece 5in long x 1½in wide and glue this around the top and bottom spars of the main frame B (see fig 14a). To finish, hinge frame C inside and frame A outside of the main frame as shown in fig 14c and open out as shown in fig 14d.

PICNIC SEAT AND TABLE

This modern style combined family picnic seat and table that can be left out in all weathers is made entirely of 1/16in thick x 5/16in wide jelutong, stained a light mahogany colour before assembly.

MATERIALS

- *Jelutong 1/16in thick x 5/16in x 60in approximately*
- *Light mahogany wood stain*

Cut six 3½in lengths of jelutong for the table-top, and two supports 2¼in long (see fig 15). Cut the ends of the supports at about 30 degrees as shown in fig 15a. Lay the top pieces face down onto a flat surface, with an end stop if possible to line up the ends 3/32in apart. Glue on the supports 1/8in from the outer edges and leave the adhesive to set.

Cut four legs, each 2½in long and cut the tops and bottoms at an angle to give an outer splay of approximately 2½in at the base when assembled (see fig 15a). Next, cut two long sides 4¼in long and trim the ends to 30 degrees. Glue these sides to the legs 1in above the bottom and check that each side is absolutely level. Cut four seat slats 3½in long (two for each side of the table) and glue to the ends of the long sides, leaving a 3/32in gap between each.

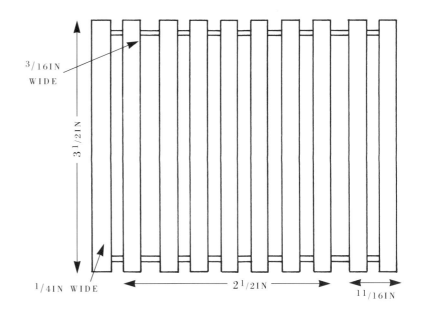

Fig 15 Overview of the picnic seat and table supports

Fig 15a Picnic seat and table assembly

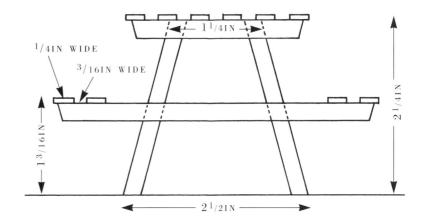

65

BENCH SEAT

This simple seat is made from ¹/₁₆in thick jelutong wood with a ¹/₄in x ¹/₈in support bar. It is recommended that all parts are colour stained with a dark oak wood stain before assembly. See photograph page 63.

MATERIALS

- *Cut the following pieces of jelutong:*
sides, two off, ¹/₁₆in thick x 3in x 2in
back ¹/₁₆in thick x 4³/₈in x ⁵/₈in
back ¹/₁₆in thick x 4¹/₂in x ⁵/₁₆in
seat, two off, ¹/₁₆in thick x 4³/₈in x ⁵/₈in
support ¹/₈in thick x ¹/₄in x 3³/₈in
- *Dark oak wood stain*

Draw out the shape of the two sides onto a piece of paper and use this as a template to transfer the design to the wood (see fig 16). It is a good idea to cut both sides together, thus any slight variances will be on both and are unlikely to be detected. Keep them together and cut the slot for the support bar. Assemble as shown in fig 16 with the sides vertical and 3in apart.

Cut two seat planks ⁵/₈in wide x 4³/₈in long and glue them onto the sides with a ¹/₁₆in gap between (see fig 16a). Cut and shape the two back pieces and glue onto the sides again with a ¹/₁₆in gap.

GARDEN CHAIR

This neat little chair is made up from two assemblies that are simply slotted one into the other. Made entirely from jelutong it can be stained, painted or left with a natural finish.

MATERIALS

- *Cut out the following pieces of jelutong:*
seat piece, two off, ³/₃₂in thick x 1in x 2¹/₂in
back piece, two off, ³/₃₂in thick x
1in x 3³/₈in
slats ¹/₃₂in thick x ³/₁₆in wide x 24in
- *Tracing and carbon paper*

Using tracing or carbon paper, transfer the two 'boomerang' shapes from figs 17 and 17c onto the pieces of ³/₃₂in thick jelutong wood. Use a fretsaw to cut out the pieces and smooth off any rough edges, rounding off the ends with fine grade abrasive paper.

Prepare a 24in strip of ³/₁₆in wide x ¹/₃₂in jelutong wood and cut thirteen lengths exactly 1³/₄in each. Make up a 1⁹/₃₂in wide template from an offcut of 4mm MDF, or similar, to maintain the correct distance to keep the back rest sides apart (see fig 17a). Keep the sides attached to the template with a rubber band around the lower halves and glue on the first six slats with a ³/₃₂in gap between each. Add the last slat that

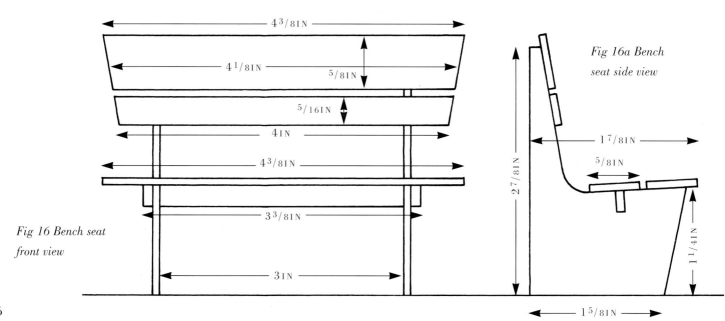

Fig 16 Bench seat front view

Fig 16a Bench seat side view

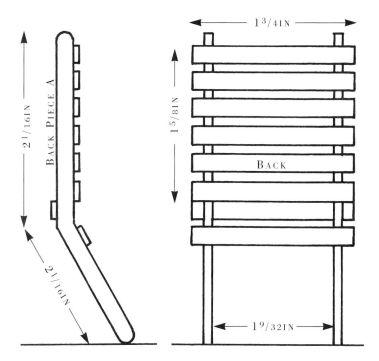

Fig 17 Side of garden chair   *Fig 17a Positioning the back rests*

supports the seat and leave to set. Remove the assembly from the template and add the final back slat as shown in fig 17.

Make a second template 1¹/₁₆in wide and make up the seat in the same way as for the backrest (see figs 17b and 17c). When the adhesive has set on both assemblies thread the seat through the backrest as shown in fig 17d.

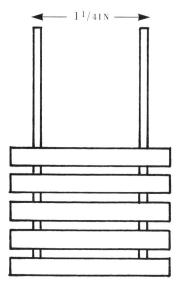

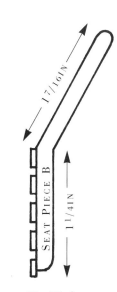

Fig 17b Slats in position for the seat   *Fig 17c Seat*

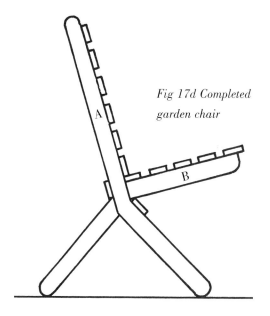

Fig 17d Completed garden chair

TIP

Be careful not let your fingers touch the plastic weld adhesive and the plastic sheet.

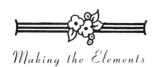

DOVECOTE

The wall-mounted dovecote shown on page 69 has been made up using that very versatile material, white plasticard sheet. 1mm thickness is used for all parts except the back and the two bottom support brackets where 2mm (1/16in) is used. You could make the dovecote in wood if you prefer, just change the adhesive and paint finish.

MATERIALS

- *1mm and 2mm white plasticard sheet*
- *Plastic weld adhesive*
- *Grey acrylic paint*
- *Fine, grey abrasive paper*

Cut out all the parts following the diagrams in figs 18 and 18a, making sure that the corners are at right angles and the edges are flat and square. Use a sharp craft knife or scalpel to carefully locate and carve the curved entrances in the top and bottom of the front. Follow the drawing of the sides and shape the top edges of the front and back to produce a suitable slope for the roof. This angle must then be reproduced onto the back edge of the roof to allow the finished assembly to lay flush against a wall.

Place the back onto a flat surface and use plastic weld adhesive to glue on one side wall. Support this and add the centre floor, followed by the second side. Finish off by adding the base. This is a good time to paint the interior with a grey acrylic paint.

Glue on the front and the ledge, followed by the roof and finish by adding the two brackets. Lightly roughen all the surfaces with a fine abrasive paper and use grey acrylic paint as a thin wash all over. Glue a very thin piece of fine, grey abrasive paper to the roof allowing about 1/16in as an overhang at the front.

BEEHIVE

What could be more natural in a country garden than a beehive, a source of food and fascination? The simple beehive on page 69 has been made up using 2mm white plasticard, glued together using plastic weld liquid adhesive.

Each side and front piece has to be trimmed at an angle and in order to keep these angles constant we suggest you draw out the shape onto a piece of stiff card and use this as a template. Use a sharp razor saw to cut the pieces, as a knife will almost certainly give problems when attempting straight lines on this thickness of material. If you do not have a saw we recommend that you score both sides of the plasticard and snap off the part required, trimming up the ragged edge as you go.

MATERIALS

- *1/16in thick white plasticard sheet*
- *Plastic weld adhesive*
- *Stiff card*
- *Short length of plastic tubing 1/8in square*
- *Fine grey glass paper*

For the sides, cut ten pieces (five for each side), 2in x 1 3/4in (see figs 19 and 19a). Trim each of these, at one end only, at an

 Fig 18 Front view of dovecote

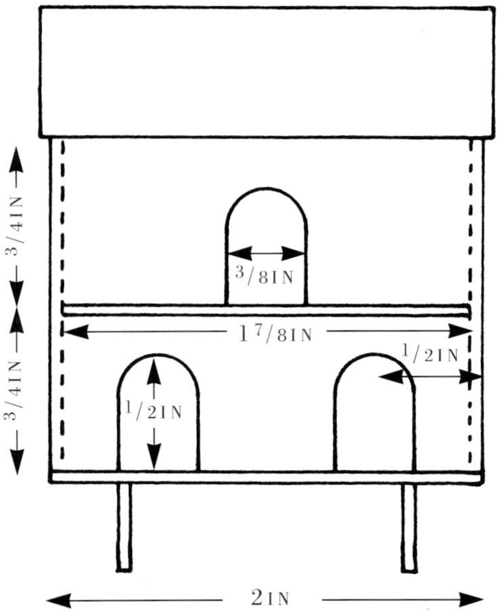

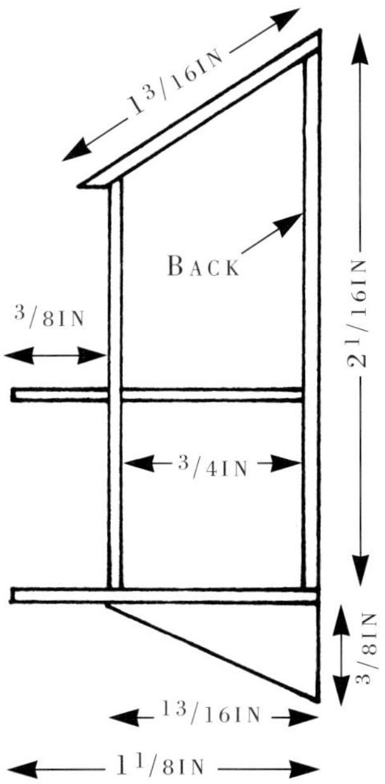

Fig 18a Side view of dovecote

The dovecote and beehive

angle so that the top edge measures 1⁷/₈in. Reduce the height of two of these pieces to ⁵/₁₆in, for the tops. Glue each piece on top of another, overlapping by ¹/₈in, keeping the back square edges flush to each other. Repeat with the next two pieces in the same manner and add the top one. Make up the other side in the same way but as a mirror image.

Cut the base 2³/₈in x 1¹⁵/₁₆in, the longest measurement running front to back. Cut two spacers 2¹/₈in long x ³/₈in wide and glue these onto the base, flush at the back and overhanging the sides by ¹/₈in.

Cut the back 2in wide x 2¹¹/₁₆in high. Draw a pencil line across the width ³/₁₆in from the top, find the centre of the top edge

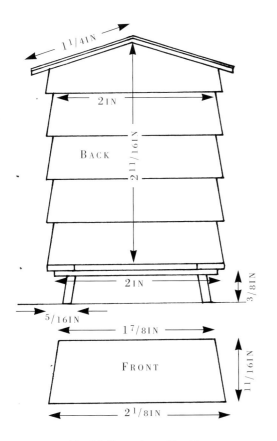

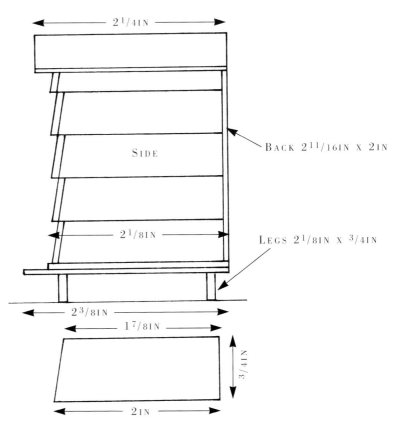

Fig 19 Front view of beehive

Fig 19a Side view of beehive

69

TIP

Stain all parts of the bird table and allow to dry before assembly to avoid 'white spots' appearing on timbers.

and draw out the angles to give a shallow pointed top. Lay the base down on a flat surface and glue the back and two sides together, the sides being flush with the edges of the two spacers at each side.

Cut and shape, as for the sides, five pieces for the front 2¹/₈in wide x ¹¹/₁₆in high. Cut so that they all taper to 2in (again a template will prove useful), and glue the lower four into position so that they overlap the thickness of the side pieces to give a flush finish. The fifth piece is trimmed to a peak by drawing one line at ⁵/₁₆in and a second at ¹/₂in. Find the centre and draw a vertical line. From where the ⁵/₁₆in line meets the edge draw a straight line to the centre at ¹/₂in on each side to produce the roof pitch. Glue this on to complete the front. You should have a ¹/₁₆in gap at the front and back to allow the 'bees' access.

Cut two pieces for the roof 1¹/₄in x 2¹/₄in and glue these so that they are flush at the back but overlap at the front. Finish off the roof by cutting and gluing on a piece of fine grey abrasive paper to mimic tarred felt, overlapping by ¹/₁₆in at the front.

Add four legs cut from ¹/₈in square plastic tubing ³/₈in long. Cut the tops and bottoms of all four with complimentary angles to give a slight splay and glue onto the base, under the main body. Paint the outside with matt emulsion and weather with a little grey acrylic paint or leave as white plastic.

BIRD TABLE

A tall bird table always looks good wherever it is placed in a garden.

MATERIALS

- *Lengths of jelutong in the following sizes: ³/₁₆in square; ¹/₃₂in thick x ¹/₈in strip; ¹/₃₂in thick x ⁵/₁₆in strip; ¹/₁₆in thick x 1in x 1¹/₄in (for table) and two off 1in x 1¹/₂in (for roof)*
- *Wire ¹/₁₆in diameter x 2¹/₂in*
- *Walnut wood stain*

Cut a 5in post from ³/₁₆in square jelutong, square off the ends and cut a V-shaped notch out of the top (see fig 20). Drill a ¹/₁₆in-diameter hole 4³/₈in above the bottom of the post and cut and glue a 1in length of ¹/₁₆in wire for the perch. Cut the roof support from the same material, 1¹/₂in long and glue this dead centre horizontally on top of the post.

The table itself is cut from ¹/₁₆in thick jelutong 1in x 1¹/₄in. Find the centre and cut a ³/₁₆in square hole to take the post and glue ¹/₃₂in thick x ¹/₈in wide jelutong strip around the edge of the table to finish off. Glue the table 4in above the bottom of the post (see fig 20a).

Cut two roof pieces from ¹/₁₆in thick jelutong, each 1¹/₂in x 1in and plane or shape one long edge of each at 45 degrees. Glue these together at the apex of the post

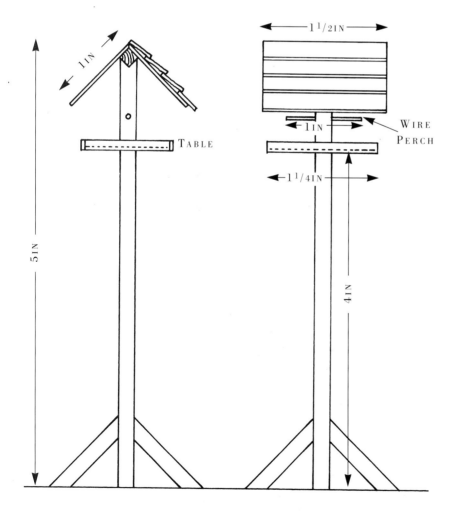

Fig 20 Bird table showing post notched into roof

Fig 20a Side view of bird table showing position of table and perch

and onto the roof support. Prepare about 13in of ¹/₃₂in thick x ⁵/₁₆in wide strip jelutong and cut eight pieces 1¹/₂in long for the roof shingles. Working on one side, glue the first piece along the bottom edge, overlapping by about ¹/₁₆in. Glue on three more, overlapping each one so that the top of the last one is at the peak of the roof. Repeat for the second side.

Cut four legs from ³/₁₆in square jelutong, each 1¹/₄in long and cut both ends of each inward at 45 degrees. Glue these to the base of the post as shown in figs 20 and 20a. Support the assembly and allow the adhesive to set. Colour your bird table with walnut wood stain diluted 50/50 with white spirit.

WELL

A well seems to be found at the bottom of every Tudor garden. This is rather larger than the one in the Rustic Garden on page 93.

MATERIALS

- *Food tin*
- *2mm MDF, two off 3¹/₂in diameter circles*
- *Jelutong in the following sizes:*
  two off ¹/₈in thick x ¹/₂in x 6in
  one off ¹/₄in x ¹/₄in x 2¹/₂in
  four off ¹/₈in thick x ¹/₄in x 2¹/₈in
  twelve off ¹/₁₆in thick x ³/₈in x 3¹/₂in

- *Round wire ¹/₁₆in diameter*
- *Old stone fibre-glass sheet*
- *Fine brown abrasive paper*
- *Wooden dowel ³/₈in diameter*

The body of the well is cut from a cocoa container, but any suitable cardboard or plastic tube with a outside diameter of 3in will do just as well. You will need a plastic lid that fits snugly on to the tube to support the outer coping stones, but before gluing this into place cut away the centre to give a

TIP

Lay both sides together and cut both notches and drill both holes at the same time to ensure they line up perfectly.

Bird table and well

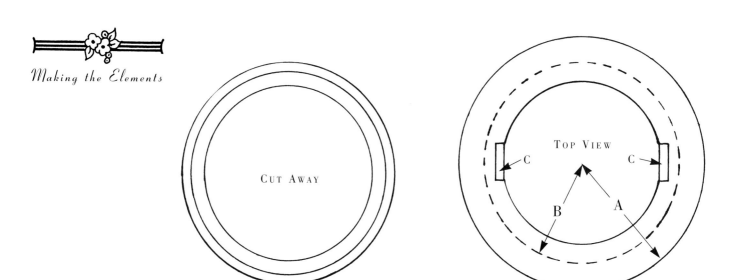

CUT AWAY

TOP VIEW

C   C

B   A

Fig 21 Making the body of the well

Fig 21a Slots cut for uprights

CUT AWAY SHADED AREA

SIDE VIEW

Fig 21b Side view

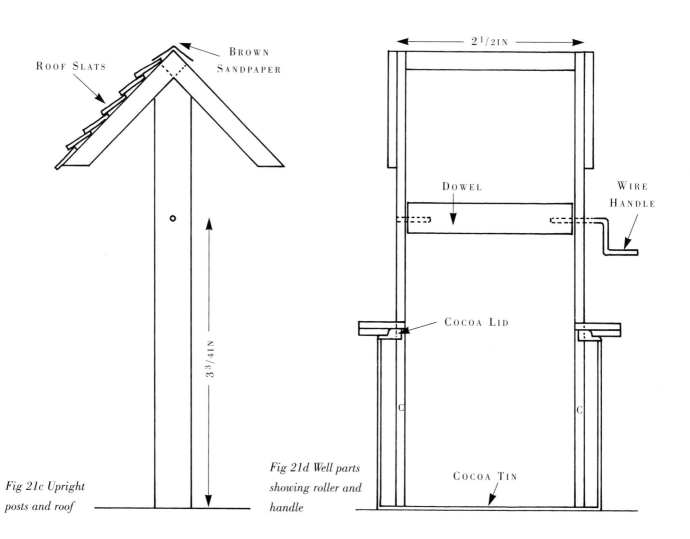

ROOF SLATS

BROWN
SANDPAPER

$3^3/4$IN

$2^1/2$IN

DOWEL

WIRE
HANDLE

COCOA LID

C   C

COCOA TIN

*Fig 21c Upright
posts and roof*

*Fig 21d Well parts
showing roller and
handle*

2¹/₄in diameter hole. If the section of tubing used does not have a base cut one from card to fit inside, and glue this into position with a clear spirit glue such as UHU.

Use a fretsaw to cut two wooden circles A and B from 2mm MDF, each with a 3¹/₂in diameter (see fig 21). Clean up the edges with medium grade abrasive paper. Remove the centres of the circles to leave a ⁵/₈in lip on circle A and a ³/₈in lip on circle B as shown in figs 21a and 21b. Use a sharp razor saw and a craft knife to remove two ¹/₂in slots C from circle A, for the uprights. Glue and clamp the two circles together so that the outer edges are flush and when set clean up with fine abrasive paper to give a smooth edge all round.

Mark up the top circle A into segments approximately ³/₄in wide and cut out along these lines to produce a V joint to the stones at the edge. Roughen up a few of the joints, chip away the edges to produce a natural finish and glue this to the top of the tube. Paint the inside of the well with a muddy green acrylic, adding a little black and brown until all the surfaces are covered.

Cut two 6in long canopy upright posts from ¹/₂in wide x ¹/₈in thick jelutong and cut a 45 degree notch out of the tops of both (see fig 21c) then drill a ¹/₁₆in diameter hole through both exactly 3³/₄in from the bottom. Stain a dark oak colour and allow to dry. Support and glue both uprights into the slots cut in the circles, with the notches at the top and the bottoms at the base of the well.

Cut the centre roof support from ¹/₄in x ¹/₄in jelutong, 2¹/₂in long (adjusting this if using a different diameter tube). Stain dark

oak and then glue this onto the cut notch, to fix both side posts together.

Cut the four roof beams each 2¹/₈in long out of ¹/₄in wide x ¹/₈in thick jelutong and trim both ends of each one at 45 degrees, so that the cuts face inward (see fig 21c). Stain as before and glue onto the side posts using a fast-setting spirit-based glue, or clamps.

Cut twelve 3¹/₂in long roof slats from ¹/₁₆in thick x ³/₈in wide jelutong, stain the same colour as the roof beams and glue six onto each side of the roof, starting at the bottom (see fig 21c and Tip box, right).

Cut a ¹/₂in wide strip of brown abrasive paper for the ridge and glue this to the top of the roof to finish off. Cut a ³/₈in diameter wooden dowel into a 2³/₁₆in length for the well roller and drill, with care, a ¹/₁₆in diameter hole into the centre of each end (see fig 21d). Stain it a dark oak colour and test fit it between the posts. Cut a ⁵/₈in length of ¹/₁₆in diameter round wire for one end of the roller and a 2in length for the handle. Bend the 2in length as shown in fig 21d to form a cranked handle.Check the length by fitting the roller into place without glue. When you are satisfied with the fit place the roller between the posts and glue the wire pin into one end and the crank handle into the other with a rapid epoxy adhesive.

Cut a length of old stone effect fibre-glass sheet 2¹/₂in wide to fit around the base of the well and glue into place. Make the join as invisible as possible and away from view. Finish off the sides by gluing on a little modelling moss or dried flowers, which can also be used to disguise the joint in the walling. Add a piece of suitable coloured string around the roller, and a bucket.

TIP

If you prefer to use a wider roof slat, say ¹/₂in, cut five not six and glue on in the same way, remembering to overlap each one. The well photographed on page 71 has been made this way.

The Formal Georgian Garden

A formal garden is often associated with the early Georgian period and usually belongs to a large country house. A regular feature of such gardens is the geometric pattern imposed on borders, hedges and plants, rather like the disciplines used by great architects such as Adam. Vast quantities of earth may have been removed to give the garden order and the house some fine views.

The magnificent fountain at the centre of this garden project is the focal point and all patterns emanate from it. The gateway shows that there is an outside world, albeit locked away, or rather that the outside world is kept at bay.

This project shows that you do not have to fill a garden with plants, pots and people. Using simple shapes you can create a wonderfully elegant garden from very basic materials. Formal doesn't have to mean inflexible as the garden elements can easily be reorganised. As you can see by the photograph on page 47, the central fountain area of this garden could contain a decorative knot garden as an alternative focal point and this could be an ideal garden to accompany a Tudor dolls' house.

The garden can stand alone of course or the main wall can be removed to place the garden against an existing dolls' house wall. Alternatively the whole garden could be fixed to a dolls' house but rotated through 180 degrees so that the main wall is positioned at the bottom of the garden.

CONSTRUCTING THE GARDEN

This is the sort of garden where templates will be really useful in achieving a good layout. Draw your garden plan out full size onto a sheet of clean white paper following the principles shown in our plan below. Make several copies of this using a photocopier if you can, and then transfer parts of each copy to separate pieces of good quality card.

Please note that for the purposes of illustration only we have bounded our garden on one side by a set of iron railings; these are not described in the text but see Suppliers on page 173.

General materials needed for constructing this garden include; PVA glue, artist's display or photo mount adhesive, instant adhesive (Super Glue), masking tape, tea bags, panel pins, dressmaking pins, template card and various paints (mainly acrylic and emulsions). Where instructions are given for general gluing it is assumed that a PVA type glue will be used.

Plan of the Formal Georgian Garden

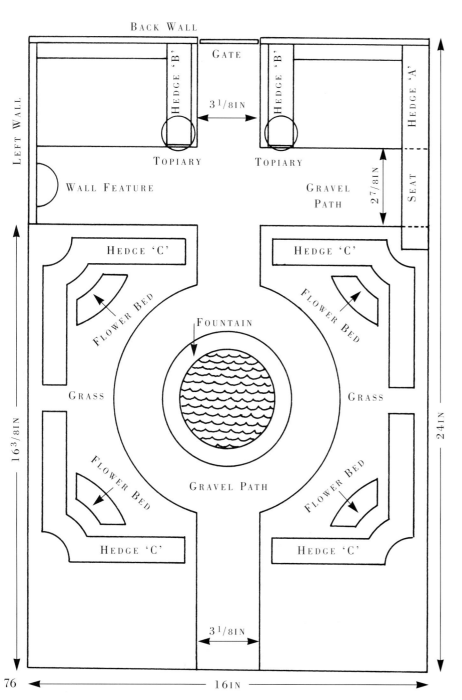

MATERIALS

MDF – 9mm
Base	24in x 16in

MDF – 6mm
Back wall outer	16in x 8in
Left wall	6in x 7³/₈in
Seat supports	(see instructions)

MDF – 2mm
Back wall inner	16in x 8in maximum (see instructions)
Coping	⁵/₈in x 16in
Spacing for inner wall	1in wide x 36in long (approx.)
Seat top	1¹/₄in x 3in

Other materials
- *Polystyrene packaging*
- *Coarse glass paper for gravel*
- *Grass covering sheet*
- *Green Oasis (floral foam)*
- *Plasticard ¹/₁₆in thick sheet*
- *1mm wire*
- *Plastic weld adhesive*
- *Green florist's wire*

Specialist supplies
(see Suppliers page 173)
- *Fibre-glass sheet of old stone wall covering*
- *Green scenic covering foam*

- *Fountain*
- *Lion's head wall feature*
- *Various pots, tubs and planters*
- *Plants*

BASE

Cut the base from 9mm MDF 24in x 16in. Trim up the edges and use a try square to check that all corners are square and at right angles to each other. Using the garden plan as a reference, take a soft pencil and mark all the elements shown on the plan onto the baseboard. You will find this easier to do if you use a T-square, compass and set square (see Tip box, right).

WALLS

Outer back wall

Cut the outer back wall from 6mm MDF 16in x 8in and square up all the corners. Draw a pencil guide line 3/16in from the bottom edge along the 16in length and drill four 1/32in-diameter holes to take panel pins. Using PVA glue, pin and glue the wall to the rear edge of the base and allow the assembly to set.

In order to give the appearance of a view through the gateway a suitable landscape picture has been cut from a magazine and fixed to this wall with spray adhesive. You may need to experiment with several pictures until the right one is found and it will be easier if you position the picture with the gateway in place.

Inner back wall

Cut the inner back wall from 2mm MDF 16in x 8in and trim 9mm, the thickness of the base, off the long edge to give a height of 7⁵/₈in (see Tip box overleaf).

Define the gateway by laying the inner wall onto a flat surface and drawing a vertical line dead centre at 8in. Draw two more lines 1³/₈in either side of this, add a horizontal line 6in from the bottom and finally use a compass to make the top of the gateway into an arch (see fig 1). This wall will be cut into irregular stonework but the gateway will be surrounded with rustic, coarsely shaped blocks. Draw a line for the blocks about 3/4in with a large key-stone in the centre of the arch, working down on each side and referring to fig 1 for guidance.

Use a soft pencil to mark up the remaining part wall with a series of horizontal lines, using measurements between 1¹/₈in

TIP

When garden features are complicated, like the gravel path, make a template for each clearly defined part, such as the round centre or 'T' shape at one end. Before making the templates add ¹/₈in to all dimensions where the gravel paths meet a grassed area to allow the grass to overlap, but do not add ¹/₈in to the ends of the pathways or where two path templates meet.

Fig 1 Positioning the gateway within the back wall

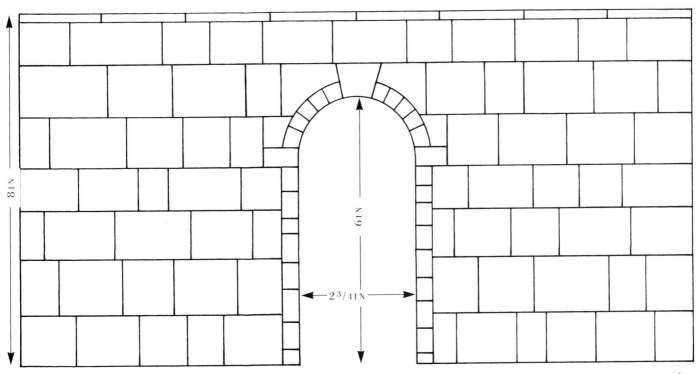

The Formal
Georgian Garden

TIP

The inner back wall height is only approximate as we are mixing metric and imperial measurements. A simpler way is to lay the 16in x 8in sheet against the inner side of the outer wall, mark off where the heights match and trim.

TIP

To avoid unsightly bulges when fitting fibre-glass sheets around right-angled corners mitre the sheet first.

and 1¼in. Start this at the top so that any odd blocks are placed at the bottom, out of sight. Finish off marking up by drawing on the vertical joints to give stones widths varying between 1½in and 1⅝in. Start marking from the centre leaving odd stones at the outer edges and remembering to stagger the joints so that each of the vertical lines are more or less at the centre of the stone below.

Use a sharp craft knife to incise V-shaped joints along all the lines, vertical, horizontal and around the archway, removing the waste. Fold a piece of fine abrasive paper into two and use this, or a small file, to smooth off the joints and soften any rough edges. Using a fretsaw with a fine blade

and, supporting the work on a bench hook, cut out the arched gateway and clean up.

Lay this wall face down onto a flat working surface and glue strips of wood to act as spacers around, and flush with, the outer edges and the gateway. Colour the front wall with a grey/ochre mixture of acrylic paints (or spray with a cellulose car spray if you prefer), adding a little extra brown to the joints. Allow this to dry thoroughly before proceeding.

The next job is to fix the two walls together and the landscape picture must be in place before you do this. Glue the inner wall onto the outer wall and clamp them together at several points to avoid warping. Pin these two walls together with fine panel pins to

ensure the joints are firm. You should now see the 'view' clearly through the gateway.

Wall coping

Cut the strip of coping ⅝in x 16in from 2mm MDF and use a pencil to mark joints at 2in intervals. Use a sharp craft knife to incise a V-shaped joint into each line, removing the waste and cleaning up as you go. Paint this to match the stones on the inner back wall and set to one side. When the paint is dry the coping can be glued and panel pinned to the top of the back wall assembly.

Left wall

Cut the wall from 6mm MDF 6in x 7⅜in and check that the sides are all at right angles. Glue this wall on top of the baseboard, butting it against the back wall and securing with masking tape until the glue has set firm. Cut a fibre-glass sheet of old stone wall covering to the same size as the wall plus ¾in all round, and fix this to the wall using a PVA glue or display mount adhesive. Wrap the excess over the top and around the sides to give a smooth finish. Add a little foliage, such as ivy, to the top of this wall to break up the hard lines. If you wish to include the lion's head wall feature as shown in our photograph it is available ready-made – see Suppliers on page 173.

PATH

Make templates for the gravel path as described in Constructing the Garden and transfer these shapes to the gravel material of your choice. There are several ways of making gravel paths and more information is given in Making the Elements page 30. We have used a coarse grade of glass paper, cut cleanly from the underside using a sharp craft knife and a steel ruler. It is important that this material is laid as flat as possible and you will achieve better adhesion by priming the baseboard with a thin coat of PVA glue brushed evenly over the surface (see Tip box, right). When this primer coat

has dried thoroughly, spread a thin layer of glue evenly over the bottom of the glass paper path and lay it into position. Add sufficient weights to keep this sheet material flat until the glue is dry.

GRASS

Make card templates for all the grassed areas, check that they fit into position and lay ⅛in over the edge of the pathways (see Tip box, below). Mark on each template the position of the flower beds and the hedges and cut these shapes out using a scalpel or craft knife with a fresh blade.

Lay the sheet of modelling grass onto a flat surface, transfer the shape of the templates onto the reverse side and cut out using a sharp craft knife or scalpel. When reversing the grass remember to reverse the templates too. Lay the cut grass sheets onto the garden and glue down using artist's display mount adhesive or an evenly spread coat of PVA glue.

FLOWER BEDS

The flower beds are made from ¼in thick pieces of Oasis (floral foam) cut to shape using a sharp craft knife. These are sprayed with display mount adhesive and covered with tea leaves (see also Making the Elements page 56). Once shaped these can be planted up away from the garden with small, low plants (see photographs) and placed into position as a final touch. Ensure the flower beds fit the cut-outs before planting up.

HEDGES AND TOPIARY

The hedges in this garden are made from polystyrene blocks 1in thick, commonly found as packaging. There are several grades of this material and a denser one with a smaller 'grain' size is much better for this type of work. Remember that polystyrene reacts to some spirit-based materials by dissolving. It is also flammable and you should not smoke or work on it near a naked flame.

TIP

You could use an artist's display mount adhesive to fix the path but there is no latitude for mistakes as it cannot be repositioned easily. If the glass paper is not the correct colour it can be sprayed with a creamy/yellow gravel-coloured paint. Remember to mask surrounding areas to protect them from any overspray.

TIP

To avoid confusion with all the various pieces of grass, number each template and mark its position on the plan, transferring this number to the underside of the pieces of grass as you work.

TIP

Care should be used when cutting polystyrene with knives. Use a gentle sawing motion for best results or alternatively use a very fine-bladed fretsaw. There are also specialist 'hot wire' tools to cut this material, available from craft shops. Polystyrene is very friable and we recommend that you work on it away from your garden project.

Fig 2 Shaped hedge 'A' (with arch)

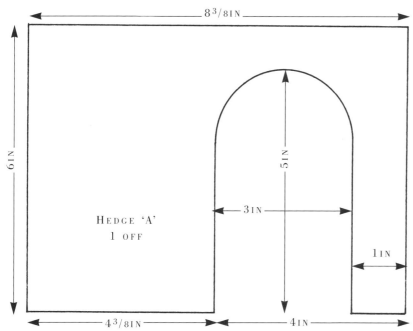

HEDGE 'A'
1 OFF

Note that the hedge shapes shown in figs 2, 2a and 2b, are half the size the finished hedges need to be, so draw them out full size (or enlarge them on a photocopier). Use an X-acto No.15 bladed saw and a keyhole saw to cut out the pieces (see Tip box).

Shaped hedge 'A' (with arch)

Cut a blank first (see fig 2) then make a card template for the archway and this time draw the outline on both sides of the block, so that you can work towards the centre. Under-cut and trim rather than over-cut the first time and do not worry about slightly ragged edges as this is a hedge after all!

Shaped hedge 'B' (with topiary)

Cut two off (see fig 2a). You may find it useful to make a card template so that the pieces are identical, alternatively try cutting both pieces at once. These two hedges will have topiary additions (see below).

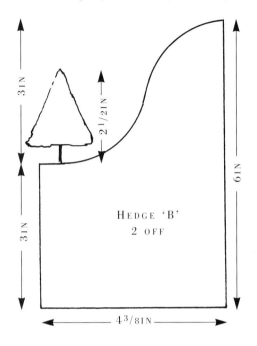

Fig 2a Shaped hedge 'B' (with topiary)

Shaped hedge 'C'

Cut four off, each 1in high (see fig 2b). Cut this from a 1in thick sheet of polystyrene with a smooth top and bottom if you can. This is a much more complicated shape and your work will definitely benefit from using a card template and working very slowly when cutting and shaping.

Fig 2b Shaped hedge 'C'

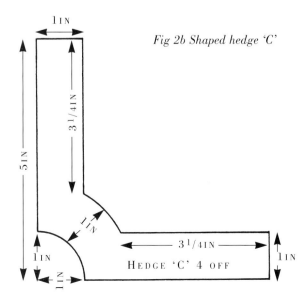

Paint all parts of the hedges, except the bases, with a green emulsion or poster paint to seal the surfaces and make sure that all the crevices are covered. When the paint is dry spray all those surfaces that will be showing with artist's display mount adhesive and cover with green scenic foam. (Scenics T45 foam is available from railway model shops.) Repeat until all the surfaces being worked are covered equally. (It is not necessary to spray or cover the tallest ends of the 'B' hedges or the back of hedge 'A'.) When covered, spray with a light coating of spray mount to seal.

Lightly glue the four 'C' hedges into the main garden and place the two shaped 'B' hedges on either side of the gate. Hedge 'A' complete with arch is fixed to the top right-hand side of the garden.

Topiary

The small pieces of topiary seen in this project are all produced from the same materials and in the same way as the hedges. Simply shape, seal, colour and sprinkle with scenic foam. Twist two or three short strands of green florist's wire to produce a stem, push this into the base of the topiary and fix it to the 'B' hedges in the same manner (see fig 2a). If you wish to include more topiary in this garden, you could easily replace the central fountain area with a knot garden (as shown on page 47). See Making the Elements page 45 for instructions.

SEAT

Although the seat looks like stone it has been made from scrap offcuts of 6mm and 2mm MDF. Cut the seat from 2mm MDF 1¼in x 3in and shape the under part of the front lip as shown in fig 3 overleaf.

The two seat supports have been reproduced full sized in fig 3. Simply trace off and transfer the shape to a piece of 6mm MDF and cut out using a fine-bladed fretsaw (see Tip box). Glue together and allow to set.

TIP

Polystyrene can react with some spray paints and we recommend that you avoid spraying directly onto uncovered surfaces unless you have tested them for adverse reactions.

TIP

The hedges can be made into moveable features by fixing two 1in panel pins into the surface of the garden and placing the base of each hedge firmly onto the pins.

TIP

Project builders can make complicated moulded edges to seats by cutting the seat ⅛in short all round and adding a commercial moulding, mitred at the corners.

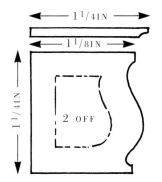

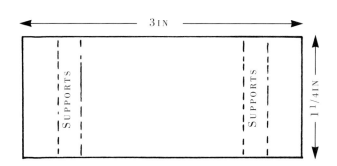

Fig 3 Making the seat

Prime the surfaces of the seat with a matt emulsion or poster paint and finish off with a grey stone-coloured paint adding a touch of green around the base of the supports. Place the finished seat in the archway of hedge 'A' or against the left wall (see photographs).

GATE

The gate has been made from ¹/₁₆in plasticard and 1mm wire. Plasticard, or plastic sheet, is available in several thicknesses and is joined together with a 'plastic weld' adhesive that actually dissolves the surface of the two pieces being joined. This type of card can easily be cut with a scalpel or craft knife, with a steel rule as a guide, but firm pressure is required to hold the material and prevent it distorting.

To work on this feature you will need a flat offcut of MDF or similar and some dressmaker's pins. Masking tape and Plasticine might also prove useful for holding parts in place. A round tin or container 2¹/₂in in diameter is also required for bending the top of the gate into shape.

Prepare four 4in lengths of 1mm wire, two lengths of 4⁵/₈in and nine lengths of 5⁷/₈in. Mark the MDF offcut with two horizontal lines 5⁷/₈in apart for the height of the gate and two vertical lines 2⁵/₈in apart (see fig 4). Fix the tin firmly onto the surface so that it will not move unless required, ¹/₁₆in below the top line and dead centre of the box you have drawn.

Cut a strip from the plastic sheet ¹/₈in wide x 13³/₈in long. Place one end onto the

bottom mark, place a pin on either side and bring the strip up around the tin and down the second side to the bottom, pinning into place again. Cut neatly off at the line.

Cut three cross pieces from the ¹/₈in wide plastic sheet strip, 2¹/₂in long and glue one into place at the bottom of the gate using plastic weld adhesive. Carefully divide 2¹/₂ inches into eleven equally spaced divisions and make a centre mark with a very sharp pointed tool on each of them. Drill eleven 1mm-diameter holes on each mark, ensuring that the holes in each cross piece line up. Using plastic weld adhesive, weld the top cross piece into place and check that it is horizontal 4¹/₁₆in from the bottom.

Insert all the wires into the second, or bottom cross piece as shown in fig 4 and

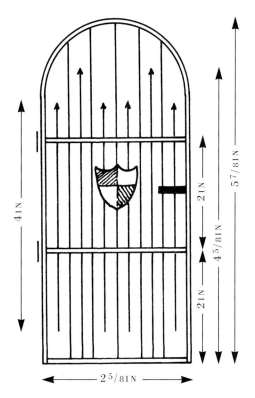

Fig 4 Making the gate

gently slide them through the holes in the upper cross piece. Trim off any that protrude below the bottom due to the curvature of the gate top. Weld in the second cross piece and, when this is dry, weld on the bottom, inserting those wires that fit. Pin the bottom into place until the plastic weld has set. Glue the shorter wires into the cross pieces and to the top of the gate using a touch of instant adhesive such as Super Glue.

Onto one side of the gate, weld on two offcuts of ¹⁄₁₆in x ¹⁄₈in plasticard to mimic hinges, and weld a small strip on the opposite side to act as a handle. Glue on Fimo or card finials (made from the

shape given in fig 5) to the tops of the wires.

Using a cellulose car spray, spray the whole assembly matt black or paint with black acrylic, finishing off with touches of brown/red for rust. When the paint is dry add a small coat of arms, cut from a magazine and glued to a piece of card. Place the gate into the arch and glue into place.

FOUNTAIN

The fountain is a ready-made one (see Suppliers on page 173) and is heavy enough to be simply placed into position, as is the large urn at the end of the garden. Plant up all pots and planters with a suitable selection of plants and shrubs.

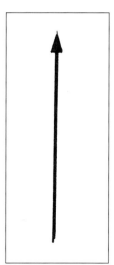

*Fig 5 The finial shape
for the gate*   83

The Rustic Garden

A country garden is both real and a dream for many people: a tiny cottage tucked away in a country lane where one can spend idyllic days basking in the sunshine is the way many of us see it. To others a cottage represents a run-down property with a leaking roof, poor sanitation and doors that let in more draughts than they keep out. Typical of a small-holder's dwelling around the beginning of the twentieth century, this type of house will still tug at folk memories long into the new millennium.

Helen Allingham captured the English country cottage and its garden so famously in her paintings that her view has become almost archetypal and it is something of this flavour that we have tried to capture in this project – a warm sunlit garden, slightly ramshackle, with a place for chickens and children. Firewood stored in a lean-to, water drawn from a well and a children's tree swing help build up a picture-book garden fronted by a picket fence. A rickety old fence around the back and sides offers little protection from weather or intruders. The design of this garden deliberately aims for an informal, almost careless style, echoed in the untilled ground and the casual planting. This cottage has not been cared for and the mortar has fallen away from the wall in places, the beams used for the framework reflect a previous use, perhaps the carcass of a ship, and the roof has definitely seen better days.

This garden would be delightful as a free-standing structure but it could easily accompany your own rustic-style dolls' house by simply removing the cottage and attaching the garden to your existing building.

CONSTRUCTING THE GARDEN

General materials needed for constructing this garden include; PVA glue, plaster filler, masking tape, stiff card, dark oak wood stain, white spirit, matt varnish, panel pins, string, Plasticine or Blu Tack, cling film (Siran wrap), artist's display mount adhesive and paints (mainly acrylic, poster and black Humbrol). Where instructions are given for general gluing it is assumed that a PVA type glue will be used.

Most of the accessories used in this garden can be obtained from the suppliers listed on page 173 or by making the items, such as the dovecote, yourself (see Making the Elements page 68).

(see Suppliers on page 173)

TIP

Prepare the two sides as rectangles 4in x 12in, clamp together and cut the 55 degree slope as one piece. Any minor variation will then be reproduced equally on both sides.

MATERIALS

MDF – 9mm

Main base	16in x 24in
Steps	2¼in x 1⅛in
	2¼in x ⅜in

MDF – 6mm

Cottage sides, two off	4in x 12in
Cottage front	9in x 14in
Cottage back	12in x 14in
Cottage roof	14in x 6in
Step	2¼in x 1⅛in
Tree base	2in x 2in
Well base, two off	2in x ¼in
two off	1½in x ¼in

MDF – 2mm

Under base	20in x 28in
Cottage foundations	¾in x 14in
Brick panels	2in x 6in
Wood shed	(see instructions)
Well base	5in x 5in
Hedge base	1in x 16in

Jelutong wood

• *As required for beams, door, window, shed, swing, well and fencing
(see instructions for details)*

Other materials

- *Acetate sheet*
- *Door furniture (such as knob or latch)*
- *Spirit-based adhesive such as UHU*
- *Rapid-set epoxy adhesive*
- *Fine twine or string*
- *Dowel pins*
- *⅜in-diameter wooden dowel*
- *Tree branches*
- *Fine sand and small rocks*
- *Oasis (floral foam)*
- *1/16-diameter wire*
- *1/6in-diameter copper tube*
- *1/32in-diameter round wire*
- *Small wooden well bucket*

Specialist supplies

(see Suppliers on page 173)

- *Mod-Roc plaster bandage*
- *Roof tiles*
- *Scenics foam*
- *White metal*

BASES

Cut the main base from 9mm MDF 16in x 24in and square up all sides. Mark the position of the cottage walls by laying the base down onto a flat surface so that the longest edge is towards you and using a try square mark a line ¼in away from the back edge. Mark two more lines at 14in and 13¾in from the left-hand edge, both about 4in long. Finally make a line ¼in from the left-hand edge, again 4in long.

Cut the secondary or under base from 2mm MDF 20in x 28in and panel pin and glue this to the underside of the main base. The purpose of this piece is to provide a platform for the additional foliage and hedging around the outer edges of the front and sides of the garden. It is important that this base is *not* allowed to curl or warp and we feel that a base thicker than 2mm might be better at preventing this happening.

Using the drawn lines as a guide, drill a series of 1/32in-diameter holes through the thickness of both bases to take panel pins when the cottage is fixed into place.

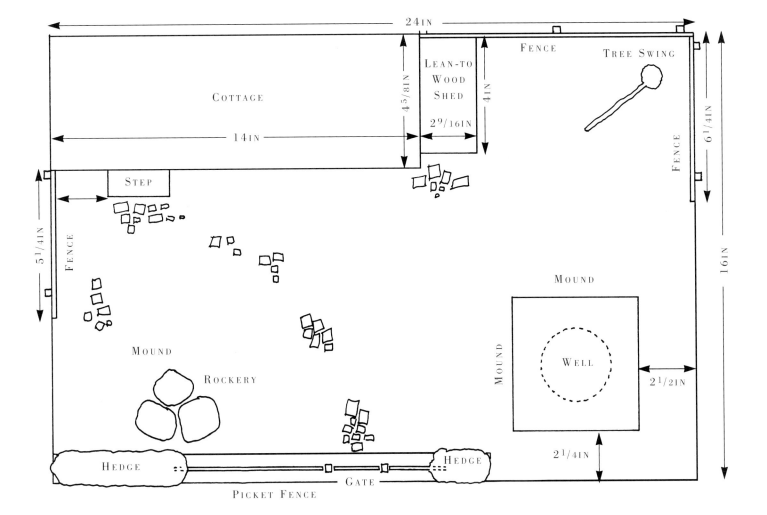

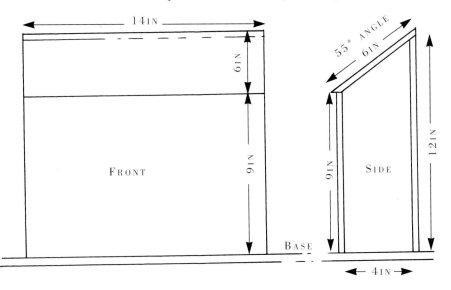

COTTAGE

Cut the back, two sides and front from 6mm MDF following the dimensions in the cutting list and square up all the sides with a small plane. Note that the two sides reduce in height at an angle of 55 degrees, from 12in at the back to 9in at the front (see fig 1 and Tip box on page 86). Using a small plane, shape the top edges of the back and front to the prescribed angle so as to allow the roof to slope down to the front.

Cut the roof 14in x 6in from 6mm MDF and shape both ends with a small plane to repeat the 55 degree angle. Note that the angles in effect 'face' each other.

Glue the two sides to the back and panel pin if necessary. Check that all parts are at right angles and support until the adhesive has set. Cut and glue a 3/8in x 6mm MDF offcut onto the baseboard so that it runs flush with the front between the walls, to act as a support to the front. Lay the front against this assembly and check that when the roof is placed into position that all edges

match with no gaps. Place roof and front to one side to work on later. Now is the time to place the partly assembled cottage onto the baseboard and glue and pin it into position. The sides are painted at the same time as the front.

Positioning the door and window

The cottage used in this project has not been built to the correct depth for a 1/12th-

Plan of the rustic garden

Fig 1 Front, roof and sides of the cottage

The Rustic Garden

TIP

If you want to make your window look a little more realistic cut out the aperture by drilling two ¹⁄₁₆in-diameter holes in opposite corners and use a fretsaw to remove the waste. Clean up and square off the corners.

TIP

Before marking up the brick pattern of the foundations, place the MDF strip in front of the cottage and mark two vertical lines where the step will be positioned as there is no need to cut bricks into this portion.

Fig 2 Position of the door and window of the cottage

scale model as it is only intended to give the garden atmosphere and a focal point. For that reason we felt that it was not necessary to make the door open or the window glass transparent, not least because that would have meant decorating the interior which is beyond the scope of this chapter. The door and the window are therefore 'dummies' but we have explained how to achieve an effect that still looks quite real.

Mark out the doorway by drawing a vertical line 2¹⁄₂in from the left-hand edge of the front, and then make a second line 2³⁄₈in from the first. Mark the bottom of the doorway with a horizontal line 1in from the bottom edge, and the top at 7¹⁄₄in (see fig 2). (The net height for the door is therefore 6¹⁄₄in.)

The window measures 2³⁄₈in high and 1⁷⁄₈in wide. Mark out the position by drawing a vertical line 2⁷⁄₈in from the right-hand edge of the cottage front with a second line 1⁷⁄₈in from this. (The second line is therefore 4³⁄₄in from the right-hand side.) The base of the window is 5in above the bottom of the front and the top 2³⁄₈in above that. As this window was not meant to be seen through we painted the surface of the wall with a matt black Humbrol paint.

Foundations

Cut and prepare a piece of 2mm MDF ³⁄₄in wide x 14in long. Lay onto a flat surface and use a sharp pencil to draw a mixed pattern of rough bricks and stones for the base of

the cottage. When you are happy with the design use a sharp craft knife to incise a series of V-shaped cuts along all the joints, using abrasive paper on the edges to indicate wear. Glue the finished strip along the bottom edge of the cottage front and place under a weight or clamp until set.

Beams

Prepare about 90in of jelutong ¹⁄₈in thick x ³⁄₈in wide in convenient length strips for the beams on the front of the cottage. Put about 24in of this to one side for use around the door and window. Use some fine abrasive paper around a sanding block and a sharp craft knife to rub down and shape the edges of the remainder of the wood strips to produce irregular, wavy edges (see Tip box page 89). Cut and glue straight-edged strips around the sides and bottom of the door and the sides and top of the window (see fig 2). Cut and glue all the shaped strips onto the cottage front.

The authentic finished colour of the woodwork beams should be a weather-worn grey or perhaps a warm soft brown with a few flecks of white to indicate lime. Tastes vary and you may prefer the colour a little darker but avoid black as this is a modern affectation and is too harsh. Finish by painting the beams with a matt varnish to protect them when covering the front with plaster later.

Brick panels

To give the cottage an aged appearance it is shown with the mortar off the walls in places revealing the 'brickwork' beneath.

Prepare a piece of 2mm MDF approximately 2in x 6in and use a sharp pencil to draw onto this a pattern of a brick bond. As this is an old cottage you could use an English bond (see Making the Elements page 34). Just make sure that the joints are staggered correctly, each joint over the centre of the brick below. Using a sharp craft knife and a steel ruler, carefully incise a very light V-shaped cut along all the

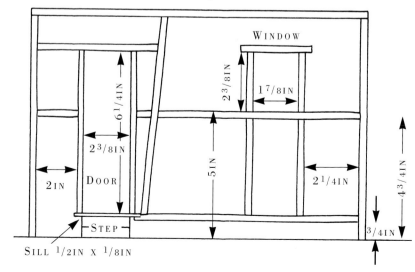

WINDOW

2³⁄₈IN

1⁷⁄₈IN

6¹⁄₄IN

2³⁄₈IN

5IN

4³⁄₄IN

2IN

DOOR

2¹⁄₄IN

STEP

3/4IN

SILL ¹⁄₂IN X ¹⁄₈IN

joints, horizontally and vertically. Introduce some ageing by distorting some joints and incising irregular cracks across a few bricks. Wash over the sheet with a light lime-coloured acrylic paint for the joints and finish off the surface of the bricks with a dark reddish-brown. Once dry, spray with matt varnish to protect the colour.

Use a razor saw to cut off blocks of bricks and a fretsaw with a fine blade to cut the remainder of the sheet into four or five irregularly shaped pieces about 1½in x 1in. These can all now be glued onto the front wall more or less horizontally, using a clear adhesive.

Rendering the front wall
If this were a real cottage the whole of the front would be covered in a mortar rendering. In our project, parts of this are shown to

have broken away to expose the bricks, but in reality we had to build up a covering of mortar around the bricks leaving them to appear as if they have been exposed by rotting plaster. The mortar covering can be built up with plaster filler but this may flake off if the surface is not properly prepared, so we have covered ours with Mod-Roc plaster-impregnated bandage.

Cut lengths of the bandage to fit the areas you wish to cover and lay them into a shallow dish filled with water. Lay the cottage front down onto a flat working surface and carefully dampen the surface using a clean paint-brush. Lay the wet

TIP
You can give the outer edges of the strips around the door and window an irregular or wavy edge if you prefer.

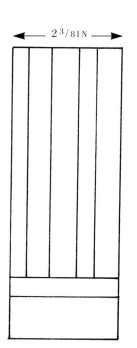

Fig 3 Measuring off lines on the door to mimic planks

bandage into position, cutting and placing it around the beams and brick panels. Continue to add layers until the bricks are slightly beneath the level of the rendering, smoothing out the layers as you work and overlapping the edges. Allow the surface to dry off but not harden and sprinkle with a little plaster filler, smoothing this off with a wet paint-brush to obtain a flat but not too perfect surface. Finally, clean any plaster from the surface of the brick panels, beams and foundations and allow to dry. Touch up any paintwork and paint around window and door apertures with a dark grey acrylic.

DOOR

Prepare a piece of $^1/_8$in thick jelutong, 6in x $2^3/_8$in and check that this will fit the door opening, adjusting as necessary. Lay this on a flat surface and measure off four vertical lines to mimic planks (see fig 3). To give the door a rustic appearance, make some of the planks $^3/_8$in wide and others $^1/_2$in. Using a sharp craft knife cut shallow V-shaped joints along each line, rubbing down with abrasive paper to indicate wear.

Prepare a second piece of $^1/_8$in thick jelutong $2^3/_8$in wide x $1^3/_{16}$in deep for the weather board that is placed along the bottom edge of the door. Using a piece of fine abrasive paper wrapped around a sanding block, bevel off the top edge to approximately 45 degrees, but take care not to make this too clearly defined. Cut a V-shaped joint at $^3/_8$in from the top edge two boards along its length and glue this to the bottom edge of the door. Add a door sill made from $^1/_8$in thick jelutong to the base of the opening, rounding off the edges to show wear. Colour the door with a spirit-based wood stain of dark oak mixed with 20 per-cent white spirit. When this is dry add your choice of door furniture, such as a knob or latch, then glue the door into its framework.

WINDOW

Cut a small piece of stiff card to fit the window aperture and use this as a template to cut a piece of acetate $2^3/_8$in x $1^7/_8$in for the window 'glass'. Make a drawing the size of the window ($1^7/_8$in x $2^3/_8$in) and add diamond lines for the lead pane dividers at $^3/_8$in intervals. Lay the acetate sheet over your drawing and using a sharp instrument gently score the diamond lines. The depth of the scoring will depend largely on the thickness of your acetate but be careful not to overdo this effect as you may cut through it – using the back edge of a knife blade would be a good idea. Paint over the marked surface with white acrylic paint and whilst it is still wet wipe over with a soft cloth to remove the surplus but leaving the paint in the score lines.

Cut four strips of $^1/_{16}$in thick x $^1/_8$in jelutong and glue these around the acetate on the reverse side of the scored lines. Glue the finished assembly into the window aperture with the jelutong strips on the outside and the paint-filled lines inside.

ADDING THE FRONT

At this stage the front can be added to the main part of the building by gluing it against the sides, using the offcuts placed inside for extra purchase. Support the front with masking tape until the adhesive has set and fill any gaps with a proprietary plaster filler (see Tip box, left).

Finish off the front and sides by painting all the plasterwork with an off-white or cream-coloured water-based poster paint or matt emulsion, carefully avoiding the beams and exposed brickwork. Gently distress the colour of the mortar by using a little brown or grey acrylic paint as a wash.

TILING THE ROOF

The roof, which was made earlier, is now covered with thin tiles made from fired clay. Ours were commercially made and we deliberately selected a batch of mixed sizes and surface finishes so as to maintain the rough, tumbledown appearance. The majority of the tiles used were $^5/_8$in x 1in. (See also Tip box, page 92.)

Glue a strip of $^1/_{32}$in x $^3/_{32}$in jelutong along the front edge of the roof to allow the leading tile to sit up slightly and so throw off the 'rain'. Tiles are then laid from the front edge up and fixed using a clear adhesive with a fast grab, such as UHU. The size of tile and the amount of overlap will determine the number of rows; here the cottage roof has eleven rows and the overlap varies between $^1/_8$in and $^1/_4$in.

STEPS

The steps leading down from the front door of the cottage onto the garden are made from MDF offcuts to simulate standard bricks (see fig 4).

Cut a piece of 9mm MDF $2^1/_4$in x $1^1/_8$in and then cut a piece of 6mm MDF to match. Cut a third piece from 9mm MDF $2^1/_4$in x $^3/_8$in to place on top (aligning the backs of all three pieces). Use a sharp pencil to mark up the 'bricks' on each piece of MDF and incise each of the marks with a V-shaped cut using a sharp scalpel or craft knife. Glue the three pieces together and place to one side until the assembly is dry. Show age and wear on the bricks and the joints using a small file or a piece of fine abrasive paper wrapped around a ruler.

Paint the step assembly with a mixture of brown and yellow acrylic paint, leaving the most worn areas a lighter colour than the surroundings. Glue the steps into position below the doorway and against the foundations, filling any gaps around the steps with a mixture of plaster filler and PVA glue.

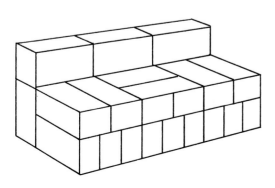

Fig 4 Making up the 'bricks' on the steps

WOOD SHED

Before wood will burn properly it must be seasoned and dry and to achieve this cottagers stored cut logs in open lean-to sheds so that the winds could carry off the moisture. These sheds were usually simple structures, easy to construct and cheap to make and as you can see from fig 5 ours is no different, except that we have built it as a separate assembly that does not rely on the outer wall for support.

Cut the back of the shed from 2mm MDF 6in high x 4in wide and shape the top edge with a small plane to an angle of 30 degrees. Prepare a strip of $^3/_{16}$in x $^3/_{16}$in square jelutong about 30in long for the four upright posts and the two roof beams. Cut two lengths $5^3/_4$in long for the back posts (the roof beam will sit on top) and trim the tops to match the 30 degree angle at the top of the back. Lay the back onto a flat surface and use glue to attach the posts to the inside of the back at each of the outer edges, flush at the bottom. The gap at the top is there to take the roof beams.

Prepare a strip of 2mm MDF $2^1/_2$in wide and about 7in long to use for both the front and the single side, cleaning up any rough edges. Measure off and cut the right-hand side piece $2^1/_2$in long and glue this onto the back at right angles, butting it against the back upright post.

The next piece to cut is the 2mm thick MDF base, which needs to be $3^3/_4$in x $2^1/_4$in. Mark off a $^3/_{16}$in square at both right-hand corners and cut these portions out to provide location points against the bottom of the right-hand posts. Glue this into position so that it butts against the back wall, between the posts and right-hand side, with the cut-outs fitting snugly around the bottom of the back posts. Check that all the parts are at right angles, then support as necessary and allow the assembly to dry thoroughly before proceeding.

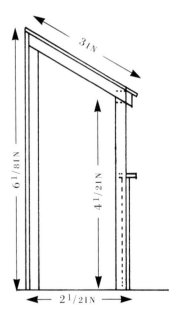

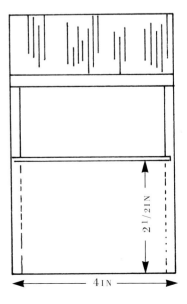

Fig 5 The wood shed

Cut the front from the 2¹/₂in wide 2mm MDF strip 3⁵/₈in long and place onto a flat surface. Cut two upright front posts 4¹/₂in long and trim the tops at 30 degrees to match those at the back (see fig 5). Glue these to the posts to either side of the front, keep the assembly flat and allow the adhesive to set.

Prepare 30in of ¹/₂in wide ¹/₁₆in thick jelutong and cut into 2¹/₂in lengths for the boards on the front of the shed. Turn the front assembly over so that the flush side is uppermost and glue on the boards starting from the right-hand edge. Cut a sill from ¹/₁₆in thick jelutong ¹/₄in wide x 4in long. Cut notches at each end on the back to allow it to sit around the posts and then glue it onto the top of the front boards.

Cut two roof beams from ³/₁₆in x ³/₁₆in square jelutong 3¹/₈in long and cut both ends with a 30 degree angle, one end fitting against the back. Glue these into position on top of the front and rear posts, laying one end flush against the back (see fig 5).

Mix a dark oak wood stain 50/50 with white spirit and colour the entire assembly, leaving to dry in an area that is properly ventilated. Staining all the parts before assembly will help you to avoid unsightly glue spots.

For the shed roof, cut a piece of stiff card 3¹/₄in x 4in and stain the underside as for the remainder of the shed assembly. Allow to dry.

Cut a piece of corrugated packing board to fit the roof, being careful not to make marks in the soft corrugations. Spray this with a light coat of matt varnish or paint over with a PVA adhesive to give it strength and glue this down onto the roof card.

Paint the roof with silver-coloured paint and add a few 'nail heads' in black with the tip of a fine brush. Finish off by using a red and brown acrylic paint mix to indicate rust on the nail heads and around the front edges of the corrugated 'iron' roof. Glue the roof into position.

Finish off the shed by cutting a number of small, trimmed branches from a real tree to resemble logs. Use a spirit-based glue, such as UHU to assemble these into a pile ready to place inside the shed, or leave them loose. Stand the shed against the cottage on final assembly.

TREE AND SWING

The tree used in this project was a branch cut from a small tree. Look for a piece about 12in tall with a branch more or less at right angles to the trunk about 2in from the top, and cut the base at right angles to the trunk (see top Tip box page 93).

Prepare a 2in x 2in base from 6mm MDF and drill a ¹/₈in-diameter hole through the centre, countersinking the underside to take a No. 6 screw. Smooth off the top edges all round into an irregular shape that can easily be disguised. Drill a shallow starter hole into the base of the branch (now your tree) and glue it down onto the tree base, securing the assembly by attaching it to the base with the screw. Glue and panel pin the tree assembly onto the baseboard as shown on the garden plan and fig 6.

Swing

Cut the swing seat from a piece of ¹/₁₆in thick jelutong 2in x 1in and drill two ¹/₁₆in-diameter holes along the centre line, each ¹/₄in in from the outer edges. Score a ragged line down the middle of the board to indicate the jointing of two planks and smooth off all the corners and edges to show wear.

In order to make the swing seat hang properly we made ours from a piece of white metal as used in casting metal miniatures. However, you can make yours from the ¹/₁₆in thick jelutong and glue a small piece of white metal, about ¹/₁₆in thick, to the underside with a spirit-based glue or a rapid fix epoxy adhesive. Use the ¹/₁₆in drill bit to continue the holes through the white metal weight.

Cut two pieces of ¹/₁₆in square jelutong 1in long and glue these across the bottom of the swing seat, front to back ³/₈in in from

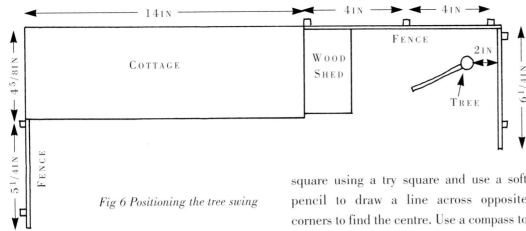

Fig 6 Positioning the tree swing

the outer edges. Bevel off the edges with a piece of fine abrasive paper and stain the whole assembly with a wood stain in a light oak colour.

String the seat to the tree with two lengths of fine twine or string which you have first rubbed through your hands in order to make it more pliable and take the newness off the surface. Cut two lengths of twine so that the seat will finish up about 2in above the ground and there is still sufficient twine to wrap around the branch two or three times. Tie a knot in one end of the twine, thread it through the hole in the seat, from the bottom, and tie it off after wrapping it around the branch. Repeat for the other side ensuring that the seat is level.

WELL

Prepare the base from a piece of 2mm MDF 5in x 5in. Check that the corners are all

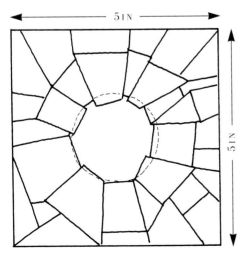

Fig 7 Making the well base with random flag stones

square using a try square and use a soft pencil to draw a line across opposite corners to find the centre. Use a compass to draw a 2in-diameter circle in the centre of the base. Using fig 7 as a guide, draw out a random pattern of stone flags, approximately 1in wide, working outwards from the centre. Once the pattern looks satisfactory use a sharp craft knife to incise V-shaped cuts for the joints around the stones. Vary the shape and depth of the cuts and soften the edges to give some modelling to the surfaces (see Tip box, centre right).

Cut a piece of 6mm MDF into a ¼in strip about 7in long and from this cut two support pieces 2in long and two pieces 1½in long. Glue these supports around the outer edge of the base on the underside.

Find a 2in-diameter food or drink can and using tin snips if it's metal, or old scissors, carefully cut a ¼in wide strip. Glue this under the central aperture in the base using a rapid-set epoxy adhesive. (We used a cleaned-up cocoa container but you could use a strip of stiff card wrapped around any suitable round object, gluing the ends together.) This ring should just sit under the well base and is hidden from view by the supports. Glue the well base assembly into position according to the garden plan.

Finish the well base by painting the inside of the ring, the well, and the base with a silk-finish black paint. Finish the paving with a grey acrylic paint mixed with a light green to simulate moss.

Well working parts

Cut two sides from ³/₁₆in thick jelutong ¾in x 3½in. Mark the centre of one end of each

TIP

Any old branch may not look realistic and a little time and patience in choosing just the right piece will be more than worth the effort. Remember that we are dealing with ¹/₁₂th scale and that the bark on the trunk must be in proportion too.

TIP

Use a piece of fine abrasive paper wrapped around a small stick to indent some of the paving around the well base.

TIP

Always wear a pair of protective gloves when cutting metal and file down any sharp edges before proceeding with assembly.

and plane both edges to 30 degrees (see fig 8). Place one side onto a flat working surface and make a mark ³/₄in from the top, dead centre. Place the second side directly beneath the first and drill a ¹/₁₆in-diameter hole through both to take the dowel pins.

Cut four supports for the sides from ³/₁₆in thick jelutong ⁷/₁₆in wide x 1⁷/₈in long. Cut each end of each piece to 45 degrees. Lay one side onto a flat surface using a wood offcut as a stop at the bottom and glue two supports into place, flush with the bottom (see fig 8). Repeat for the second side.

Cut two roof parts from ¹/₁₆in thick jelutong 4¹/₂in x 1³/₁₆in and trim the inner edges at 30 degrees using a small plane. Fix a 4¹/₂in strip of masking tape along the top of one part of the roof and glue the second roof part to it. Use the masking tape to hold them together and support both pieces in an upside-down position until set. Support each side with Plasticine or Blu Tack in the upright position 3⁹/₁₆in apart and glue the roof onto both.

Cut a 3¹/₂in length of ³/₈in-diameter wooden dowel for the well roller and drill a ¹/₁₆in-diameter hole into the centre of each end, about ³/₈in deep. Cut a piece of ¹/₁₆in-diameter wire ³/₄in long and a second piece about 2in long. Use two pairs of pliers (or one pair and a small vice) to bend the second piece of wire into the shape of a car starting handle. One tail should be about ³/₄in long, the other can be trimmed to ¹/₂in.

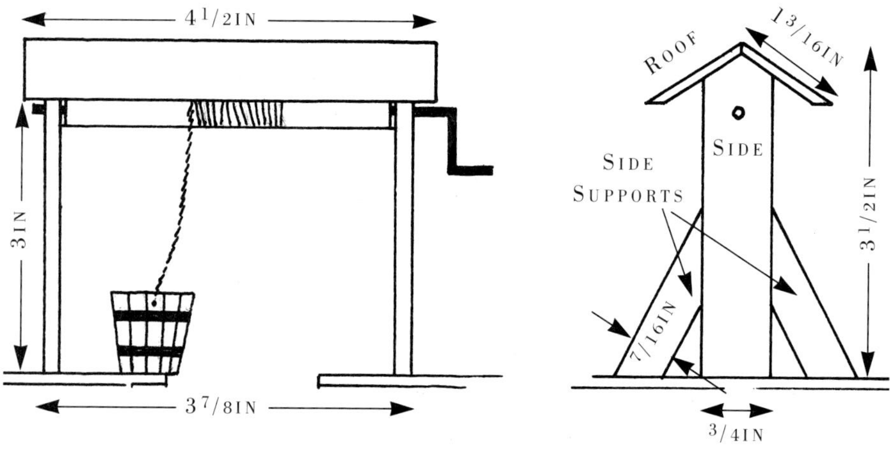

Add a little rapid-set epoxy adhesive to the holes in both ends of the roller and place it between the two well sides. Insert the short wire through the pre-drilled hole and the wire handle through the other side, into the roller. Check that the roller moves freely and then allow the glue to set.

Colour all the wooden parts with an oak wood stain mixed 50/50 with white spirit and allow this to dry. Wind a 9in length of string, coloured with a little weak-coloured wood stain, around the centre roller and tie on a small wooden bucket to the other end. Place the assembly to one side until the garden has been built up.

GARDEN SURFACE

As you can see the surface of this garden is rough and uneven, it has no formal arrangement and you can really add anything you wish to give that rough tumbledown appearance. The surface is built up using Mod-Roc modelling bandage over a base made from any moulded waste material, such as polystyrene, newspaper, tissue or Oasis (floral foam). In this project the ground level has been raised on the left side of the door and moulded around the base of the tree and the well so that these two features become part of the landscape.

Start by masking off those areas which will not be covered with modelling bandage, such as the hedge and fence. You can do this with an offcut of 2mm MDF fixed into place with tape or modelling wax that is removed when the Mod-Roc has dried out. Protect the front of the house and the well from splashes of plaster by covering with a piece of cling film (Siran wrap) and holding this in place with masking tape.

Draw the higher ground areas onto the baseboard and lay the moulded waste materials into position, fixing with glue or masking tape. Make these undulations gradual and taper them off to flow down into the main areas. Place some material around the tree so that the groundwork can be built up over its base.

Fig 8 The well working parts

4¹/₂IN

3IN

3⁷/₈IN

ROOF   1³/₁₆IN

SIDE

SIDE SUPPORTS

⁷/₁₆IN

3¹/₂IN

³/₄IN

Cut the Mod-Roc bandage into pieces about 6in long and lay them into a shallow dish of water. Start laying it at the back of the garden and work forwards, laying the bandage down flat and smoothing it with wet fingers. Add a little plaster filler or sawdust as you work and brush this onto the surface to obtain the levels and finish you require. When all the groundwork has been added allow the site to dry thoroughly before proceeding with painting.

Mod-Roc plaster bandage should be painted using water-based paints not enamels. Paint the whole of the earth area a scrubby grass green colour and when this is dry it can be covered with more texture as required. To finish, simply paint PVA adhesive over the chosen areas, sprinkle with fine sand and foam from Woodland Scenics (available from good craft shops) and add some small stones or pebbles. Remove protective coverings and masking tape and add typical country-garden plants (see photographs).

FENCES AND HEDGES
The fencing is all made from jelutong wood: in the event that this is not available see Making the Elements for alternatives.

Back and side fences
Cut seven 4in long posts from $^1/_4$in square jelutong, with the bottom ends cut square. Drill a $^1/_{32}$in-diameter hole $^3/_{16}$in from the bottom of each, dead centre. Roughly plane the tops to a 30 degree angle, which should face away from the fence on assembly.

With the garden baseboard on a flat surface, place one post in an upright position $^1/_2$in from the top right-hand corner, on the side (see fig 6 and the garden plan). Push a panel pin through the hole to mark the base and pre-drill a $^1/_{32}$in-diameter hole, $^1/_4$in deep into the base. Place a second post 4in away from the first and pre-drill a second hole. Repeat for the other corner at the back of the base, this time with two extra posts each spaced at 4in intervals.

Place the last two posts on the left-hand side of the baseboard $^1/_2$in and 4in away from the front of the cottage, pre-drilling holes as before. Firmly panel pin all the posts into position, do not glue, and secure in an upright position using a grip wax or re-usable adhesive, such as Blu Tack.

Prepare about 40in of fence railing from $^1/_8$in thick x $^1/_4$in jelutong and cut two lengths to fit between the end of the cottage and the right-hand corner of the garden, approximately 10in each. Cut two more for each section of fencing, overlapping the ends of the posts by $^1/_4$in. Use a rapid-set spirit adhesive such as UHU to glue the bottom rails to all the fences, resting them on and flush with the base. Glue the second set of rails $2^1/_2$in above the first, secure these and allow the glue to set.

Remove the three sets of rails and posts at this stage of the assembly as you will find them easier to work on if they are laid onto a flat working surface. Cut and prepare fifty $4^1/_4$in long strips of $^1/_{16}$in thick x $^1/_2$in jelutong for fence panel uprights. About half of these strips should be distressed by chipping and filing the ends, and shaving

TIP
Most fences are designed to keep intruders out and livestock in. For well designed houses keep fences neat and tidy with the best side facing away from the house. Hedges are a useful alternative to fences and can easily be removed for garden maintenance.

95

pieces off the sides. Mix these in with the straight ones and assemble in a random way. Glue the first panel upright against the rails and work your way along the section. Overlap some of the boards by 1/16in, leave one or two out entirely and place a few at extreme angles to give an unkempt appearance (see fig 9 and photograph).

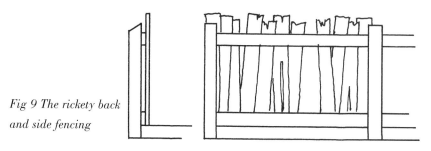

Fig 9 The rickety back and side fencing

Finally, stain the completed assemblies with a wood stain in dark oak mixed 50/50 with white spirit. Allow this to dry and apply a second coat of stain to some of the upright panels and along the bottom of all of them. When the assemblies are thoroughly dry, glue and panel pin to the baseboard.

Front hedges

Prepare a base from 2mm MDF 16in x 1in, clean up the edges and lay onto a flat surface. Paint the surface with a mixture of brown and green acrylic paint.

From a sheet of dense grain polystyrene packaging material cut two blocks for the hedges. For the left-hand hedge cut a piece 3/4in wide x 2 1/4in high x 5in long. For the right-hand hedge cut a piece 3/4in wide x 1 1/4in high x 2 1/2in. Shape these blocks into the outline of a hedge using a sharp craft knife (see fig 10). Seal the surfaces of the two polystyrene blocks of hedge with any dark-coloured matt emulsion and allow to dry, then paint the entire surface with a

Fig 10 The front hedges, picket fence and gate

green acrylic paint and allow to dry. Use a fine brush to cover the surface with PVA glue or spray with artist's display mount adhesive and then sprinkle the surface with Woodland Scenics fine green foam. Brush off any surplus and repeat if necessary.

Mark the position of these two hedges onto the base strip (the shorter hedge to the right) and cover this area with masking tape. Cover the remaining area with PVA glue and whilst this is still tacky cover the surface with scenic foam and the sand used in the garden. Remove the masking tape and glue the left-hand hedge onto the base strip but leave the right-hand hedge until the final assembly of the garden in case any adjustments need to be made.

Front picket fence and gate

Cut sixteen 2in pieces of 1/8in thick x 1/4in jelutong, for fence uprights and use a razor saw and mitre block to shape one end of each into 45 degree points, leaving a net length of 2in (see fig 10).

Cut two pieces of 1/8in thick x 1/4in jelutong 5 1/4in long and two more pieces 2 1/4in long for rails and cut one end of each to a narrow point, about 1/2in long, which will be used to fix the fence into the hedge. Cut two gate rails and one gate brace from pieces of 1/8in x 1/4in jelutong, each 1 3/4in long.

Cut two fence posts from 1/4in x 1/4in jelutong, each 2 1/4in long and shape the tops by cutting at 45 degree angles in all four directions. Cut two pieces of 1/16in copper tube each 3/8in long and file a 'flat' onto the side. Cut two pieces of 1/32in-diameter round wire 1/2in long and bend each at right angles to produce the L-shaped hinges for the gate.

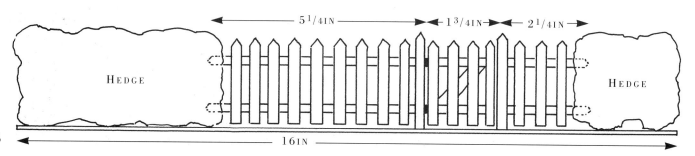

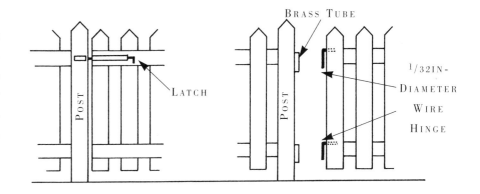

Fig 11 Gate assembly

Make a spacing template (A) from a strip of card ³/₄in wide x 6in long and pin this onto a flat surface. Make a second template strip (B) ³/₈in wide and about 6in long. Lay the two 5in rails on either side of the spacing template (A) ensuring that the ends are level with each other and secure in place using dressmaker's pins. Place template (B) below the bottom rail and firmly pin into position. The bottom edge of the uprights should match that of the second template.

Starting with the longer of the two fences and working from the right-hand end, place one upright vertically, flush with the ends of the rails and in line with the bottom template, but do not glue this into position. Place a spot of quick grab glue such as UHU on both rails to the left of this upright and fix the second upright into position. Place a third upright beside the second, and then glue the fourth into position. Remove the first upright and proceed like this until all nine uprights are glued onto the assembly (see fig 10). Repeat the procedure for the right-hand end of the fence, this time starting from the left-hand edge, with the points on the right-hand side. Use templates as before to ensure correct spacing.

Make up the gate parts (see fig 11) using the spacing templates but this time uprights are glued to both the outer edges and a brace is added from right to left, the ends being cut at angles to fit between the rails. Drill ¹/₃₂in-diameter holes into the ends of both gate rails on the left-hand side and glue in the L-shaped pieces of wire. Add a latch if required using 1mm wire and tubing.

Lay the gate onto a flat surface and place the posts on either side so that the bottom of the gate is ¹/₈in above the bottom of the posts. Mark the position of the wire hinges on one post and use Super Glue or rapid-set epoxy adhesive to fix the two pieces of copper tubing (the flattened side of the tube to the post). Glue the posts to the two fences with a gap of ¹/₈in between the bottom of the fence and that of the posts.

Paint all the picket fence and gate parts with white acrylic paint and add streaks and weathering with a watered-down mixture of brown and grey.

Attach the left-hand fence to the hedge by pushing the fencing rails into the polystyrene, being careful to keep the fence upright at all times. Attach the right-hand fence to its hedge in the same manner and lay this onto the base. Check that there is sufficient space for the gate to swing on its hinges and then glue this hedge and fence into place using a PVA glue (avoid spirit-based glues as they may dissolve the polystyrene). Allow to dry, then assemble the gate into the gap between the two fencing assemblies.

To complete your rustic garden, add accessories and plant up in a suitably relaxed country manner, referring to the photographs for ideas.

The Edwardian Summer House

This garden is a place for rest and recreation, not requiring too much in the way of maintenance work – that's if you do not consider mowing the lawn and weeding, work.

The summer house is situated above the garden level to provide a focal point for this simple but effective project. We say simple but it is deceptive as there is a wealth of features placed on a several levels with many textures. The smooth lawns give way to a paved path which leads the eye to a rough rockery full of natural shapes and on to a decorative summer house. The paths, lawns, rockery, steps, seating and ordered flower beds come together to produce a striking contemporary geometric design full of angles and straight lines.

The garden is also multi-functional: the broad grassed areas can be used for small ball games such as croquet; the rockery gives the opportunity for the enthusiast to grow alpine plants and the summer house provides shelter from the sun as well as the rain – a place to take tea, read a book or contemplate the scene below.

The size of this garden is not fixed and it may be adapted to fit an existing house – period or contemporary – or be made as a tabletop scene, simply adjust one or more sizes on the plan and alter accordingly. A separate list of materials is given for the summer house, making it easy to build this structure as a dominant feature in a garden of your own design.

CONSTRUCTING THE GARDEN

General materials needed for constructing this garden include; PVA glue, masking tape, tea bags, panel pins, scrap polystyrene, fine sand and various paints. Where instructions are given for general gluing it is assumed that a PVA type glue will be used.

MATERIALS

MDF – 9mm

Steps	A	$2^{1}/_{4}$in x $^{3}/_{4}$in
	B	$2^{1}/_{4}$in x $^{1}/_{4}$in x $1^{7}/_{8}$in (shaped, see instructions)
	C	$2^{1}/_{4}$in x $2^{3}/_{4}$in x $1^{1}/_{8}$in (shaped, see instructions)
	D	3in x $2^{3}/_{4}$in
Lawn bases		14in x 14in

MDF – 6mm

Base	16in x 16in
Wall A	$14^{1}/_{4}$in x 7in
Wall B	14in x 7in
Walls C (low)	2in x 25in total (plus offcuts)

MDF – 2mm

Crazy paving platform		14in x $8^{1}/_{2}$in sheet (cut as on garden plan)
Step treads	A	$2^{5}/_{16}$in x $^{3}/_{4}$in
	B	$2^{1}/_{2}$in x $^{3}/_{4}$in x $1^{7}/_{8}$in (shaped, see instructions)
	C	$2^{5}/_{8}$in x $2^{3}/_{4}$in x $1^{1}/_{8}$in (shaped, see instructions)
	D	$3^{1}/_{16}$in x $2^{3}/_{4}$in
Path		13in x 2in (see instructions)

> **TIP**
>
> *The base for the lawn can be made from 2mm MDF with $^{1}/_{4}$in formers or packing placed underneath to give height. This is more economical and 2mm will prove easier to cut than 9mm.*

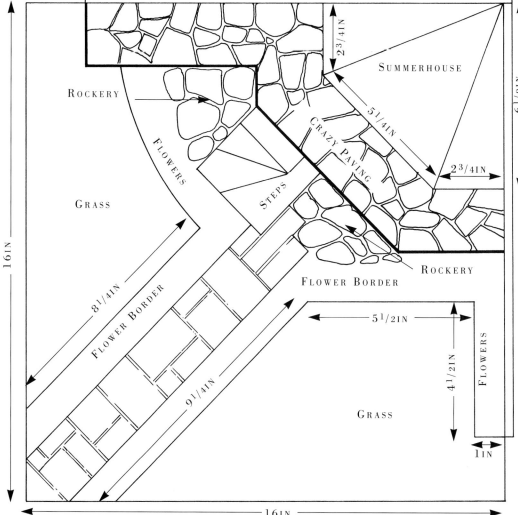

Jelutong wood
- *^{1}/$_4$in x ^{1}/$_4$in x 65in for the formers for the
raised area*

Other materials
- *Polystyrene packaging*
- *Rocks 20–25 pieces approximately
1 cubic inch each*
- *Grass matting*
- *Oasis (floral foam)*

Specialist supplies
(see Suppliers page 173)
- *Brick wall fibre-glass sheet,
any traditional bond*
- *Grey stone-patterned fibre-glass
moulded sheet*
- *DAS modelling clay (see Tip box
page 103)*

SUMMER HOUSE MATERIALS

(see page 105)

BASE

Cut the base from 6mm MDF, 16in x 16in
and square off. Mark which corner will have
the brick walls attached and draw a line
from this point for the pathway across the
diagonal. Measure off two more lines, 1in
either side of the centre of the first and
mark with a firm pencil line – these lines
delineate the width of the path.

BACK WALLS

Cut both A and B walls from 6mm MDF
following the sizes given in the cutting list
and drill three or four ^{1}/$_{32}$in-diameter holes
to take panel pins along the bottom edge of
each one, ^{1}/$_8$in up from the bottom. Glue
with PVA adhesive and pin walls A and B to
the base. Wall B is located flush to the back
corner, whilst wall A overlaps B to make a
neat joint. Hold both walls in position with
masking tape until the adhesive has set.

Measure off the amount of fibre-glass
brick sheeting required for each wall and
add ^{3}/$_4$in to the tops and sides. Mitre the
corners and glue onto the surface of the

walls using PVA glue or artist's display
mount adhesive, carrying the sheet over and
around the edges to finish off.

UPPER PAVED AREA – PREPARATION

Cut out the crazy paving platform from a
sheet of 2mm MDF, 14in x 8^1/$_2$in (see fig 1).
Lay the platform onto the baseboard and
draw a guide line around the shape. These
lines indicate the position of the 2in supporting walls that are laid inside the line.

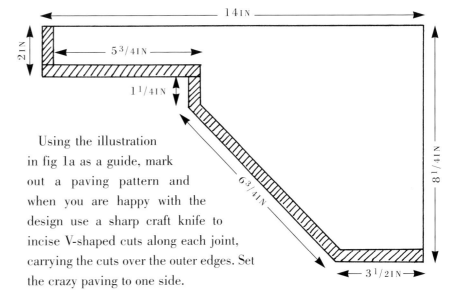

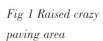

*Fig 1 Raised crazy
paving area*

Using the illustration
in fig 1a as a guide, mark
out a paving pattern and
when you are happy with the
design use a sharp craft knife to
incise V-shaped cuts along each joint,
carrying the cuts over the outer edges. Set
the crazy paving to one side.

LOW WALLS

In 6mm MDF cut the 2in low walls that are
placed under the crazy paving platform (see
shading in fig 1). Each wall butts against
the next and three require angled joints to
make a neat finish (see Tip box page 103).

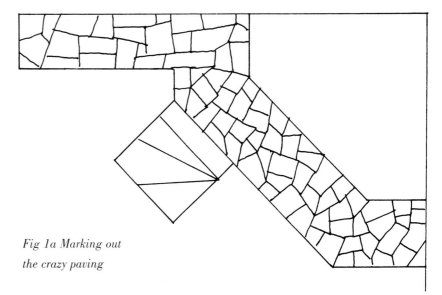

*Fig 1a Marking out
the crazy paving*

TIP

*The summer house will
sit onto the paved area
and it will look more
realistic if the paving is
cut around its outline.*

Glue the five pieces into place flush with the guide line and glue two or three 6mm x 2in MDF offcuts onto the baseboard, for support at the back of the assembly to give stability and strength (see fig 1). Finish off the assembly by gluing on a grey stone-patterned fibre-glass moulded sheet (see Suppliers page 173) and trim the top edge dead flush.

UPPER PAVED AREA – FINISHING OFF

Spray (with cellulose car paint) or brush paint (with acrylic) the area of crazy paving with a mixture of grey and khaki colouring and add a touch of blue and green to some areas. Keep the colouring uneven at all times to make it appear more natural and emphasise the joints with a little black or brown colouring. Remember to paint the outer edges to match. Glue a few pieces of lichen to the joints. Glue and pin the paving into place, flush against the two back walls and the front supporting wall. Punch down any pin heads, then fill and touch up any damaged paintwork.

STEPS

These are garden steps and absolute accuracy is not a requirement, that way if they end up being a little out of shape it will only add to the character of the garden. All four steps are built up from 9mm MDF (see cutting list). A and D are cut as rectangles with right-angled edges but steps B and C have one edge cut at an angle (see figs 2 and 2a). Cut tread D so that it is flush with three sides but overlaps the long clear (front) side

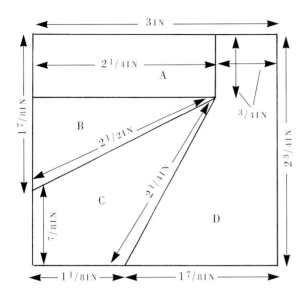

Fig 2 Plan of the four steps

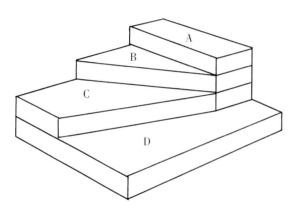

Fig 2a Step shapes with treads in place

the colour off the outer edges to indicate wear. Finish off by adding a strip of stone walling sheet to the face of each step, under the tread. Glue the step assembly into place on the baseboard.

ROCKERY

The rockery is built around the steps onto a base of scrap polystyrene blocks. Once these have been shaped with a craft knife, glue them into place on either side of the steps using PVA glue or decorator's filler. Spirit-based glues should *not* be used as they will dissolve the material and may give off noxious fumes.

We have used DAS modelling clay (see Basic Tools and Materials for alternatives) to build up the secondary base into which the small natural rocks are pressed. The area you are working on should be covered to a depth of about ³/₈in. You can either find small rocks in your area or buy some from a garden centre.

Start by placing the larger rocks at the bottom and gently press them into the clay so that they are held firmly. Add more rocks until you have pattern that fills the area satisfactorily. Then, carefully remove all the rocks, remembering where they belong in the pattern and without disturbing the clay. Place the garden in a warm area and allow the clay to dry out – this may take twenty-four hours (see also the rockery in Making the Elements page 37).

When the rockery base is thoroughly dry use a spirit-based adhesive (UHU) to glue all the rocks into their places and add a little extra moist clay between the joints. Allow the whole rockery to dry off and then paint the clay used as a jointing compound with 'earth' colour acrylic paint, being careful not to colour any rocks. The surface of the 'earth' will be covered with tea dust in the usual way, see flower beds below.

PAVED PATHWAY

The pathway runs from one corner of the garden to the centre of the rockery to meet

---

TIP

To make a correct angled joint, measure the total angle using an adjustable square and a protractor, divide by two, mark and then cut.

TIP

DAS modelling clay slowly dries once it is exposed to the air so you should avoid working on large areas at one time. To keep the clay pliable, place a damp cloth over unfinished areas until you are ready.

---

by ¹/₁₆in and lay this on top of the step. Place step C on top of this tread and mark around it with a pencil, cutting off the waste. Lay step C on its tread and draw a line ¹/₁₆in away from the front edge to where it meets step B, then cut off the waste. Now, lay tread C onto step C and place step B onto this assembly, mark around the top step and cut off the waste. Repeat this procedure for treads B and A.

Once you have cut and shaped the treads the steps should be glued together with PVA adhesive and clamped until the adhesive has set. Glue on the treads and when the adhesive has set hard finish off with a little abrasive paper or a file, rounding off the edges to introduce wear and tear.

Paint the steps assembly using light grey and khaki acrylic colours, working a little black into the corners and rubbing some of

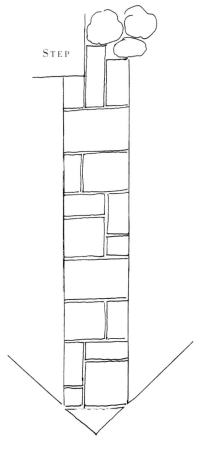

STEP

Fig 3 Positioning the paving stones on the paved pathway

the steps, along the centre lines we drew earlier on the baseboard. Cut the following paving stones from 2mm MDF using a hand saw and do not worry if the lines are not perfect as a little inaccuracy will help to give the appearance of real stones.

Two off	2in x 1¹/₄in
Four off	1¹/₄in x 1¹/₄in
Seven off	1¹/₄in x ⁵/₈in
Two off	⁵/₈in x ⁵/₈in
Two off	⁵/₈in x ⁷/₈in
One off	1¹/₄in x ³/₈in
One off	1⁵/₈in x 1in

Smooth off any ragged edges and round off the corners on some stones to introduce a natural appearance. Lay and glue all the paving stones along the path following the diagram in fig 3, leaving very small ¹/₃₂in gaps between each which are then filled with thin rolls of moist DAS modelling clay. Smooth off the clay and cover with fine sand, press this into the surface and allow it to dry.

Finish off with a soft brush and paint the paving with a mixture of grey and khaki acrylic paints, adding a little darker colouring to the joints and allowing stones to show different shades. Any loose sand can be safely painted onto the pathway as it will give a more realistic finish.

GRASS BASES

If you follow the cutting list in the materials section you will see that the grass bases are made from 9mm MDF (see also Tip box on page 105). Cut each lawn base following the diagram in fig 4. Place the two bases into position on the baseboard and carefully make a pencil mark around them, but do not fix at this stage.

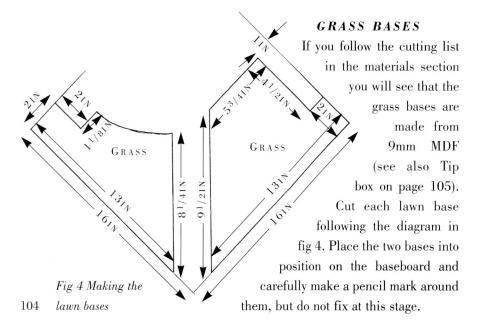

Fig 4 Making the lawn bases

FLOWER BEDS

Cut the flower beds from a green-coloured block of Oasis (floral foam), ³/₈in thick to fit along each side of the path and glue into place. Shape the edges with a craft knife to resemble an earth border profile, then cut and shape further sections to fit against the edges of the rockery and against the right wall.

You can make the job easier by preparing a template and cutting the foam to fit that. Alternatively you could add small pieces of foam which are glued together until the area is built up to the shape required.

Please note that the main photograph on page 98 shows an additional flower bed along one front edge of the garden. This can be included if you wish by altering the right-hand lawn size slightly and making the bed from Oasis as described above.

Use a small paint-brush to cover the surface of the Oasis and the 'earth' between the rocks on your rockery with white PVA glue and allow this to become tacky before covering with tea dust from a tea bag. Press the tea down onto the surface to make sure that it adheres but avoid pressing too hard or the dust will lift off. When dry, brush off any loose dust from the surfaces and place more glue and dust on any areas left uncovered. Clean up the area ready to position the grass bases, adding low plants to the flower beds and alpines to the rockery when ready.

GRASS

Lay the grass matting face down onto a smooth work surface with the lawn bases face down on top. Draw round each of the bases with a felt-tip pen and cut out the shapes, slightly oversize, with a sharp pair of scissors.

Glue the matting down onto each of the lawn bases and leave them face down to dry. When dry, trim off any excess matting using a sharp craft knife. You can now glue the grassed bases down onto their positions on the baseboard.

SUMMER HOUSE

This charming little structure is the focal point of the garden.

SUMMER HOUSE MATERIALS

4mm hardboard

Back wall A   9in x 6¹/8in
(shaped, see instructions)

Back wall B   9in x 6in (shaped, see instructions)

Base C   6in x 6in square (shaped, see instructions)

MDF – 2mm

Roof side, two off   7³/8in x 2⁵/8in
(shaped, see instructions)

Roof centre   7³/8in x 5¹/2in (shaped, see instructions)

Jelutong wood

Side frame uprights,
four off   ³/16in x ³/16in x 4¹/2in

Side frame bottom rail,
four off   ¹/8in x ¹/4in x 2¹/16in

Side frame top rail,
two off   ¹/8in x ¹/4in x 2¹/16in

Frame top (1),
two off   ³/32in thick x ³/8in x ³/8in

Frame top (2),
two off   ³/32in thick x ¹/4in x ³/8in

Frame lintel D and F,
two off   ¹/8in thick x 2³/8in x ³/4in
(shaped, see instructions)

Frame lintel E   ¹/8in thick x 5in x
³/4in (shaped)

Frame lintel G (1),
two off   ¹/8in thick x 2³/8in x ¹/8in

Top lintel G (2)   ¹/8in thick x 5in x ¹/8in

Seat support former,
two off   ¹/8in x ³/32in x 5in

Seat, two off   ³/32in thick x 1¹/4in x 5¹/2in

Roof support formers,
four off   ³/32in x ¹/4in x 7in

Other materials

• *Four stair spindles minimum 2¹/2in long*
• *Shiplap cladding, two off*
9in x 6in (shaped)
• *Oak floor boards ¹/2in wide, to cover a*
6in x 6in shaped area
• *Sheet of 150gsm grey card for roof*

Walls and base assembly

Cut out both back walls, A and B and note that A is approximately 4mm wider (or the thickness of the material used) to allow for the overlap (see fig 5). Measure off the angle that reduces the height of both to 5⁵/8in at the front and then cut, making sure that the two front corners match in height.

Draw a line ¹/4in in from each outer front edge as a location mark for the frame and the shiplap cladding. Cut the base C from the same material, ensuring that all the

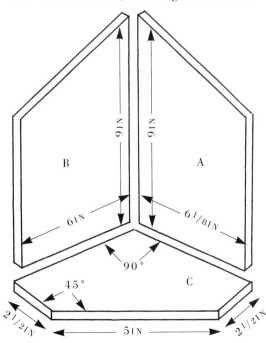

Fig 5 Making the summer house walls

corners are at right angles. Mark out the front 2¹/₂in in from each corner for the cut off, then carefully saw this piece off and clean up all the edges. Glue walls A and B together allowing A to overlap, using the base as a guide to the right angle. Then, glue the walls to the base.

Measure off and cut two pieces of shiplap cladding to fit the inner walls, ensuring that the panels match. Remove, paint or spray with a white, satin-finish paint and leave to dry. Glue to the inside of the walls, after laying the flooring for a neat finish.

Summer house flooring

Draw a pencil line from the back corner to the centre of the front as a guide to laying the floor boards. Draw a line ¹/₄in in from the left-hand and right-hand outer edges where the bottom rails are located. Select sufficient fine-grained ¹/₂in wide boards and cut each board off neatly at the front and against the two lines. Glue these into place using a spirit-based adhesive such as UHU, working from the centre line outwards and towards the corners. When the boards are laid and the adhesive has set, cover all with masking tape to protect until the painting and other assembly work is finished.

Seating

Cut two seat support formers from ¹/₈in x ³/₃₂in jelutong and cut the inner corners at 45 degrees to form a right angle. Colour with 50/50 white spirit and oak stain mixture and when dry glue onto the shiplap back at a height of 1¹/₂in from the base.

Cut two seats from ³/₃₂in x 1¹/₄in wide jelutong and cut the inner corners at 45 degrees to form a complete right angle (see fig 6). Colour with 50/50 white spirit and oak stain and when dry fix into place onto the two support formers and the back with a fast grab adhesive such as UHU.

Frames

Trim four spindles to 2¹/₄in and cut four side frame rails from ¹/₈in thick x ¹/₄in wide

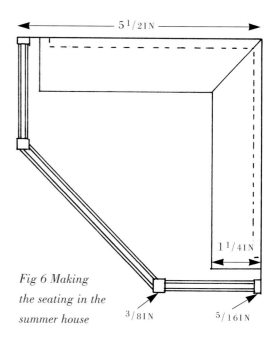

Fig 6 Making the seating in the summer house

jelutong, each 2¹/₁₆in long. Cut four side frame uprights from ³/₁₆in square jelutong and lay all the parts onto a clean flat surface. Assemble with the rails and spindles to make two assemblies (see fig 7).

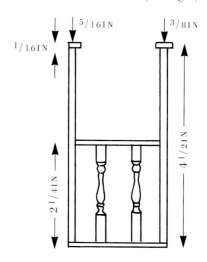

Fig 7 Making the summer house rails and spindles (left side)

Round off the top corners of the frame tops and glue onto the frame uprights. Note the ³/₈in x ³/₈in pieces are at the front, not against the back wall. The shorter edge tops are against the walls. Paint the assemblies with a white satin-finish paint and glue into place against the back walls.

Lintels

Cut the blanks for the decorative lintels from ¹/₈in thick x 3¹/₈in x ³/₄in jelutong and plane the inner ends so that they match when assembled at an angle. Fretsaw the cut-outs on each piece as shown in fig 8.

Cut the three top lintels G from $\frac{1}{8}$in x $\frac{1}{4}$in jelutong and glue on top of the decorative lintels, D, E and F. Finish off all the assembled lintels with white satin-finish paint and glue onto the side frames. Support the assemblies with masking tape until the adhesive has set.

Roof

Cut the three roof parts from 2mm MDF (see cutting list). Use a small plane or fine abrasive paper wrapped around a cork block to bevel the inner matching edges to produce a smooth fit. Cut four roof support formers from $\frac{3}{32}$in thick x $\frac{1}{4}$in jelutong, 7in long. Bevel the top surfaces to match the inner side of the roof when assembled. 'Dry' fit all the parts to avoid any problems later and plane off the top of the walls if necessary to obtain a good fit. When you are satisfied, paint the under surfaces of the roof and the supports with a white satin-finish paint. As soon as the paint is dry assemble the roof on top of the walls and lintels.

Roof tiling

Take the sheet of grey card and cut off a strip $\frac{1}{2}$in wide, then with the remainder measure off a series of lines $\frac{3}{4}$in apart (see fig 9, page 37 if necessary). Turn the card around at right angles and mark off again at $\frac{3}{4}$in intervals. Cut the card into a series of $\frac{3}{4}$in wide strips. Using a pair of scissors cut a slit up each of the marks no more than $\frac{5}{8}$in. Leave one $\frac{3}{4}$in strip uncut and glue this along the three front edges of the roof.

Cut and glue a strip of cut tiles to the front edge of the roof over the blank strip, starting with the left-hand section. Glue a second strip onto the first leaving a gap of exactly $\frac{1}{2}$in, staggering the joins exactly as you would on a real roof and repeating the process until you reach the top of the roof.

Take the $\frac{1}{2}$in strip of card and lightly

score a line down the centre. Gently fold this over to form a ridge tile and then cut and glue the strip on where the three roof parts meet.

The roof can be given a weathered appearance by cutting a portion off one or two tiles and by adding a little white and brown paint to some of the joints in the tiles. Use a minimal amount of paint on a nearly dry brush and stipple on the colour. Finally, place the summer house into position to finish your garden project.

The accessories shown with this garden, particularly the lion's head wall feature, the wooden trellis and the flower tubs and ornaments, can be obtained from the Suppliers listed on page 173.

Fig 8 Making the lintels for the summer house

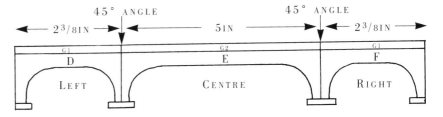

The Terrace House Backyard

Many readers will remember the backyard: a small area at the back of a terraced house never quite big enough to cope with all the demands placed upon it. Large industrial towns had substantial developments of small artisans' cottages and houses that were built in a series of blocks, back to back, with backyards that led to an alley running down the middle. If nothing else the yard was a breathing space, a place to put out the day's washing, store the bath and somewhere for the children to play. During the Second World War, a period so many miniaturists are now busily re-creating, the yard was put to use in a different ways – growing vegetables, housing a bomb shelter, keeping a few rabbits to supplement the meagre food rations.

The backyard created here is probably set between the wars, somewhere around the 1930s. This garden is essentially a working space, containing a shed for storage, the outside and only WC or toilet and a rabbit hutch. At the end of the yard is a gate leading into an alley. The outside WC, or privy, was for many households the only toilet with running water – indoor plumbing did not arrive for some until as late as the 1950s. As a consequence bathing was a weekly luxury taken in front of the kitchen range using a portable bath, kept hanging in the yard.

The condition of the building and paintwork was often poor, tending to make a backyard look more than a little run-down and we have continued this plain, utilitarian style throughout the project.

CONSTRUCTING THE GARDEN

Follow the garden plan for the layout of the elements. General materials needed for construction include; PVA glue, artist's display mount adhesive, rapid-set clear adhesive (UHU), wood stain, white spirit, various paints, clear varnish, tea bags, panel pins, dressmaker's pins, stiff card, masking tape, Vaseline (petroleum jelly), wallpaper paste and plaster filler. Where instructions are given for general gluing use a PVA type glue.

Jelutong wood

Shed, privy, fencing and gate — ¹/₁₆in thick strips x ¹/₂in x 24in total (see instructions)

Privy seat — ¹/₈in thick x 3in x 2in

The following sizes of jelutong are required for most of the small components, such as the shed and the rabbit hutch, and the exact lengths can be determined from the text accompanying the individual piece: ¹/₄in x ¹/₈in; ³/₈in x ¹/₄in; ¹/₈in x ¹/₈in; ³/₁₆in x ³/₁₆in; ³/₈in x ¹/₈in; ³/₃₂in x ³/₃₂in

Other materials

- *Perspex (plexiglass) or acrylic sheet*
- *Polystyrene blocks (from packaging)*
- *Door furniture for house and privy door*
- *¹/₃₂in thick and ¹/₁₆in thick plasticard*
- *Brick-patterned paper sheet*
- *Corrugated cardboard*
- *Mod-Roc modelling bandage*
- *³/₃₂in wooden dowel, short length*
- *Thin twine*
- *L-shaped moulding (see page 120)*

- *Fine wire mesh, 6in x 6in approximately*
- *Plants, weeds and foliage*
- *Garden tools and accessories*

LEAN-TO SHED MATERIALS

(see page 117)

BASE

Prepare the base from 9mm MDF 24in x 12in, square up all the edges and lay this down onto your work surface ready for the building.

THE HOUSE EXTENSION

The first task is to build up the back of the house and the extension onto the baseboard to provide a suitable setting. This is not meant to be a real dolls' house and only represents the position your own house might occupy. If you do not have a house but would like to build this unit onto the garden there is a door and windows printed on page 113. Enlarge on a photocopier by 141% and glue to the walls. Alternatively, doors and windows can be purpose made to the correct sizes and corresponding apertures cut for them.

TIP

When using brick-patterned paper sheets, size the walls with wallpaper paste first and then paste the paper. Allow two or three minutes for the paper to absorb the paste and then apply to the walls.

Plan of the terrace house backyard

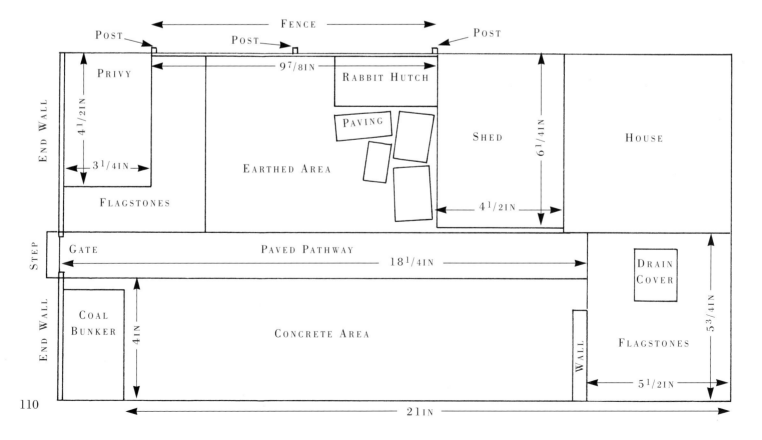

Walls

Cut out walls A, B and C from 6mm MDF and mark the back of each with the appropriate letter. You will see that wall A reduces in height from 15³/₄in to 12³/₄in, where it meets wall B (see figs 1 and 1a).

The extension

The building sits on top of the baseboard and is glued and panel pinned into position. Start by laying wall A onto the back wall C and mark the outer edge as a location point for wall B (see fig 1). Draw a second line ¹/₈in in and parallel to the left of the first.

Drill three equally spaced ¹/₃₂in-diameter holes down the second line to take panel pins. Drill three ¹/₃₂in-diameter holes down the right-hand edge of wall A, ¹/₈in in from the edge to take panel pins. Chamfer the top edge of wall B at an angle to match the slope on A – this will enable the roof to sit perfectly. At this stage any apertures for windows or doors should be cut out from all the walls. If you are gluing on 'mock' components mark the locations.

Hold wall B in a suitable bench vice and glue and pin wall A to it as shown in fig 1. Glue the assembly of the two walls onto wall C against the mark made earlier. Check all is level and at right angles and hammer home panel pins through from the back, allowing the adhesive to set.

Cut and prepare the roof D from 6mm MDF, noting that both ends are chamfered. Glue the roof onto the building assembly allowing the top to sit flush and the bottom to overhang. Lay the finished assembly down onto the baseboard as shown in fig 1 and make a pencil mark around it. Drill a series of ¹/₃₂in-diameter holes ¹/₈in inside these lines for panel pins. Glue and pin the completed assembly to the baseboard.

To finish off the extension, measure off all the walls and cut sufficient brick-patterned paper sheeting to cover them plus about ³/₄in overlap all round. Glue with a suitable adhesive such as wallpaper paste and fix into position, carefully removing any bubbles as you work.

Doors and windows

To complete the extension, **either** enlarge the window and door drawings provided in fig 1b on page 113 and glue these into position with display mount adhesive (see Tip box overleaf), **or** buy ready-made wooden windows and doors, painting them with a white acrylic paint mixed with a little brown ochre. When dry add the glazing and glue the assemblies into the apertures cut earlier.

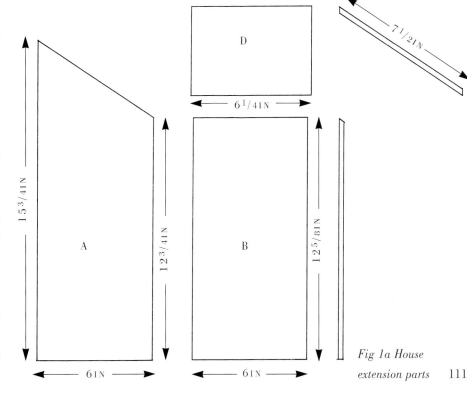

*Fig 1 House extension –
three-dimensional plan*

*Fig 1a House
extension parts*

Roof

The roof covering has been made up from $^1/_{32}$in thick plasticard cut into strips in order to make imitation slates. The card is supplied in white or black and will need to be painted grey but a surprising number of effects can be achieved and it will look very close to $^1/_{12}$th scale when it is finished.

Use an HB pencil to mark up the plasticard into $^3/_4$in wide strips. Turn the card round and draw the tile divisions at right angles to the first set of lines, again at $^3/_4$in intervals. First cut the sheet into $^3/_4$in long strips, then cut up each marked division to no more than $^5/_8$in, to leave each tile attached by $^1/_8$in at one edge. Keep one strip uncut to use as a support under the first row of cut slates. To introduce character into the roof and give it a run-down appearance, trim the edges of some tiles as if they have been chipped or broken but be careful not to overdo this effect or make it appear too uniform. Prepare sufficient strips in this way to cover the roof, remembering that each row overlaps the one below – you should need about fifteen.

Use a clear spirit-based adhesive (UHU) to glue the first uncut strip along the front edge of the roof, trimming off at each end. This will lift the bottom row very slightly upward to throw off the 'rain'. Now glue a strip of tiles on top of the first but overlapping the front edge by $^1/_8$in. Prepare the third row, remembering to stagger the joints. If you have done this correctly the two outer tiles will be half the normal width. Glue this row over the one below, overlapping by $^1/_8$in. Repeat with alternating rows until you reach the ridge, or top of the roof.

PAVING

The backyard has three sets of paved areas including a concrete area, and a few paving slabs of odd sizes around the rabbit hutch. All are made from 2mm MDF and can be cut from one sheet measuring 48in x 12in. (Note that this sheet is also sufficient to make the shed, coal bunker and privy.)

Paving area 1 – outside the back door

Cut a piece of MDF $5^3/_4$in x $5^1/_2$in. Lay the blank sheet down onto a flat surface and starting from the left-hand edge mark up with 2in x $1^1/_2$in paving stones down both of the two longer sides. This should leave $^1/_4$in slabs to the front with a $1^1/_2$in gap down the middle (see fig 2). Into this gap we are going to place an inspection cover for the drains measuring $2^1/_2$in x $1^1/_2$in.

Mark up the centre portion with the size of the cover $^1/_2$in in from the back edge and divide the remaining space into two slabs, making sure that the joints with the outer slabs are staggered. With a sharp craft knife cut V-shaped joints along all the marks where two slabs meet but not around the inspection cover. Cut a vertical line $^1/_{16}$in deep around the location of the cover and gently remove the surface with a sharp chisel. Additional half V-shaped cuts can be added. Refer to fig 2 and the photograph on page 109 for fitting the correct way round. Use a sharp craft knife to score around the inspection cover area and remove this portion using a fretsaw.

Paint the paving around the drain with a grey acrylic mixed with a little brown. Emphasise any cracks with a darker brown.

To make the drain cover, cut a piece of

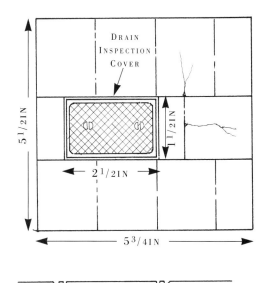

Fig 2 The paving area outside the back door

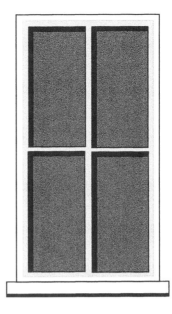

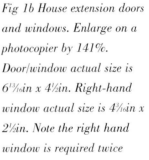

*Fig 1b House extension doors
and windows. Enlarge on a
photocopier by 141%.
Door/window actual size is
6¹³⁄₁₆in x 4½in. Right-hand
window actual size is 4³⁄₁₆in x
2½in. Note the right hand
window is required twice*

¹⁄₁₆in thick black plasticard to fit the aperture for the cover and use this to cut a second piece from ¹⁄₃₂in thick plasticard. Glue the first piece into the aperture and mark up the second, thinner piece as follows: using the back edge of a craft knife blade gently score a double line ¹⁄₁₆in around the edges and fill the centre with a series of lines drawn in a diamond pattern. Cut out two semicircular hand grips ³⁄₈in in from each end, dead centre (see fig 2).

The drain cover is 'cast iron' weathered to almost matt black. If you have used jelutong instead of plasticard it will require painting. When the black paint is dry paint the two handle details with a darker shade and rub a little pencil lead over the surface and buff up. Glue into position.

Paving area 2 – long pathway and concrete area

The pathway runs from the house to the back gate and is paved in irregularly cracked paving. The concrete beside it, having been laid directly onto earth without a suitable foundation, has cracked in at least two places. Both of these areas are made and fitted in one piece.

Cut the whole area in one piece from 2mm MDF 18¹⁄₄in x 5³⁄₄in and use a pencil to mark out the paved area along the inner edge 1³⁄₄in wide. Mark out the twelve random paving divisions of the path approximately 1¹⁄₂in long, starting from the bottom end where the gate is located, remembering to stagger the joins as you work to the right hand, or the building end. Use a sharp craft knife to cut V-shaped joints along all the paving edges and especially where it meets the concrete. Place to one side for painting and finishing later.

Paving area 3 – around privy

The privy (which is constructed later) is built up onto a concrete and paved slab and is located at the bottom of the garden, close

> **TIP**
> *Make shallow V-shaped cuts across several of the paving slabs to indicate cracks but be careful not to overdo this effect. Repeat this for the concrete area but this time the cracks should be a little wider and spread in a random way across the narrow measurement (see photograph on page 115).*

113

*The Terrace House
Backyard*

to the alley. Cut the slab from 2mm MDF 5½in x 6in and square off the corners. Lay the slab down onto a smooth work surface and measure off a space 4⅝in x 3¼in for the privy (see fig 3). Mark this area up with a pencil and leave this without paving stones as it will be under the privy. Mark up the remainder with paving slabs 1½in wide along the long side and 2in along the shorter. Use a sharp craft knife to make V-shaped cuts along all the joints and leave to one side for painting and finishing later.

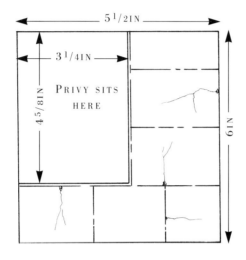

Fig 3 The paving area around the privy

Paving area 4 – around rabbit hutch

Cut four pairs of slabs from 2mm MDF, making each pair a different size but do not exceed 2in x 2in. The second set of slabs will be used when the earth around the rabbit hutch is made up. Place both sets to one side.

CONCRETE BLOCK WALL

Concrete blocks, sometimes known as breeze or building blocks, make the task of building walls so much quicker because they are much larger than a normal house brick. These have been made from a close-grained polystyrene sheet used as a packing material. Use a very sharp craft knife, razor saw or 'hot wire' cutter to make nine blocks, 1in x ¾in x ½in.

For the mortar joints cut from a sheet of stiff card three strips ⅜in wide x 3⅛in

long. Cut seven further strips ⅜in x ¾in. Lay one of the longer strips onto a flat surface and glue three blocks onto this (½in side down), separating each of them with a ⅜in x ¾in piece of card. Lay another long strip of card followed by another row of blocks, separated again with card. Note that the joints are staggered and that there are half blocks at the ends of this row. Finish off the top row.

Paint this wall with white matt emulsion until all the joints between the bricks are covered, then colour with a little brown spirit wood stain for a weathered effect.

FENCE

The fence down the left-hand side of the garden has been made so that it may be fixed into place at any time after the remainder of the garden has been built.

Cut three posts from ⅜in x ¼in jelutong, each 4in long. Drill a 1/32in-diameter hole into the side of each post to take a panel pin, about ⅛in up from the bottom. Place one of the posts against the baseboard, butting up against the position where the edge of the shed will be (see garden plan). Push a panel pin through the hole to mark the base and drill a 1/32in-diameter hole. Repeat this for a second post against the privy. The third post should be placed equidistant between the shed and the privy with another 1/32in-diameter hole drilled for fixing. Check the distance between the shed and the privy is 9⅞in (adjust if necessary) and cut two rails from ⅛in thick x ¼in jelutong. Lay the three posts face up on a flat work surface and line them up together. Using a set square make a pencil mark across all three, 3/16in from the top and ⅜in from the bottom.

Mix a wood stain in light oak 50/50 with white spirit and paint this over all the fence parts and set to one side until the stain is dry.

Lay the posts face up on your work surface and glue both the top and bottom rails into position (see fig 4). Check that the

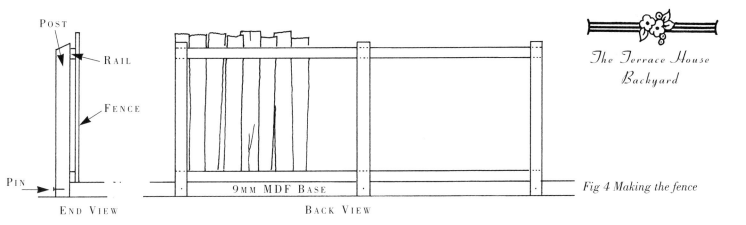

POST

RAIL

FENCE

PIN

END VIEW

9MM MDF BASE

BACK VIEW

The Terrace House
Backyard

Fig 4 Making the fence

posts are upright and that the fence sits neatly between the two outbuildings.

Cut twenty-two fence upright slats from $^1/_{16}$in thick x $^1/_2$in jelutong each $4^1/_4$in long and stain them all with the same mixture as used for the posts and rails. Assemble the slats onto the face of the fence rails commencing at the left-hand end. The top of each slat should overlap the top rail by about $^3/_{16}$in but this should vary slightly from slat to slat in order to give the fence a 'home-made' look. The finished fence can be pinned and glued to the base using the pre-drilled holes whenever you are ready.

EARTHED AREA

Almost every garden has a place that no one really knows what to do with and this one is no exception. Apart from the rabbit hutch it is home to nothing apart from rubbish, weeds

115

and insects and it is only roughly even. A slight hump has formed, almost certainly from the indiscriminate dumping of weeds and household rubbish.

Mask off the surrounding area using stiff card and masking tape, leaving only that to be covered in 'earth'. Take several small pieces of dampened kitchen paper and screw them up together to form the basis of the hump. Secure this to the base with masking tape, close to the position of the fence, and cover with strips of dampened Mod-Roc plaster bandage. Continue with wet bandage until the entire area is covered unevenly, about 1/2in at the highest.

Take one set of the four odd slabs of paving you made earlier and lightly grease the bases with Vaseline (petroleum jelly). Impress these four odd slabs into position around the hutch whilst the plaster is still wet and do not remove them until the earth is covered.

Whilst the Mod-Roc is still damp cover the whole of this area generously with plaster filler and with a wet 1/2in paint-brush smooth the filler and bandage, moulding it into shape over the hump as you progress. Set to one side and allow the bandage to dry thoroughly making sure that the four slabs are *not* fixed into position.

Paint the entire area with light earth brown acrylic as a base colour. Then cover the entire area with artist's display mount adhesive spray or brush on PVA glue and cover the area with loose tea from tea bags. Allow this to dry, brush off any surplus and repeat until you are satisfied with the finish. When this is dry the masking can be removed along with the four slabs which will be painted shortly.

END WALLS AND STEP

Cut the end walls E and F from 6mm MDF, according to the cutting list. Clean up and ensure that the corners are at right angles. Drill two 1/32in-diameter holes along the bottom of each piece 1/8in up from the bottom to take panel pins. Cut the step, again

from 6mm MDF, 2 1/8in x 1in and place to one side for finishing. Mark both walls with a 9mm wide line along the bottom where they butt against the base.

PAINTING THE PAVING AND CONCRETE

Paint all the paving with a grey acrylic to which you have added a little brown. Emphasise all of the cracks with a darker brown paint, using a fine brush. Colour the four odd slabs around the rabbit hutch similarly and glue these into position. Paint the concrete area with a grey acrylic paint mixed with a light sand colour and allow the two colours to streak a little. Colour in the cracks with a darker brown and add any lichen or weeds at this stage. Glue all the paved areas into position on the baseboard.

FINISHING THE END WALLS AND STEP

Measure off the two end walls and cover both with the brick-patterned sheeting but do not cover the bottom where the wall meets the base. Wrap the sheet around both of the ends and allow at least 3/4in extra to cover the top, then cover the back to finish off neatly. Use a PVA adhesive to fix the sheet or a spray display mount adhesive. When dry, place both walls against the base and pin and glue into position. Paint nail heads to disguise them.

Paint the step with a dirty grey-coloured acrylic with dark streaks to resemble worn stone and glue into position between the two walls so that the sill is on the outside.

GATE

This is a dummy or non-working feature, which may be stained with a 50/50 light oak and white spirit mixture or painted off-white. Stain or paint all parts before assembly (see Tip box right).

Cut two pieces for the frame from 1/8in x 1/4in jelutong each 3in long. Stain or paint them as above and glue into position either side of the gap between the back walls (see

> **TIP**
>
> *Cut the Mod-Roc to short workable lengths and dampen in a shallow dish of clean water.*

> **TIP**
>
> *Brushing a thin coat of PVA adhesive onto bare wood will allow plaster fillers and Mod-Roc bandage to adhere more permanently. Alternatively, roughen the smooth surface of MDF with a coarse abrasive paper and mix a little PVA glue into the filler.*

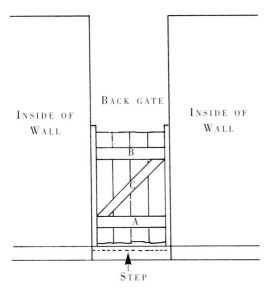

INSIDE OF WALL   BACK GATE   INSIDE OF WALL

B

C

A

STEP

Fig 5 Making the gate

fig 5). Cut three pieces of jelutong (A, B and C) ¹/₄in x ¹/₁₆in each 2¹/₈in long. Glue one piece (A) ¹/₂in up from the base in the centre of the frame uprights and the second (B) ¹/₂in from the top. Cut the third piece (C) so that it fits as a diagonal ledge between the top and bottom (see fig 5).

Cut the panels from jelutong ¹/₁₆in thick x ¹/₂in x 2³/₄in long and roughen up the bottom edges with a saw or file. Glue all panels to the gate framework.

CLOTHES LINE POSTS

Cut two posts from ¹/₄in x ¹/₄in jelutong wood both 7¹/₂in long and shape the tops at 45 degrees on two sides to a point. Drill a ³/₃₂in-diameter hole through each post, ¹/₄in from the top, turn the posts over and then drill a second hole ¹/₂in from the top. Cut four pieces of ³/₃₂in-diameter wooden dowel each ⁵/₈in long and glue these equidistant through the holes. Stain all the assemblies with a light oak spirit wood stain and leave to dry.

Drill a ³/₃₂in-diameter hole into the base of each post and insert a ⁵/₈in long panel pin after cutting off the head. Drill ¹/₃₂in-diameter holes into the base outside the lean-to and by the back wall and insert the posts on their pins. Loop a piece of thin twine between the two posts to complete the washing line.

LEAN-TO SHED

In some ways this is a straightforward shed, except that it has been erected against the side of a building and it uses that wall instead of one of its own (probably because it is a poorly made edifice and it needs at least one that is reliable). If you examine a real shed you will see that it usually consists of a framework made from square-section battens that are faced with wooden strips and the whole thing is mounted on a base, this is very similar.

MATERIALS

MDF – 2mm

Base	6in x 4¹/₂in
Sides, two off	4¹/₂in x 7in
Roof	6³/₈in x 5in

Jelutong wood

Window	¹/₁₆in x ¹/₁₆in x 10in
Sill	¹/₁₆in thick x ¹/₄in x 2¹/₈in
Beams	³/₁₆in x ³/₁₆in x 90in
Fascia boards	¹/₁₆in thick x ¹/₂in x 70in
Door boards	¹/₁₆in thick x ¹/₂in x 24in
Door brace and ledges	¹/₁₆in thick x ¹/₂in x 12in

Other materials

- *Acetate/Perspex (plexiglass) 2in x 2³/₈in*
- *Fine grey abrasive paper 14in x 3in approximately*
- *Door hardware and handle*

BASE

Cut the shed base from 2mm MDF 6in x 4¹/₂in ensuring that all the edges are dead square. Mark the MDF piece with a sharp craft knife at ¹/₂in intervals all across the width to represent boards and then stain with dark oak spirit wood stain. Set to one side and allow this to dry.

MAIN FRAME

Prepare about 90in of ³/₁₆in x ³/₁₆in jelutong ready for all the framework beams (see figs 6, 6a and 6b overleaf).

(see figs 6, 6a and 6b overleaf)

TIP

It may be necessary to adjust the width of the two outer upright pieces of the gate, so do this before attempting assembly by trying all the parts before gluing.

117

Side 1

This side is furthest away and is not covered on the outside for this project, although you may add a covering if you wish. Cut a piece of 2mm MDF 4½in wide by 7in and lay this onto a flat surface. Measure and mark 6in up the left-hand side and draw a line to the opposite corner in order to produce the roof slope, then cut along this line. Mark the centre at 2¼in and draw a vertical line to use as a guide when placing the centre beams. Prepare a second piece of 2mm MDF to the same dimensions for use as a template when building the opposite side.

Lay the side down onto a flat surface with the 6in side to the left and cut two roof beams, each 5in long (see fig 6). Glue one of these to the top edge of the side along the roof slope (set the other to one side for now). It must be flush with the top and right-hand edge but overhang at the front by ¼in. Trim the right-hand end of the roof beam to match the back edge of the side and cut the front of it to produce a vertical edge.

Cut four upright beams 6¾in long, two for each of the outer edges and two for the second side. Note that these should be glued into position 2mm above the bottom to allow the base to locate under it. Glue

these on flush to the two outer edges of the side.

Cut two beams 4in long and glue one of these horizontally between the two uprights, at the bottom and the second spaced 3in above that (see fig 6a). Add a 3in vertical beam in the centre between the bottom and middle beams, adding a second 2⅞in long cut to fit between the centre and the roof beams. Glue this assembly to the shorter end of the base with the beams on the inside. Check that it is vertical and support until the adhesive has set.

Side 2

This is the side that is nearest to the garden and it contains the door and because of this the framework is slightly more complicated. For ease of working you may find it easier to transfer the shape of the 2mm MDF template to a piece of card (see Tip box).

Glue the previously cut roof and outer upright beams into place as for side 1 and add a spot of adhesive where they join. Check that they are 2mm above the bottom of the template. Cut two ⅜in long beams as spacers and glue one 2mm above the bottom and the second 3in above that against the left-hand upright. Cut a third upright approximately 6⅝in long and trim the top

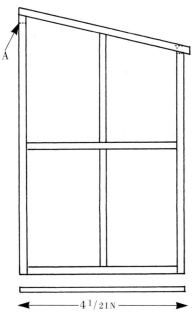

Fig 6a Making the shed – side

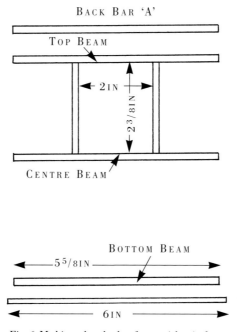

BACK BAR 'A'

TOP BEAM

2IN

2⅜IN

CENTRE BEAM

BOTTOM BEAM

5⅝IN

6IN

Fig 6 Making the shed – front with window

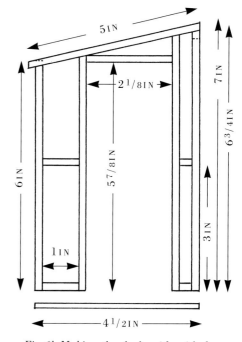

5IN

2⅛IN

7IN

6IN

5⅞IN

6¾IN

3IN

1IN

4½IN

Fig 6b Making the shed – side with door

so that it fits snugly against the two 3/8in spacers and the roof beam and glue this into place, supporting the joints with pins (see fig 6b previous page).

Cut two more spacer beams 1in long and glue these against the right-hand upright, the first 2mm from the bottom and the second 3in above that. Then, cut a fourth upright approximately 6 1/4in long so that it fits against the two 1in spacers and under the roof beam. Trim to fit if necessary and glue into place. Finally, cut a 2 1/8in cross beam to place above the door and glue this flush with the top of the inner right-hand beam.

When the assembly has set take out the pins, carefully remove the assembly from the template and turn it over so that the shorter side is now on your left.

Covering side 2

We left side 1 uncovered but you may cover it if you wish. For side 2, prepare the door and fascia boards from 1/16in thick jelutong wood x 1/2in wide (see Tip box). Working from the left or shorter side, glue the first upright board into place leaving it overlapping the front by 1/16in. Add two more boards to finish around the doorway and continue with one more cut level to the top of the door and a second to reach the roof line. Glue two boards horizontally above the doorway shaping the upper one to match the roof line. Allow the assembly adhesive to set and do not handle until you are sure the frame will not distort.

Front

Cut three front beams out of 3/16in x 3/16in jelutong, 5 5/8in long and glue the first onto the base flush with the front edge (see fig 6). Erect and glue the side 2 assembly onto the base, support in this position and add the second beam 3in above the bottom one to match those on each of the sides. Add the top beam across the roof line and hold the lean-to assembly together with masking tape until firm.

Cut two beams out of 3/16in x 3/16in jelutong, each 2 3/8in long and glue these vertically between the centre and the top beams at the front to enclose the window (see fig 6). Each one should be 1 5/8in from each end and can be assembled around the 'glass' window. Insert a piece of Perspex (plexiglass) 2in x 2 3/8in and a build a 1/16in x 1/16in frame all round to keep it in place, adding a 1/4in x 2 1/8in sill at the bottom front.

Glue the rough-stained 1/16in x 1/2in (varied widths) boards vertically over the front beams and around the window.

ROOF

Cut the roof from 2mm MDF 6 3/8in x 5in and square up the edges. Cut two pieces of grey-coloured abrasive paper, 2 3/4in x 6 3/4in. Glue one to the front edges overlapping by 3/16in at front and sides. Bend these ends down, cutting the corners to allow this.

Glue the second piece over this, overlapping the sides by 3/16in and the top end by 3/8in, bending the outer edges down and the top edge upwards. This should sit neatly on the roof beams and the assembly can then be glued into place if you wish to do so.

DOOR

Prepare four 1/2in boards each 5 3/4in long and lay these down flat, edge to edge, onto a smooth surface. Prepare a 12in length of 1/2in x 1/16in thick jelutong suitably stained to match the other boards and cut two ledge pieces, each 2in long. Glue these horizontally across the boards 3/4in from the bottom and 1in from the top (see fig 7). Cut and add the brace at an angle between these two ledges, running from one edge to the other, cutting the ends at an angle to provide a snug fit and then glue into place.

Add suitable hardware or a handle to the door and glue the door into position. Hinge if required using miniature hinges or a piece of masking tape between the frame and the ledges.

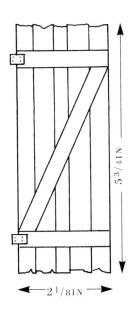

Fig 7 Inside of shed door

COAL BUNKER

This has been made almost entirely from 2mm MDF as the material is easy to work with and will mimic a concrete casting when painted.

Cut all the pieces following the dimensions given in fig 8, cleaning up the edges and making sure that they are all square. Use a fine fretsaw or sharp craft knife to cut the shute aperture at the front and the top fill aperture on the top following the dimensions given. The two apertures have sliding covers located inside a $^3/_{32}$in, L-shaped moulding (see Tip box) and you will need 15in of this (see fig 8a).

Lay two strips $2^3/_8$in long up the front part of the bunker $1^3/_8$in apart, with the rebate turned in to form the channel in which the door will slide (see fig 8a). Cut one piece of moulding $1^3/_8$in wide with both ends cut at 45 degrees. Glue this onto the top so that the rebate is $^1/_{16}$in below the bottom end of the aperture, to act as a stop. Cut two more pieces, each with one end cut at 45 degrees, so that they join at the stop and finish at the top end of the bunker and glue into place.

Lay the bottom of the bunker onto a flat surface and 'dry fit' all the parts. When you are confident, glue all the parts together, with the exception of the top, and allow the adhesive to set.

To add the 'bolts', drill two $^1/_{32}$in-diameter holes about $^1/_8$in from the edge, $^3/_4$in in

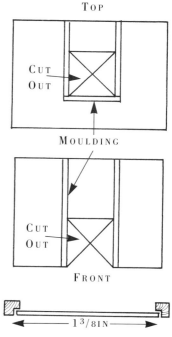

SECTION THROUGH MOULDING

Fig 8a The mounting around the apertures of the coal bunker

from the top and the bottom, and do this to the front edges also. Cut the heads off some small panel pins to leave about $^1/_8$in of the pin and glue these into the holes.

Cut two sliding doors from $^1/_{32}$in thick ply (or plasticard). The front door is $1^5/_{16}$in

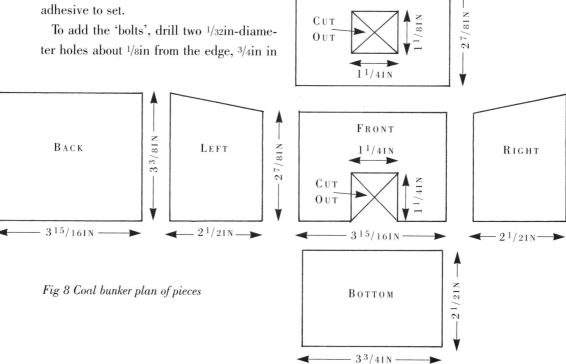

Fig 8 Coal bunker plan of pieces

The Terrace House
Backyard

wide x 1⁵/₈in high and the top one is 1⁵/₁₆in wide x ¹/₄in high. Check that these fit the slides. Make up two rectangular strap handles from a piece of scrap metal and using a rapid-set epoxy adhesive, glue onto each of the doors and place to one side.

To paint the coal bunker, spray the entire assembly with a grey primer paint and allow to dry, then sand down and spray again until a smooth finish is obtained. Once thoroughly dry gently buff up the pin heads. Using a nearly dry brush, load it with a little black acrylic paint and smudge black around the openings and joints of the bunker.

Paint or spray the two doors with a silver paint mixed with a little grey to produce a metallic galvanised finish. When dry add a

little black around the edges before placing into their respective slides. Finally fill the bunker with loose coal and place the top into position and glue down if required.

THE PRIVY

The entire structure of this feature is made from 2mm MDF, the inner surface of which has been grooved to look like planks.

Cut the base, sides, back, front, roof and door lintel to the dimensions shown in fig 9. Note that the structure is higher at the front than the back and that the roof slopes down. Measure off the angle on the two sides and cut together so that they match.

Paint the inner side of the walls and roof with matt white emulsion into which you have mixed a little brown ochre. When this

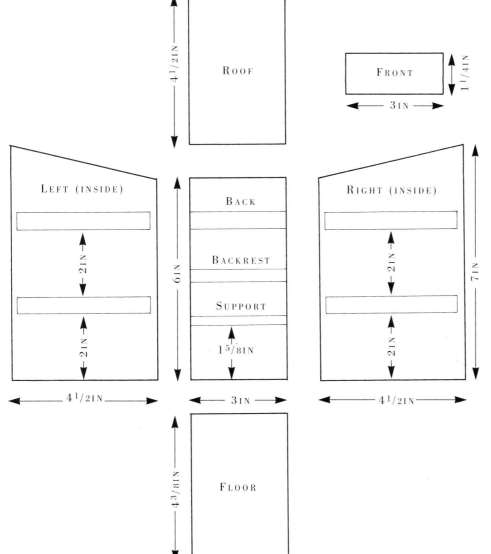

Fig 9 Constructing the privy

> **TIP**
> *Plastic replica coal made for the model railway hobby is ideal to fill the bunker. To add realism, glue several pieces together into a small heap and place around the bottom door, making it look as if it had spilled out. Any surplus can be contained in the bunker or a bucket.*

is dry use a nearly dry brush loaded with a little grey acrylic, to tone it down and introduce a little 'dirt' into the corners.

Divide the floor into a series of rough paving flagstones and mark the joints with a light V-shaped cut. Paint with a dirty grey/brown acrylic mixture and allow to dry. From a strip of $1/16$in thick x $1/2$in jelutong, cut four pieces $4^{1}/8$in long and glue these battens to the insides of the two walls 2in up from the bottom and 2in apart (see fig 9). Cut one more piece 3in long and glue this to the back wall to match the higher of those on the sides ($4^{1}/2$in above the floor). Paint the inside an off-white emulsion or poster paint, adding streaks of grey as required.

Cut a strip 3in long and glue this to the back wall $1^{5}/8$in from the floor to act as a support for the loo seat. Colour with a wood stain. Cut the back rest from $5/8$in x 3in wide x $1/16$in thick jelutong, stain light oak and glue into place 1in above the loo seat battens on the back wall.

The privy or closet

This simple toilet seat is typical of an outside privy and consists, basically, of a box with a hole cut into the top of the seat that is positioned across the bowl. Out of $1/8$in thick jelutong cut a top, 2in x 3in and a front board, $1^{5}/8$in x 3in. Mark off a line $3/16$in in from the back of the top and cut a fine V-shaped groove along this to indicate a hinge.

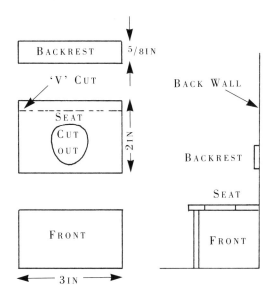

Fig 10 Building the loo

Find the centre of the remaining portion of the top, now $1^{13}/_{16}$in x 3in, and draw on to it the shape of the toilet bowl. This will be about $3/4$in from front to back and $5/8$in wide (see fig 10). Cut out the shape and use a fine abrasive paper to shape the inner edge all round.

Finish off the top by polishing to a smooth surface. Colour all the wood with a very light oak wood stain mixed 25/75 with white spirit and when dry add a little wax polish to the top only.

Privy assembly

Place all the parts onto a flat surface and lay them out as in fig 9. Using a jig or a bench stop with a back rest, glue the base of the privy to the back and then add the left side. This will leave the base inside the privy. Check that the sides are square and hold the parts together with masking tape until the adhesive has set.

Assemble the top of the loo onto its support former and the front board. When the adhesive has set add the right-hand wall, followed by the door lintel. Check that the roof will sit onto the assembly without the roof batten fouling front or back and, if desired, add plumbing at this stage, such as a high-level cistern and pipe work. Touch up any paintwork as required.

The entire outer surfaces are then covered with $1/2$in wide x $1/16$in thick jelutong planks, laid vertically, that have previously been coloured with dark oak spirit wood stain. The rougher these planks are the better the effect. Add the appearance of nail heads using a sharp HB pencil point.

Privy door and frame

Prepare a strip of 'L' section moulding by gluing $1/4$in x $1/8$in strip jelutong to $3/32$in x $3/32$in jelutong (see fig 11). (This moulding may be available ready-made from a specialist stockist.) Glue a strip of this 'L' section all around the doorway. The door is $2^3/4$in wide and is made up from $1/16$in thick jelutong strips nominally $1/2$in wide. Cut six strips $5^1/4$in long and use a small block plane to reduce the width of some of them until they measure a total of $2^3/4$in when placed side by side.

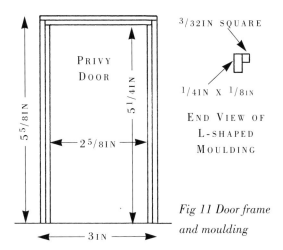

Fig 11 Door frame and moulding

Prepare two door braces out of jelutong $1/16$in thick x $1/2$in x $2^5/8$in long and third piece 3in long. Stain the strips and the braces with oak wood stain mixed 50/50 with white spirit (or paint). Lay the strips down on a flat surface and glue together lengthwise to form the door, leaving under a weight to set (see fig 12 overleaf).

Cut the $3/8$in diamond shape out of the centre of the door about $3/4$in from the top and make the bottom of the boards rough and ragged with wear. Turn the door over so that the inside faces up and glue on the two braces $2^1/2$in apart and $3/4$in from the

123

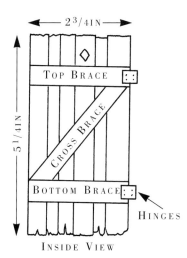

Fig 12 Privy door construction

bottom. Cut the cross brace to fit and glue into position. Stain all cut ends of timber to match. Glue the door into position, shut or open, and add a black painted door latch.

Privy roof

We finished the roof off by adding corrugated 'iron' made from a piece of corrugated packing paper glued onto a piece of thin card. Spraying or painting this first with clear varnish will give it more strength before adding silver paint toned down with a little grey, for weathering. Use a fine-tipped black felt-tip pen to add 'nail' heads at 1in intervals and streak a little red/brown paint from these heads to indicate rust.

RABBIT HUTCH

The main assembly parts are made from 2mm MDF and the framing is built up with 1/8in x 1/8in jelutong, except part (8). Cut the MDF parts to the dimensions shown in figs 13 and 13a, cleaning up all the edges. Cut jelutong parts (1) and (2), each 2³/8in long and part (8) 1¹/4in long x ¹/8in x ³/16in deep. The remainder of the parts are cut to fit.

Start assembly by gluing the right-hand side and the partition to the base, joining these two with part (8) using a rapid-set clear adhesive such as UHU (see fig 13a right). Cut parts (4) and (6) by measuring this off against the partition, copying the angles. Part (3) is the same length as part (4) less ¹/4in. Glue parts (1), (2), (3) and (4) onto the base to make the front frame. Calculate the sizes of parts (5) and (7) by checking them against the partition and complete the end assembly with part (6).

Cut the door from ¹/32in jelutong, 1¹/2in x 1¹/4in and cut vertical grooves into the surface to resemble small planks, add the head of a small nail for a knob and glue into place.

Spread glue onto the inner surfaces of the base and cover with very fine sawdust. Cut two pieces of fine wire mesh (mesh size

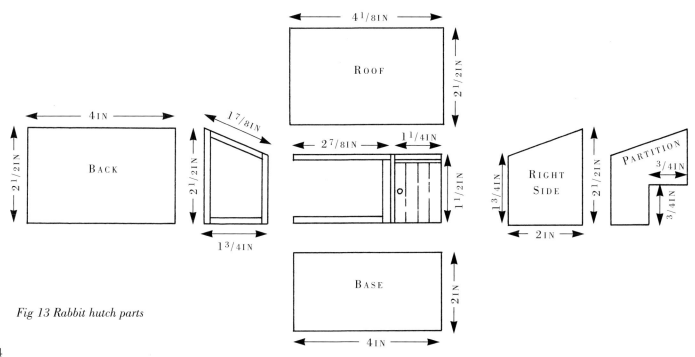

Fig 13 Rabbit hutch parts

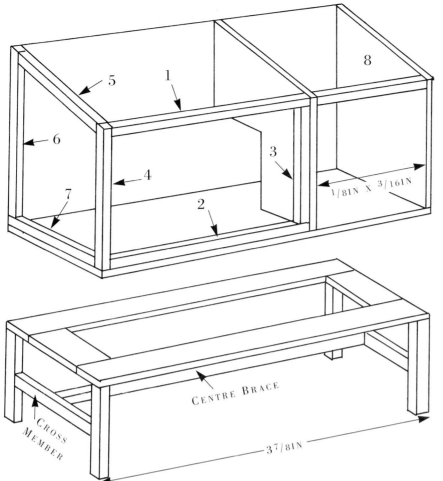

1/8IN X 3/16IN

Fig 13a Rabbit hutch assembly

CENTRE BRACE

CROSS MEMBER

3 7/8IN

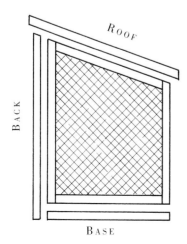

ROOF

BACK

BASE

Fig 14 Rabbit hutch side view with wire mesh

approximately 3/32in) the same size as the left-hand side and the left front and glue these pieces to the outside of the framework on the left-hand side. Glue on the back and the roof (see fig 14). Finish off the roof by gluing on a piece of fine, grey abrasive paper, overlapping this and gluing under all the edges to produce a neat finish.

Leg assembly

Prepare two strips of 3/8in x 1/8in thick jelutong 37/8in long and two strips 11/8in long. Lay these four parts face down and glue together to form a frame as shown in fig 13a. Cut four legs from 1/8in x 1/8in jelutong, each 11/4in long, two cross members 15/8in long and a centre brace 35/8in long. Lay two legs down onto a flat surface and glue on the cross brace 1/2in up from the bottom. Repeat for the second set and allow the adhesive to set hard. Lay the top assemble down onto the work surface and add one set of legs to each end, at the same time joining the two with the centre brace.

Your terrace house backyard is now ready for its finishing touches. This utilitarian backyard has few decorative plants but a sense of period detail can be achieved with various tools and accessories, such as a tin bath and mangle. Other items we have used include a spade and fork, broom, watering can and dustbin (see Suppliers, page 173).

> **TIP**
> *You can make a door hinge by following the instructions for pin hinging in the greenhouse in the Vegetable Garden page 137, however you will need to thicken the top and bottom edges of the door with a batten.*

The Vegetable Garden

People have been growing vegetables since time immemorial and cultivated food gardens have been recorded since the Middle Ages. The difference between then and now is that what was once the means of survival is now often nothing more than a recreational pastime. For the most part we now have someone else do our vegetable gardening for us – the supermarket buyer.

The basic requirements for producing vegetables are a plot of earth, somewhere to pot up seedlings, preferably under cover, and a small area protected from the frosts to bring on early supplies of delicate plants. The addition of a hothouse or greenhouse allows control over the growing conditions of vegetables more used to a foreign climate.

In the past, large estates would have had boilers installed to heat their greenhouses and the gardeners would have regulated the temperature by roof vents. Dry sheds would have been used for storage of vegetables throughout the winter. Today, we have smaller gardens and tend to use oil-fired heaters and an airing cupboard for propagation and storage.

As you can see this garden has all basic elements – a sheltered work bench, a cold frame, two vegetable patches and a small greenhouse. The walls and fence provide shelter from the winds and help to keep up the temperature in the garden. The garden is basically a free-standing structure but you could easily adapt the basic features to design a vegetable garden to suit your own dolls' house.

CONSTRUCTING THE GARDEN

General materials needed for constructing this garden include; PVA glue, spray mount and photo mount adhesive, masking tape, panel pins, acrylic paints, plaster filler, wood stain, white spirit, stiff card, dressmaking pins and tea bags. Where instructions are given for general gluing it is assumed that a PVA type glue will be used.

Refer to the garden plan for the location of all assemblies. The left-hand corner of the garden features a greenhouse, although you could make extra cold frames or a shed if you wish.

MATERIALS

MDF – 9mm

Base	18in x 14in

MDF – 6mm

Back	18^{1}/4in x 9in
Side	14in x 9in
Top level A	18in x 6in
Formers	48in x ^{5}/8in
Step (a), one off	1^{3}/4in x 1^{1}/2in
Step (b), one off	1^{3}/4in x ^{3}/4in

MDF – 2mm

Top level paving	18in x 6in
Lower level B	18in x 8in
Tread (a), one off	1^{3}/4in x 1^{5}/8in
Tread (b), one off	1^{3}/4in x ^{7}/8in
Cold frame base	3^{1}/2in x 2^{3}/8in
Work bench top	6in x 2in

Jelutong wood

Work bench area and roof	^{1}/16in x ^{3}/4in x 36in (see instructions)

Work bench roof lining (to support glazing)	^{1}/8in x ^{1}/8in square cut two off 5^{3}/4in and two off 5in

Post (1)	^{1}/4in x ^{1}/4in x 7^{3}/8in
Post (2)	^{1}/4in x ^{1}/4in x 5in
Legs, three off	^{1}/4in x ^{1}/4in x 2^{3}/4in
Wall cladding	^{1}/16in x ^{3}/4in x 80in
Wall battens	^{1}/4in x ^{1}/8in x 36in
Cold frame	^{1}/16in x ^{1}/8in x 15in
	^{1}/8in x ^{1}/8in x 6in
Shelves, four off	^{1}/8in x ^{3}/4in x 4in
Shelf supports, eight off	^{1}/8in x ^{3}/16in x ^{1}/2in

Brickwork

- Brick strips (for low walls), four strips each one brick high x 18in long (see Making the Elements page 32)
- Brick slips x 70 bricks for cold frame (see Suppliers page 173)
- Brick wall fibre-glass sheet covering approximately 300 square inches

Other materials

- Perspex (plexiglass) ^{1}/16in thick for the bench roof 5^{3}/4in x 4^{3}/4in
- Acetate for cold frame 2^{1}/8in x 2^{3}/4in
- 1mm diameter wire 24in
- Oasis (floral foam) one large block
- Sheet of clapboard siding 10^{1}/2in x 3^{1}/2in (for fence – optional)
- Polystyrene block 10in x 4in x 1in thick
- Brick patterned paper
- Fine grass sheet
- Knob or latch for greenhouse
- Plants

Specialist supplies
(see Suppliers page 173)

- Scenic model foam, green
- Garden tools and accessories
- Pots, tubs and hanging basket

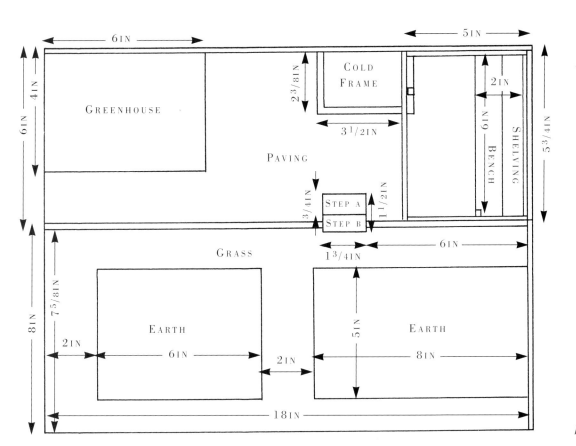

6IN

4IN

6IN

GREENHOUSE

2³/8IN

COLD
FRAME

5IN

2IN

6IN

BENCH

5³/4IN

SHELVING

PAVING

3¹/2IN

3/4IN

1¹/2IN

STEP A

STEP B

8IN

7⁵/8IN

GRASS

1³/4IN

6IN

2IN

EARTH

6IN

2IN

5IN

EARTH

8IN

2IN

18IN

Plan of the vegetable garden

MATERIALS FOR THE GREENHOUSE

(see page 135)

BASE

Cut the base from 9mm MDF 18in x 14in and square up all the sides at right angles. Mark up the position of all the formers for the upper level before proceeding.

BACK AND SIDE WALLS

Cut the back and side walls from 6mm MDF according to the cutting list and then drill four equally spaced $1/32$in-diameter holes, $3/16$in from the bottom of each to take panel pins. Glue and pin the back onto the baseboard allowing the $1/4$in overlap on the right-hand side. Glue and pin the side wall to the baseboard, ensuring that it butts up against the back wall. Check that both are square and secure with masking tape until the adhesive has set.

Using acrylic paint, cover the outer ends and the tops of both walls with a red brick colour to match the brick-patterned sheeting you will be using and when this is dry

cut out the brick sheeting to fit both walls and glue into position.

TOP LEVEL

This level is laid on top of formers to give it the necessary height. Secure the top level piece (A) of MDF in a suitable vice and cut out the $1^3/4$in x $1^1/8$in aperture ready for the steps, 6in from the right-hand edge as shown in fig 1. Clean up any rough edges.

Lay this piece on top of the base, check that it is facing the correct way and draw around the edges to indicate the exact positions of the formers. Cut sufficient $5/8$in formers out of 6mm MDF to fit around the outer edges. Glue these to the baseboard, not forgetting to lay them around the step

Fig 1 Positioning the formers for supporting the top level

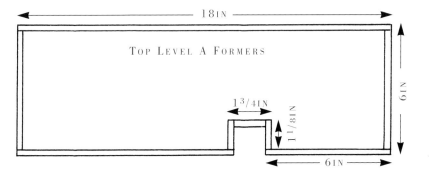

18IN

TOP LEVEL A FORMERS

6IN

1³/4IN

1¹/8IN

6IN

Fig 2 Marking out the vegetable beds

aperture (not across). Glue the top level on top of the formers and weight down until the adhesive has set.

Glue the piece of 6mm MDF for step (a) into the aperture of the top level and then glue step (b) on top of this. Glue the two treads (a) and (b) to the steps in the same fashion and when set firm, sand slight depressions in both to indicate a little wear and tear.

LOWER LEVEL

From 2mm MDF cut a piece 18in x 8in (B) and mark out the vegetable patches as shown in fig 2. The left-hand bed is 5in x 6in and the right hand is 5in x 8in and is open at one end, butting against the wall. Cut out the beds using a fretsaw or a sharp craft knife.

Cut out the step recess 1¾in wide x 1in deep so that the bottom step, which protrudes out from the top level, fits neatly. The position of this cut-out should be 6in from the right-hand edge (see fig 2 and check before cutting). Glue this onto the baseboard using a PVA wood adhesive, ensuring that the front edges are flush and that the right-hand bed fits against the wall. Weight or pin down until dry. The plants will be added later.

LOW BRICK WALL

Take the strips of bricks that you have made following the instructions on page 32 in Making the Elements and cut two pieces to fit in front of the upper level, on either side of the steps (see fig 3). Lightly dampen the strips and mix a little plaster filler with white PVA glue. Lay the first strip down on a clean, lightly oiled work surface, with the bricks facing up and glue the next layer into position, keeping the walls flat. Proceed like this until you have built up four rows for each side and then allow the assembly to dry out.

Paint the two brick walls a nice red brick colour and when dry glue them into position against the upper level so that they enclose the steps.

PAVING

The ground covering for the top level of the garden should be ⅛in thick, so if you are intending to use a material thinner than the one we have you should increase the thickness by using an art card or similar. The paving stones shown in Making the Elements would be an ideal covering, but here an irregular paving has been made up from a sheet of 2mm MDF.

Cut and shape the piece of MDF to fit the upper level and with a sharp pencil mark out the irregular paving (see fig 4). When you are happy with the design make a series of V-shaped cuts with a sharp scalpel or craft knife along all of the joints and remove the waste (see Tip box, left).

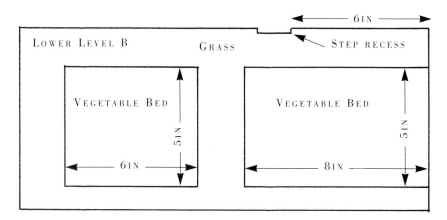

Fig 3 The low brick wall

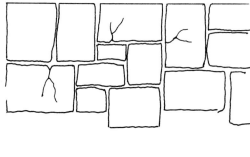

Fig 4 Creating the paving effect on the top level

Use khaki and grey spray paints when painting the paving to obtain a stone effect. When the surface is dry paint in the joints and cracks with a streaky dark brown or black. Finish by gluing on a few weeds and lichen. Glue your completed paving down onto the top level, behind the low brick wall.

COLD FRAME

The walls for the cold frame situated on the back wall, have been built with 'real' bricks onto which are placed a piece of framed acetate. In effect this is a window, known as a light. Cut a piece of 2mm MDF 3¹/₂in x 2³/₈in to form the base and on which to assemble the bricks. The outer dimensions of the frame are 3¹/₂in wide x 2⁵/₁₆in deep,

left wall 1³/₄in high, right wall 2¹/₄in. These measurements do not include the 2mm MDF base (see fig 5 overleaf).

Select sufficient bricks and build up the framework onto the MDF base. Don't forget to dampen the bricks as you work as this will aid adhesion. Arrange the bricks so that they interlock at the corners and so produce a proper interlocking bond. The wall illustrated has been built using the standard stretcher bond but you could use another pattern if you wish. Note that the frame has a plain 2mm MDF back inserted and butts against the wall.

To make the cold frame window or 'light', cut a piece of waste 2mm MDF x 1⁵/₈in to fit snugly into the back of the assembled frame

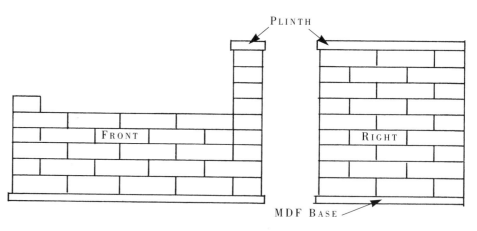

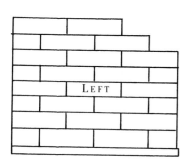

Fig 5 The cold frame walls
(shown partially built)

TIP

*Before assembling any
woodwork, stain all
parts and cut ends
with a proprietary
walnut-coloured wood
stain diluted 50/50 with
white spirit, as this will
avoid any unsightly
spots on areas that
become sealed with glue.
Allow stain to dry
thoroughly before using
any adhesives.*

TIP

*Use a piece of waste
wood ¹/₄in wide as a
template to fix the
support around the
inside of the roof.*

and glue to the top of this a piece of ¹/₈in square jelutong. Glue another piece of ¹/₈in square jelutong to the top of the front wall against which the glass frame will rest.

Cut a piece of acetate 2¹/₈in x 2⁵/₈in and check that this will fit snugly inside the cold frame walls. Make and glue a frame from the ¹/₁₆in x ¹/₈in jelutong to fit over the top and add a centre glazing bar to complete (see fig 6).

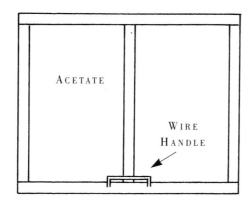

Fig 6 The cold frame window

Using a pair of pliers, carefully bend a small piece of wire offcut about ¹/₂in long, to form a handle for the cold frame, and glue this to the bottom of the glass frame. Glue an offcut of jelutong ¹/₈in thick x ³/₈in x 3¹/₂in onto the top of the right-hand wall to act as a plinth, supporting one of the posts for the work bench roof.

Cut a piece of Oasis (floral foam) ⁷/₈in thick to fit snugly inside the completed cold frame. Remove and cover this with a thin layer of PVA glue and sprinkle the contents of a tea bag over the surface. Brush off any surplus and carefully place the foam back inside the frame.

WORK BENCH AREA
Work bench roof

Cut two pieces of ¹/₈in thick x ³/₄in jelutong 5³/₄in long and a further two pieces each 5in long and glue together to make a frame. Make sure this is dead square and when set glue four pieces of ¹/₈in square jelutong inside the frame ¹/₄in from the top to form a support for the glazing (see fig 7). Cut a piece of thin card to fit snugly inside the roof frame and use this as a template to mark out and cut the Perspex (plexiglass) sheet.

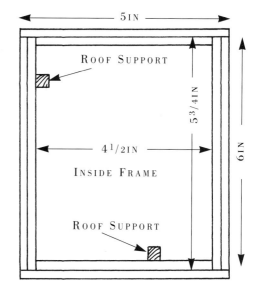

Fig 7 The work bench area roof

Work bench

Take the work bench top (the 6in x 2in piece of 2mm MDF) and cut out a notch ¹/₄in x ¹/₄in from the bottom right-hand corner to take the post (see fig 8). Using the ¹/₁₆in thick x ³/₄in jelutong bench surround material (see cutting list) cut one piece 6¹/₈in long and another 2in long. Cut one

Fig 8 The work bench top

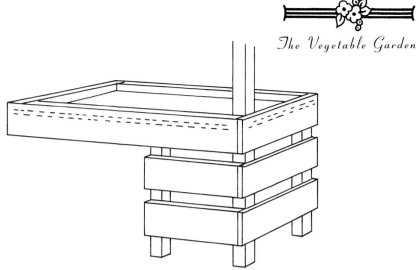

post from ¹/₄in x ¹/₄in jelutong 7³/₄in long and glue this into the notch, leaving 2³/₄in on the underside. Assemble the two pieces of the bench surround leaving ¹/₈in protruding above the work bench surface. Clamp the assembly and allow to set.

Cut two post legs from ¹/₄in x ¹/₄in jelutong, 2³/₄in long. Cut four pieces of ¹/₁₆in thick x ³/₄in jelutong each 2in long. Glue the two posts in place and add the four surround rails as shown in fig 9. Glue the bottom rails ³/₁₆in from the bottom and leave a gap of ³/₁₆in between the rails. Set this assembly to one side along with the roof frame until the wall cladding is complete.

Wall cladding

Cut the following support pieces for the wall cladding using ¹/₄in x ¹/₈in thick jelutong (see fig 10): one off 7⁵/₈in (A), one off 6¹⁵/₁₆in (B), one off ³/₄in (C) and four off 4³/₁₆in (D, E, F, G).

Glue pieces A, B, C and D onto the back wall and E, F and G onto the right-hand wall. Note that the spacing between uprights

Fig 9 The work bench support rails

Fig 10 Fixing the support pieces for the wall cladding

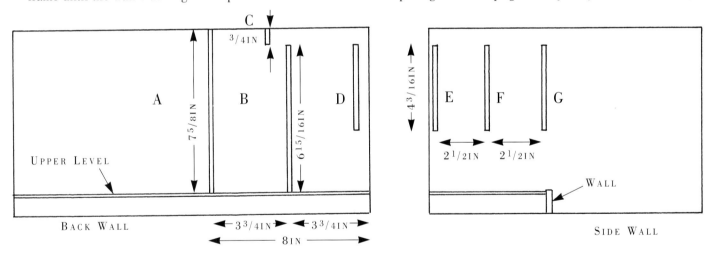

Fig 11 Attaching the wall cladding

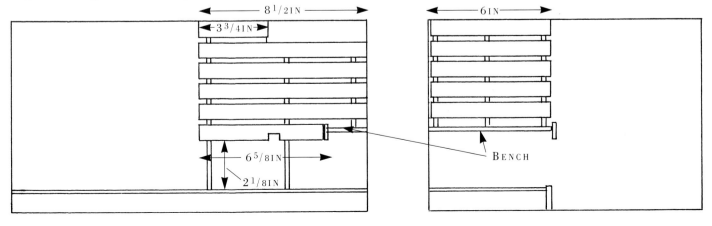

TIP

*To allow the fence to be
free-standing, glue two
pieces of 6mm MDF
10in long x 2in wide
together to form a long
L-shape and then glue
the fencing strip to the
upright of the L. That
way your hedge can
stand behind it and they
can both be moved
whilst you work on the
garden.*

*Fig 12 Fixing the
shelving and hooks on
the wall cladding*

A, B and D is 3³/₄in. Between E, F and G the spacing is 2¹/₂in. The position of the bench top is marked at 2⁷/₈in above ground level.

Cut the following pieces for the wall cladding using ¹/₁₆in thick x ³/₄in jelutong (see fig 11 on page 133): four off 8¹/₂in, four off 6in, one off 3³/₄in and one off 6⁵/₈in. Cut a ¹/₈in notch in this last piece to take the bench surround.

Assemble all the pieces onto the wall with the right-hand cladding reaching into the corner and allowing it to overlap the supports by ¹/₈in. Allow 2¹/₈in between the bottom piece of cladding and ground level (see fig 11). All strips of cladding are ³/₁₆in apart. Cut the roof support post from ¹/₄in x ¹/₄in square jelutong, 5in long.

Shelving and hooks

Cut four shelves each 4in long from ¹/₈in thick x ³/₄in jelutong. Cut eight shelf supports, each ¹/₈in thick x ³/₁₆in wide x ¹/₂in long. Cut eight pieces of 1mm-diameter wire each ⁷/₈in long.

Drill a small hole into the centre of each of the shelf supports on the ³/₁₆in width and glue the wire into this. Hold each of the supports by the attached wire and push them through the gap between the wall cladding. Twist the wire in a clockwise direction until the supports are vertical and

then position the wires to hold the shelving (see fig 12). Bend ten pieces of wire into S shapes and hook over the cladding to hold baskets, drying vegetables and tools.

Work bench final assembly

Carefully place the work bench against the right-hand wall and locate the top into the notch that was made in the back wall cladding. The bench assembly sits on top of the paving. Place the completed roof onto the top of the bench support post and insert the second support between the roof and the cold frame wall. Glue the roof to the supports and the wall cladding and drop the Perspex (plexiglass) glazing into place.

FENCE

This is an optional feature, not shown in all the illustrations. To make, first prepare a 10in length of fence from clapboard siding, 3¹/₂in high when stood on end. Stain with dark oak wood stain, mixed 50/50 with white spirit. When dry, add 'nail heads' to alternate boards 1¹/₂in from the bottom and 1in from the top by making a small round indentation using a sharp HB pencil. Position the fencing on the left-hand side of the garden (see photograph right) and glue and panel pin to the baseboard and back wall (see also Tip box, left).

HEDGE

This too is an optional feature, not shown in all the illustrations. To make, first cut a piece of polystyrene 10in long x 4in high and round off the corners – don't worry if the top is a little uneven, so are most real hedges! Paint the entire surface a medium brown acrylic colour ensuring that all the crevices are covered and no polystyrene shows through (see also Making the Elements page 44). As the hedge is behind the fence it will not be seen and a simple base made from art board can be attached using long panel pins and glue, if required. Do not use spirit-based glues as these may melt the polystyrene. Spray the surface with display

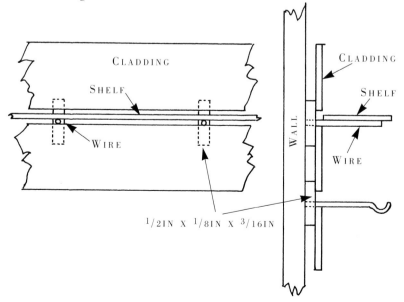

CLADDING

SHELF

WIRE

CLADDING

SHELF

WALL

WIRE

¹/₂IN X ¹/₈IN X ³/₁₆IN

mount spray adhesive and cover liberally with green scenic foam until completely covered. Remove any surplus by brushing or shaking when dry and then paint.

PLANTING

The ground on the lower level between the vegetable beds is covered with fine grass sheet (obtainable from craft shops) but green scatter could also be used. Follow the garden plan for the area to be covered, gluing on the grass sheet when ready.

Cut two ^{1}/4in blocks of Oasis (floral foam) to fit into the vegetable beds and paint the surface with brown acrylic. Cover both beds with a thin layer of PVA glue and spread the contents of two tea bags over the surfaces. Brush off the surplus and insert the prepared blocks into the beds. They are now ready for planting out with vegetables (see list of Suppliers on page 173). Our beds have been planted out in rows and runner beans added to give realistic height to the planting.

GREENHOUSE

The greenhouse occupies the left-hand corner of the garden but you could change this for another feature if you wish.

MATERIALS

MDF – 2mm

Base	6in x 4in
Back	3^1/8in x 5^5/8in
Side (A)	2^7/8in x 4in
Side (B)	2^7/8in x 1^3/4in
Front	2^7/8in x 6in

Jelutong wood

Main frames	^{3}/16in x ^{3}/16in x 40in
Sills	^{1}/16in thick x ^{1}/4in x 12in
Left-hand door post	^{3}/16in x ^{3}/16in x 6^1/2in
Door lintel	^{3}/16in x ^{3}/16in x 2^1/8in
Front stiles, door	^{1}/16in thick x ^{1}/4in x 13in (approx.)
Door inner panel	^{1}/16in thick x 1^{13}/16in x 2^9/16in

Rear stiles, door	¹/₁₆in thick x ¹/₈in x 16in
Door panel	¹/₁₆in thick x 2⁵/₈in x 2in
Door inner frame stiles	¹/₁₆in thick x ¹/₁₆in x 16in
Window and skylight frames	¹/₁₆in thick x ¹/₈in x 108in (approx.)
Roof frame	⁵/₃₂in x ⁵/₃₂in x 24in (approx.) ¹/₈in x ¹/₈in x 24in
Side frame infill	¹/₁₆in thick x 2in x 1in
Racking, four off	³/₃₂in x ³/₃₂in x 2¹/₂in
Racking slats	¹/₁₆in thick x ¹/₄in x 33in (approx.)

Other materials
- *Perspex (plexiglass) or acetate sheet*
- *Brick-patterned paper sheet*

First-stage assembly
Cut the base, back, front and sides A and B from 2mm MDF (see cutting list), ensuring that all the sides are at right angles and cleaning up any rough edges. Cut two upright frame pieces from jelutong 5³/₄in

long and cut the tops to a 25 degree angle to match the roof slope. Lay the front face down and glue the frame uprights to the back so that the angled cuts face down to the front. Cut two more frame uprights each 2⁷/₈in long and glue 2in in from either end, also on the inside (see fig 13).

Cut the door post 6¹/₂in long, shaping the top at a 25 degree angle to fit, and glue this to the inside of side B. Glue one 2⁷/₈in frame upright to the centre of the inside of side A. Cut the two back frame uprights 7¹/₂in long, shaping the tops to slope at 25 degrees. Lay the back face down and glue the uprights to the outer edges of the back.

Glue the front assembly onto the base with the upright supports located on each corner. Glue side B onto the base, locating it against the front upright and repeat for side A. Finally assemble the back onto the baseboard and glue this to sides A and B.

Cut the door lintel from ³/₁₆in square jelutong and glue between the back and side uprights, checking that all the 25 degree angles of the uprights are continuous. Cut the frame infill from ¹/₁₆in thick jelutong at the same angle to fit and glue into place above the door lintel and against the rear upright. Prepare a 15in length of sill material from ¹/₁₆in x ¹/₄in jelutong and cut off 6¹/₄in length for the front piece. Cut a notch at either end so that it will fit around the

Fig 13 First stage assembly of the greenhouse frame

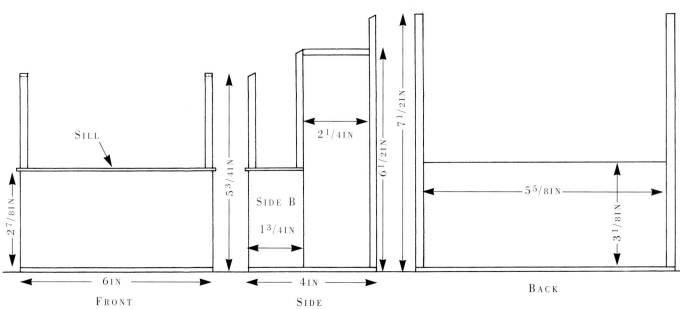

SILL

2⁷/₈IN

6IN

FRONT

5³/₄IN

2¹/₄IN

SIDE B

1³/₄IN

6¹/₂IN

7¹/₂IN

4IN

SIDE

5⁵/₈IN

3¹/₈IN

BACK

upright and glue into place (see fig 14). Cut the two side sills, 4in and 1¾in long, notch to fit and glue into place. Trim off excess to leave squared ends.

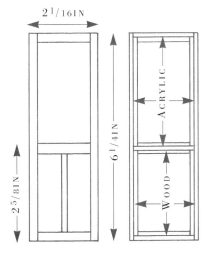

Fig 15 *The greenhouse door construction*

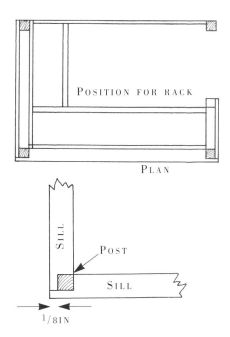

Fig 14 *Cutting the greenhouse sills*

Door

The door is made as a framework built onto the front of the panel. Small strips are added to the back for support. The finished size is 2¹⁄₁₆in wide x 6¼in high.

Cut the door panel from ¹⁄₁₆in thick jelutong 1¹³⁄₁₆in wide x 2⁹⁄₁₆in high. Cut two upright front stiles from 1¼in x ¹⁄₁₆in thick jelutong, 6¼in long and cut three cross stiles 1⁹⁄₁₆in long. Cut one centre upright 2³⁄₈in long from ¹⁄₈in x ¹⁄₁₆in thick jelutong.

If possible use a bench jig with at least one right-angled corner to assist with the assembly. Lay the parts face down and glue the two upright and the three cross stiles together (see fig 15). Cut the bottom panel from ¹⁄₁₆in thick jelutong and glue the door panel to the back of the assembly. Turn this over and add the centre upright so that it lays flush with the front of the door. Add the rear door stiles all around the outside of the door – these are all cut to fit from ¹⁄₁₆in x ¹⁄₁₆in square jelutong. The centre stile glued ¹⁄₁₆in below the top of the one at the front is to support the acetate.

Cut a piece from the Perspex (plexiglass) sheet, 1¹³⁄₁₆in wide x 3¼in high to fit the upper door panel and glue into the rebate formed by the addition of the back stiles.

Cut the ends off two fine dressmaking pins (or use fine wire) to produce two lengths each about ³⁄₈in. Drive one of these into the top of the door ¹⁄₈in in from the right-hand edge and the second ¹⁄₈in in from the bottom right-hand edge. Remove the pins and use masking tape to fix the door into position (see fig 16). With the door in this position drill a ¹⁄₃₂in-diameter hole up through the base and the top lintel (before inserting the infill) to line up with the pin hole in the door. Insert both pins and remove the masking tape, adjusting and gluing the pins into position once the door has been painted. Add a door knob or latch to finish off.

Front window frames

Cut two long frame pieces from ¹⁄₁₆in x ¹⁄₈in jelutong each 5⁵⁄₈in long. Check that this measurement matches the distance between the two frame uprights and adjust if necessary. Cut five uprights from ¹⁄₁₆in thick x ⁵⁄₃₂in jelutong, each 2¹³⁄₁₆in long.

Lay all the parts onto a flat working surface and assemble the two end uprights, checking that the corners of the assembly are at right angles (see fig 17). Add the three inner uprights, equally spaced. Cut a piece of acetate to fit the frame and glue

Fig 16 *Fixing the greenhouse door in position*

TIP

Ease off the hinged edge of the door to prevent it sticking and, if required, add a stop plate to prevent the door being opened inward.

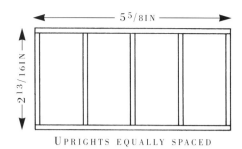

Fig 17 The front window frame

this to the back. When the assembly is completed it can be glued between the uprights, flush with the back.

Side window frames

The side frames are made slightly differently to the front in that the uprights extend from top to bottom and do not sit on the lower parts.

Cut one right-hand side frame from ¹/₁₆in x ¹/₁₆in jelutong 2⁷/₈in long and a second 3¹/₂in (see fig 18). Cut the bottom piece 1in

> **TIP**
>
> *Do not glue any acetate to frames until the assembly has been painted.*

long and the top 1¹/₄in long. Glue in the two side frames and add the bottom so that they all fit between the two main uprights, to the back. The top piece of this frame is angled to match the roof and must be trimmed to fit. Make up a small template from stiff card, transfer the design to the Perspex then cut out and glue to the inside.

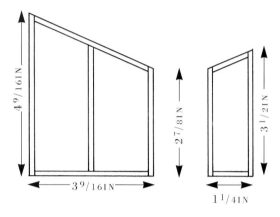

Fig 18 The side window frames

Make up the pieces for the left-hand side window frame from ¹/₁₆in thick jelutong. Note the largest upright is 4⁹/₁₆in and the smaller is 2⁷/₈in. Cut the bottom cross piece 3⁵/₁₆in and the top 3⁵/₈in to fit the frame. Cut a centre upright to fit, 3³/₈in long. Glue all the parts into position.

Roof – skylight

For the outer frame of the skylight, cut two pieces from ¹/₁₆in thick x ⁵/₁₆in jelutong, one 6¹/₄in long and two 4⁵/₈in long. Lay onto a flat surface and glue together to form the support frame (see fig 19). From ¹/₈in x ¹/₈in jelutong cut two pieces 6¹/₄in long and two

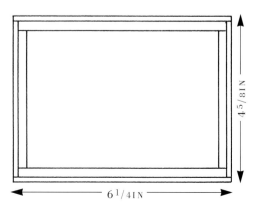

Fig 19 The outer frame of the greenhouse skylight

4⁵/8in long, and glue on top of the support frame along the outer edges.

The inner skylight frame is made from ¹/16in thick x ¹/8in jelutong and is designed to sit inside the skylight outer frame and can be left loose if required. Cut the top and bottom members from ¹/16in x ¹/8in jelutong, each 5⁷/8in long and five uprights 4in long. Place the parts face down onto a flat surface and glue together to form a framework (see fig 20), making sure that the centre uprights match those of the lower front window to form a continuous line. Cut four cross pieces, each 1³/8in long and glue between the uprights in the centre of the frame. Lay the assembly onto the Perspex (plexiglass) sheet, and mark and cut a piece to fit. The finished frame can now be laid in position.

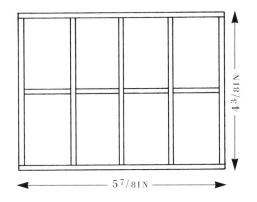

Fig 20 The central frame of the greenhouse skylight

FINISHING OFF

Complete all the painting before gluing the Perspex (plexiglass) into position. Remove the door and the skylight, paint with white acrylic and leave to dry. Paint all the uprights and window frames with the same colour. Give all parts a light rub down with fine abrasive paper and re-paint to give a satin finish. Glue on all the cut and prepared Perspex parts using UHU.

Paint the door with white acrylic and re-hang, gluing the pins into position to secure. The paintwork on the greenhouse shown has been 'weathered' by picking up a little brown paint on a small brush and leaving a streaked finish.

The unglazed part of the greenhouse is covered with brick-patterned sheeting. Cut a piece 2⁷/8in x 13in to cover the front and sides. Glue it to the front and then the sides, wrapping one end around the back and finishing off neatly at the doorway. A little grey paint along the some of the mortar lines and the bottom edge will indicate weathering and improve the look of the sheeting.

Racking

This is the staging or shelving within the greenhouse. Cut four legs in ³/16in x ³/16in jelutong, 2¹/2in long. Cut the main framing stretchers from ¹/4in x ¹/16in thick jelutong: A – 5¹/2in and B – 2³/16in. Cut the secondary stretchers from ¹/8in x ¹/8in jelutong: C – 6in and D – 3¹¹/16in. Cut nineteen slats from ¹/4in x ¹/16in jelutong 1⁹/16in long.

Cut a piece of stiff card or a ¹/16in thick jelutong offcut, 1in wide and lay the longest main and secondary stretchers down onto a flat surface with the card between them to maintain an even distance (see fig 21). Note that these stretchers are offset. Start gluing on the slats with the end flush with the edge laid on the ¹/8in stretcher. Leave a ¹/8in gap between each one and allow the adhesive to set before starting the next stage. Lay the two short stretchers into position and glue on the remaining slats.

Apply dark oak wood stain mixed 50/50 with white spirit to all the racking and the four legs and allow to dry. Glue the four legs into position under the racking and glue the assembly inside the greenhouse.

To finish off your vegetable garden choose a selection of tools and equipment to reflect the purpose of the garden. Plant up some seed trays, pots and perhaps a hanging basket to show plants in various stages of growth.

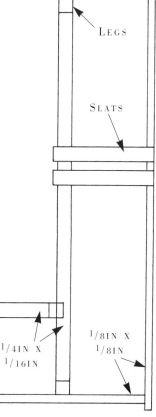

Fig 21 Making the greenhouse racking

A Victorian Roof Garden with Conservatory

During the Georgian and Victorian eras the opening of trade routes across the warmer climates of the world and expeditions undertaken by naturalists resulted in many strange plants being brought back to Britain. The glass hothouse became a necessity for these plants and eventually a decorative feature of many gardens. The Victorians built them in contemporary architectural styles, very often on an extremely large scale. The owners of smaller houses with more modest gardens also wanted to share in this new hobby, so the conservatory came into being.

Today we tend to have greenhouses for plants and conservatories for people, and the addition of a conservatory, particularly in a Victorian style, has become the latest accessory for the modern house, providing a light and airy extra room. The size constraints of town houses, often built in terraces, usually results in a small back garden with little space for extension and whilst modern planning regulations can forbid expanding a building in any lateral direction, clever architects are managing to add conservatories to roofs.

Many dolls' houses come with a flat roof which provides an ideal location for a roof garden project. The conservatory we used was a kit, but as this is a free-standing item several changes, including the addition of glazing, were made in order to make it fit against our mock building.

141

CONSTRUCTING THE GARDEN

Follow the garden plan for the positioning of all the elements.

General materials needed for constructing this garden include; PVA glue, artist's display mount or photo mount adhesive, panel pins, stiff card, paints, tea bags, dressmaking pins, wood stain and white spirit.

Where instructions are given for general gluing it is assumed that a PVA type glue will be used.

MATERIALS

MDF – 9mm

Base		16in x 19in
Chimney stack	A	14in x 2⅝in
	B	7⅛in x 2⅝in
	C	6⅞in 2⅝in
	D	6½in x 2⅝in
Chimney stack cap		3in x 1½in

MDF – 6mm

House sides, two off	11¾in x 7½in
House front A	7⅛in x 3½in
House front B	7⅛in x 12½in

Plan of the Victorian roof garden with conservatory

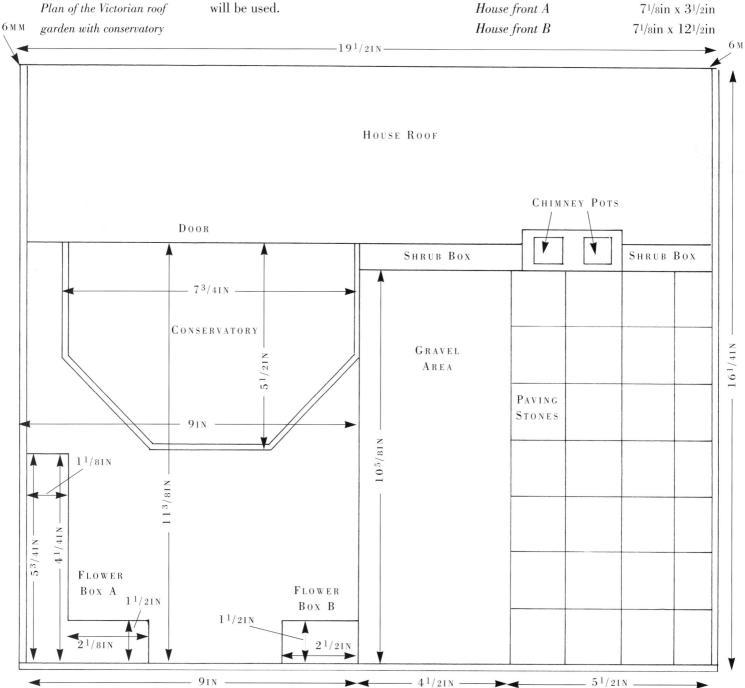

House guide	strip x 16in
House roof	7^{1}/$_{4}$in x 19in
Low balustrade wall	2^{1}/$_{4}$in x 51^{1}/$_{2}$in

MDF – 2mm

Low balustrade coping	^{1}/$_{2}$in x 52in
Door blank	6^{7}/$_{8}$in x 2^{3}/$_{4}$in

Jelutong wood

Trellis	^{3}/$_{16}$in x ^{3}/$_{16}$in x 40in
	approx. (see instructions)
	^{1}/$_{8}$in x ^{1}/$_{32}$in thick x 85in
	approx. (see instructions)
Door stiles	^{3}/$_{8}$in x ^{1}/$_{16}$in thick
	x 28in approx. (see instructions)
Roof soffit boards	^{3}/$_{4}$in x ^{1}/$_{16}$in thick
	x 15in (see instructions)
Door frame	^{1}/$_{4}$in x ^{1}/$_{8}$in thick x 20in
Flower boxes	^{1}/$_{8}$in x 1in x 25in approx.
	(see instructions)
Sills	^{3}/$_{16}$in x ^{1}/$_{16}$in thick x 4in

Paving materials

- Tiles ^{1}/$_{2}$in square: 90 black; 90 terracotta; 20 white
- Paving stones (See Making the Elements page 26): twenty-one off 1^{1}/$_{2}$in x 1^{1}/$_{2}$in; seven off 1^{1}/$_{2}$in x 1in

Other materials

- Acetate sheet (for glazing)
- Door knob
- Oasis (floral foam)
- Plants
- Brick-patterned paper sheet
- Tile-patterned paper for roof

Specialist supplies

(see Suppliers page 173)
- Conservatory kit
- Fibre-glass gravel paper sheet
- Two chimney pots

BASE

Cut the base from 9mm MDF 16in x 19in and use a try square to check that all the edges are at right angles to each other. Draw guide lines for both sides of the house, at the back of the base, 6mm from each edge about 7in long. Drill several equally spaced ^{1}/$_{32}$in-diameter holes for panel pins inside this line.

HOUSE
Sides

Cut and prepare both sides from 6mm MDF 11^{3}/$_{4}$in x 7^{1}/$_{2}$in and measure off the 45 degree angle shown in fig 1, checking that the back edge is 11^{3}/$_{4}$in and that at the

TIP

Roof gardens have the advantage of not requiring surrounding scenery, apart from the sky and a few tall trees. Sky scenes, prepared and mounted on a suitable board, can be placed behind the conservatory to heighten the illusion that the garden has been built onto a real roof.

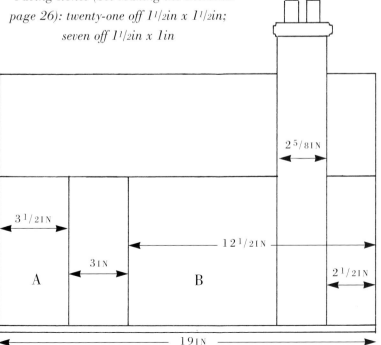

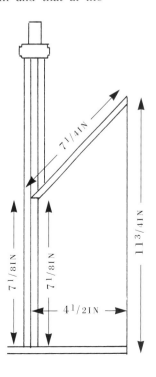

Fig 1 Making the house

front it measures 7¹/₂in at the highest point, tapering to 7¹/₈in. Use PVA wood adhesive to glue both sides on to the baseboard and secure with panel pins into the holes previously made. Support both sides at 90 degrees to the baseboard until the adhesive has set firm.

Front

Cut and prepare front pieces A and B from 6mm MDF and using a small plane chamfer the top edges to 45 degrees, sloping to the front surface (see fig 1).

Lay a steel rule or straight edge across the bottom front edges of both sides and draw a guide line between them on the baseboard. Cut the 6mm guide strip into two pieces 3¹/₂in and 12¹/₂in long. Glue the strips along the inside of this line, with the ends against each of the side walls to leave a 3in gap. Glue the front walls into place, against the sides and guide, leaving a 3in gap between them for the doorway.

Roof

Cut and prepare the roof from 6mm MDF 7¹/₄in x 19in and square off the edges. Use a small plane to shape the two long edges at 45 degrees, noting that the angles face each other as shown in fig 1. Draw a guide line along each of the outer edges ¹/₈in from the edge and drill two ¹/₃₂in-diameter holes for panel pins through each line. Glue and pin the roof into position on top of the sides and fronts, ensuring that it is flush with the back edge.

Chimney stack

Using 9mm MDF, cut one length 14in long x 2⁵/₈in wide (A) and one 7¹/₈in long x 2⁵/₈in wide (B). Glue these two together one on top of the other with the bottoms flush, clamp-ing together until set (see fig 2). Check that the part assembly fits against the front of the house, the longer piece to the front and shorter piece fitting under the lip of the roof. Cut a third piece of 9mm MDF 2⁵/₈in wide and 6⁷/₈in long (C), this time with one end cut to 45 degrees. Glue this to part (A)

above the roof line with the 45 degree cut resting on top of the roof lip. Cut a fourth part (D) from the same material 2⁵/₈in wide x 6¹/₂in long, again with a 45 degree cut at the bottom where it meets the roof line. Glue this to the stack assembly and clamp until dry. Trim off the top edge if necessary to produce a flat surface.

Chimney stack cap

Cut a piece of 9mm MDF 3in x 1¹/₂in and draw a cutting line ¹/₈in in around all the edges on the top surface and repeat on the under side. Draw a second series of lines around all the edges, top and bottom, again at ¹/₈in. Fix the piece into a small vice and use a fine tenon saw to remove the waste following the guide line, to produce a part shown in fig 2. Alternatively, use a powered bench saw to remove the waste evenly all round. Glue this part to the top of the stack.

Using wallpaper paste, cover the entire stack assembly with a brick finish paper sheet (this will match the front of the house) and glue on the two chimney pots.

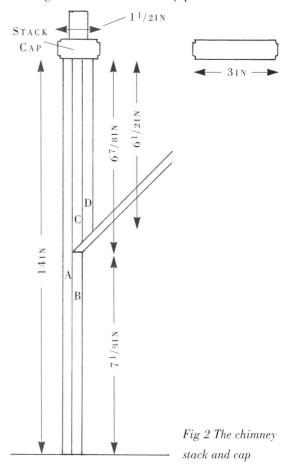

*Fig 2 The chimney
stack and cap*

Door and doorway

To form a door lining, cut two pieces of $^1/_4$in x $^1/_8$in thick jelutong 3in long and two pieces $6^7/_8$in long, and glue these into place between the front walls (see fig 3).

Cut a piece of 6mm MDF for the door blank, $6^7/_8$in high x $2^3/_4$in wide and check that this fits the opening without any gaps, trimming one or both of the dimensions if necessary. Remove the door and lay flat onto a work surface.

Cut the door stiles from $^1/_{16}$in x $^3/_8$in wide jelutong, as follows: two pieces $6^7/_8$in for the

TIP

You could use a ready-made door and frame, just remember to adjust the size of the aperture in the house front if necessary before cutting out.

Fig 3 The door and doorway

145

outer frame (a) and one $6\frac{1}{8}$in for the centre frame (b). Cut two 2in lengths for the top and bottom frame (c) and one $1\frac{7}{8}$in long for cross frame (d). Glue parts (a) through to (d) onto the MDF door blank as shown in fig 3, then place the door assembly under a weight until the glue has set hard.

Paint the door and its frame with a matt finish white acrylic paint mixed with a little brown to produce an off-white colour. Glue the door into the doorway and add a door knob to finish off.

Roof soffits

Cut two plain $7\frac{1}{4}$in long soffit boards from $\frac{1}{16}$in thick x $\frac{1}{2}$in wide jelutong, cutting the ends at 45 degrees. Paint these with an off-white acrylic paint and glue on to the edges of the roof after adding the house and roof covering (see below).

House and roof covering

Cut and paste brick-patterned paper to fit the front and sides of the house, trimming this around the doorway and chimney stack and wrapping it inside the building at the

*Fig 4 Shaping the
conservatory roof*

back for a neat finish. Cover the roof with a suitable tile-patterned paper sheet, working around the chimney stack and finishing off neatly at the edges. Glue on the painted soffit boards.

CONSERVATORY

The conservatory was supplied as a kit (see Suppliers page 173). In order to make it fit our roof and building it was assembled minus the end panels and the end roof joists, but otherwise to the manufacturer's instructions. See fig 4 for roof amendments as the main roof span should be cut at the same angle as the house roof to provide a neat fit and the door should be fixed into the centre panel at the front.

For the outer glazing two $\frac{1}{16}$in thick x $\frac{1}{8}$in strips of jelutong each 5in long were painted white and cut to length on site to fit between the top centre beam and the side walls. Five pieces of $\frac{1}{16}$in thick x $\frac{1}{8}$in strip jelutong were cut to fit the inside of each of the decorative panels and glued just below the window panes to give support to the acetate glazing.

The whole assembly should be painted white before it is attached to the garden project and we suggest that the best way to achieve this is to use a cellulose car spray undercoat or primer to seal the surface and finish off with a satin-finish white.

Before fixing the conservatory into place draw the area the base covers (inside measurement) onto a sheet of stiff white card or paper. Divide this into tiled squares $\frac{1}{2}$in wide and use a fine-tipped, black felt-tip pen to ink in the joints. Glue this card down onto the baseboard and place the conservatory over it.

Cut and glue acetate sheet to fit inside the four decorative side panels and door. The acetate glazing for the roof can be added later but this is a very good time to cut the sheets to fit (make a template if necessary).

The conservatory is assembled onto the roof against the left-hand side of the building with the roof doorway in the centre.

BALUSTRADE WALLS

The balustrade walls are a vital part of the project – stopping the occupants falling off the roof! Cut and prepare three strips of $2^{1}/_{4}$in 6mm MDF to fit around the front and two sides of the garden. Paint the inner sides with an off-white matt emulsion or poster paint and the outer surfaces a matt grey. Cut the balustrade coping from $^{1}/_{2}$in x 2mm MDF and score with a shallow V-shaped cut every inch. Cut lengths to match the balustrade walls, running it the full length of the left-hand side and beyond the trellis on the right. Mitre the joint where the sides meet the front and glue into place with a slight overlap to the front.

For the front corner posts, cut two pieces of jelutong $2^{1}/_{4}$in long x $^{1}/_{4}$in x $^{1}/_{16}$in thick, add under the coping and glue on. Finish by painting with a grey acrylic colour with a few brown streaks to indicate weathering.

FLOOR TILING

Use the tile layout in fig 5 and draw a line around the area to be tiled on the base. Mark off the two spaces to be occupied by the flower boxes and pin in the templates (see Tip box). The tiles we used were $^{1}/_{2}$in square but the diagonal of a square is greater than the measurement of a side and that, plus the size of any gap left between each tile, may affect the numbers actually used in your garden.

Cut the half-size white tiles along the gravel path edge first and work towards the left hand wall (facing the area). That way you can cut and lay odd-sized tiles against the wall where it will notice least. Use a razor saw to cut the tiles accurately. After fitting the conservatory you may find there is a small gap, about $^{1}/_{8}$in between it and the tiled area. This can be filled with three small fillets cut from $^{1}/_{16}$in thick x $^{1}/_{8}$in jelutong strip, first painted white to match.

Follow the plan in fig 5 and glue all the tiles into place, alternating black with terracotta rows and placing half tiles of white around the edges. Take great care *not*

to allow any adhesive onto the face of the tiles.

FLOWER BOXES

The two boxes to the front of the garden under the balustrade wall are made up using $^{1}/_{8}$in thick jelutong 1in wide. For the L-shaped box A, cut one end $^{7}/_{8}$in and the second $1^{1}/_{4}$in (see fig 5). The four sides are cut as follows: $5^{3}/_{4}$in, $4^{1}/_{4}$in, $3^{1}/_{8}$in and $2^{1}/_{4}$in. It is important that all ends of the pieces are cut square and at right angles otherwise the box will not assemble correctly. Place all the parts onto a flat surface or jig and assemble together using a PVA adhesive, then support and allow the glue to set.

Cut the parts for the rectangular flower box B, again using $^{1}/_{8}$in thick jelutong 1in wide. Cut two sides $1^{1}/_{4}$in each and two $2^{1}/_{8}$in (see fig 5). Assemble and glue the parts together as for box A. There are no bases to these boxes.

> **TIP**
> *Cut two templates from stiff card the same size as the bases of the flower boxes. Pin these firmly into place and remove after gluing down all the tiles.*

Fig 5 The black and red tiled area around the conservatory

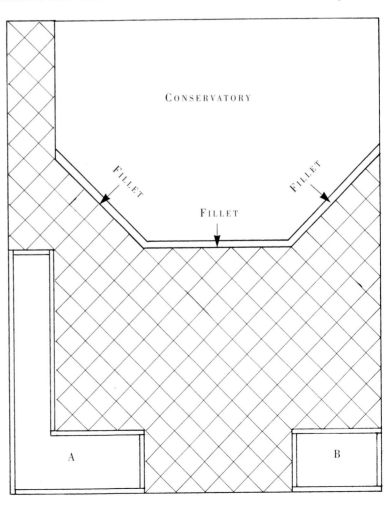

CONSERVATORY

FILLET

FILLET

FILLET

A

B

*A Victorian
Roof Garden with
Conservatory*

TIP

*You may have assembled
your chimney stack or
wall in a slightly
different position to ours
so it is a good idea to
check the measurements
of shrub boxes C and D
before cutting out these
two containers as they
look so much better
when they fit snugly.*

TIP

*To maintain a straight
edge to paving draw a
guide line directly onto
the baseboard 5¹/₂in
from the right-hand side
and pin a piece of card
or thin wood along it,
keeping it to the left of
the line.*

Remove any rough edges from both boxes, clean up and prepare for painting by sealing with a thin coat of emulsion or poster paint. Finish off with a white satin-finish paint. Glue the boxes into position (see fig 5), after first removing any templates you have used.

Cut pieces of Oasis (floral foam) as an exact fit for the boxes (the piece for box A can be cut in two parts). Away from the garden, shape the Oasis tops with a sharp craft knife. Spray the top surfaces with display mount or photo mount adhesive and sprinkle over the contents of one or two tea bags. Repeat until the surfaces are covered, brush off any surplus and place them into their respective boxes. Fill with appropriate, low growing flowers when all other tasks are finished.

SHRUB BOXES

Strictly speaking these are not four-sided boxes but three-sided, with the sides and front supported by Oasis (floral foam), however four-sided boxes can easily be made up if you wish. Make up two boxes C and D from ³/₃₂in thick jelutong 1in wide, to sit either side of the chimney stack (see Tip box top left). Cut four end pieces ⁵/₈in wide. For box C cut the front 4³/₄in long and for box D cut two 2⁷/₁₆in long. Check that all ends are neat and square and at right angles and then glue together to form two U-shaped boxes. Place them on their sides, and leave to dry.

When the two assemblies are fixed together finish off with a thin primer coat of emulsion and a top coat of satin-finish white paint. These can now be placed flush with the back wall.

Cut Oasis (floral foam) to fit each box, remove and shape the top surface using a sharp craft knife. Spray the top surface with artist's display mount adhesive and cover with the contents from a tea bag, brushing off any residue and repeating as required. Place the foam into the boxes ready for adding plants.

PAVING

You will need twenty-one paving slabs 1¹/₂in x 1¹/₂in and seven 1¹/₂in x 1in to fill the paved area under the pergola. During the making of paving you may find that some of them suffer from shrinkage when they dry out, resulting in you needing rather more to finish the given area. You can overcome this by adding four small slabs, to the front under the front balustrade wall where they will not be noticed. These last four could be oddments, or they could be cut down from standard paving using a sharp razor saw. See Making the Elements page 27 for casting slabs and colouring these to resemble stone flags.

Brush a thin coat of PVA modelling glue onto the whole area in order to seal it, and allow this to dry. Place a small spot of glue under each paving slab and lay each one down following the pattern shown in the garden plan on page 142, keeping all the edges square. Maintain a very small gap between each side of each slab with thin pieces of card or paper. Leave the area blank at the back to the right of the chimney stack into which we have placed a shrub box. When the slabs have set firmly fill any large gaps with a proprietary plaster filler and use an acrylic colour on this to match the slabs.

GRAVEL

The gravel used in this roof garden project was cut from a sheet of fibre-glass gravel finish (see Suppliers on page 173), a material which is very realistic and very easy to use. The area to be covered with gravel runs directly from the front of the garden to the house (see the garden plan on page 142) and is approximately 4¹/₂in wide and 10⁵/₈in long. You will need to check both these measurements carefully against your model after laying the paving and the tiles and amend if necessary as the gravel paper sheet should fit snugly against the tiles on the left, the paving on the right and the boxes at the back. When the sheet has been cut to size simply glue down with a PVA adhesive (see also Tip box, right).

TRELLIS AND PERGOLA

This assembly sits on top of the side balustrade wall, supported by the chimney stack and with one post supporting it at the front. Photocopy or trace fig 6 to the same size onto a piece of stiff white paper and pin this drawing firmly to a flat working surface ready to assemble the trellis and pergola onto it. Please note that fig 6 shows the side of the trellis that faces into the garden. Lightly cover the drawing with Vaseline (petroleum jelly) to avoid accidentally gluing parts to it, wiping off any surplus. In assembling the trellis the crossed strips are laid on the back of the posts.

To make the trellis and pergola you will need the following extra materials: PVA wood glue or clear adhesive and a tray of dressmaking pins, preferably about $3/4$in long with large coloured heads. Four strips of stiff card or wood will be needed as spacer guides, $1/2$in wide – cut two $1^7/8$in long and two $2^1/2$in long.

Cut six posts from $3/16$in x $3/16$in jelutong, each 5in long and cut one $6^7/8$in long for the front support. Cut a further two pieces from the same material $11^1/2$in long for the top beams running from front to back. The base support rails are also cut from $3/16$in x $3/16$in jelutong and you will need two $1^7/8$in long and two $2^1/2$in long. There is no base support for the centre section but it is recommended that a $1^1/2$in length of $3/16$in square jelutong is cut to act as a spacing guide and discarded once the assembly is complete. Cut a short roof end support from $3/16$in square jelutong $1^1/2$in long.

The five top beams are cut from $5/16$in x $3/16$in jelutong, each $5^5/8$in long. The horizontal trellis strips are all made from $1/8$in x $3/32$in thick jelutong. Cut eight off $2^7/8$in and six off $4^7/8$in long. Now, cut the vertical strips from the same material, six off $5^1/8$in long and for the shorter pieces, four off $1^7/8$in long. Cut two short sills or hand rails from $3/16$in x $1/16$in jelutong, each $1^7/8$in long. Stain all the parts with wood stain in a light oak colour diluted 50/50 with white spirit, and place the parts to one side until thoroughly dry.

Place each of the six 5in vertical posts onto your drawing and fix into place by placing a series of dressmaking pins on

TIP

Gravelled areas can also be simulated by using fine stones sprinkled over a pre-glued sheet of coarse glass paper that has been suitably coloured.

Fig 6 Constructing the trellis (inner view)

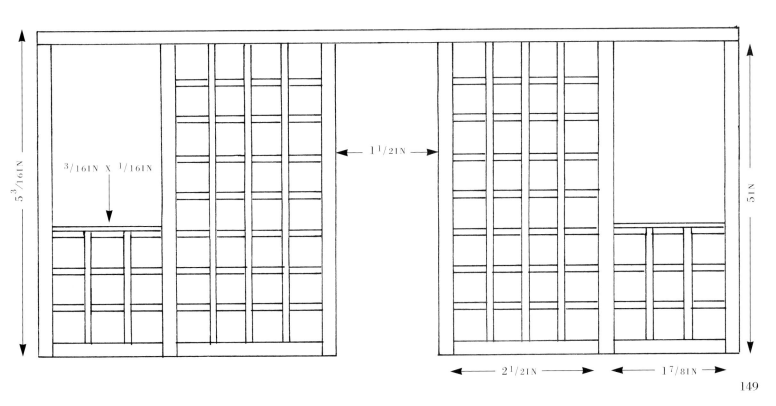

either side. Glue one long top beam into place, pin securely so that it does not move and check that all the posts are vertical before proceeding with the assembly. Glue the bottom support rails into place and follow this with the two sills, checking that all the components are horizontal to the posts and equally spaced.

The next stage is to fix the thin trellis strips onto the posts. Start with the vertical ones and working from the left-hand side glue the two short ones with a ¹/₂in gap between them. These should lie on top of the base support and just under the sill. Repeat for the right-hand side. Follow this by gluing the three strips into each of the larger vertical spaces, placing the strips on top of the beams and using the spacer cards to maintain even gaps and supporting the work with pins.

Once this assembly is workable, glue on all the horizontal strips following the drawing and using the spacer card to keep it all evenly spaced. The fourth horizontal strips should lie just under the sills.

When the assembly is ready and the glue has thoroughly dried, carefully remove it from the drawing and clean up any rough edges. Place it on top of the low balustrade wall on the right-hand side of the garden, add the support under the roof line and glue the whole assembly into place on the wall (see fig 7a).

The long support or front post (6⁷/₈in) is placed against the inside of the front wall, 5¹/₈in away from the trellis assembly. Use a razor saw to cut a notch in the coping stone at this point, or alternatively cut a notch out of the post so that it will lay flush with the wall (see fig 7b).

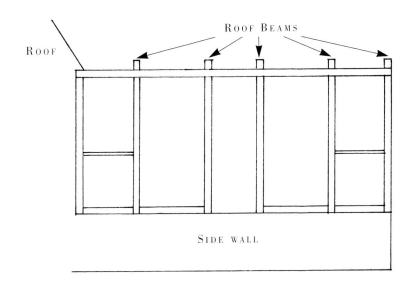

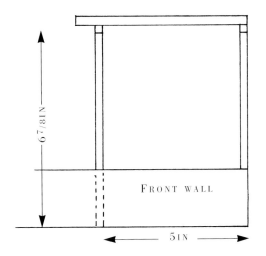

Fig 7b Positioning the front post of the pergola against the inside front wall

Glue the second roof beam 11³/₈in on top of this post with the other end fixed to the side of chimney stack. The front post that supports this beam sits on top of the paving so it is a good idea to check that the beam is horizontal and that the height is constant with the main trellis work.

Glue the pergola roof beams so that the one at the front is flush with the tops of the two posts with a ¹/₄in overlap to the inside of the garden. You will see that each beam

is positioned directly over an upright post (see fig 7c).

To complete your Victorian roof garden choose and position accessories that will enhance the period (see photographs for ideas and the list of Suppliers on page 173). Plant up the flower and shrub boxes with low-growing, bedding-type plants and add the necessary specimen and climbing plants around the rest of the garden.

Roses, clematis, honeysuckle, grape vine and ivy would make ideal climbing plants to drape over the pergola, while specimen plants to adorn pots and trellis work could include wisteria, laburnum or standard roses. You could emulate the Victorians by including exotic and unusual plants, such as cannas, tree ferns or even bananas. You may be able to find unusual plants at dolls' house fairs or you could try making your own, particularly the large-leaved varieties (see Making the Elements page 57).

Fig 7a Positioning the pergola on the low balustrade wall

TIP

Put the trellis into place and check the best position for the support before gluing into place.

Fig 7c Attaching the pergola beams

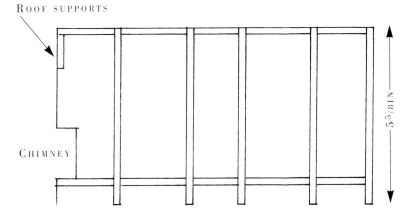

151

The Georgian Courtyard Garden

Georgian town houses were often built in terraces (row houses) on narrow plots of land, within easy reach of the town centre, and the space given over to the garden was correspondingly small. A front or rear courtyard was not unusual – very often this area would be a simple basement. A courtyard garden for a Georgian house was a very formal affair, designed more to impress visitors and passers-by than for comfort or practical ease. It was a feature intended to show the latest ideas and fashions of the age.

It is very important not to include too many features in a garden of this sort. Keep in mind that the occupants are people impressed by the simple lines of Palladio, an Italian architect whose influence was popular among the Georgians. In keeping with the period the decorative touches are supplied by elegant planters and carved pots which have been used to adorn the upper terrace. A sweep of steps carried the occupants down from street level into the garden. An important focal point of this miniature courtyard is the water display against the back wall. Supported by a brick surround, it contains water plants and features a Greek marble statuette in a niche. The area below the house has been paved with York flagstones.

Many dolls' houses are tall slim buildings and a courtyard garden placed in front will set it off very well. The garden may be placed to one side or even at the back of the house, or you could make it as a 'stand alone' garden, complete in itself.

TIP

*Adding a decorative
ironwork railing to the
steps will enhance this
project. The use of
wooden banisters and
railings should be
avoided however as they
are too heavy for a
house of this type.*

TIP

*With a little skill a
fretsaw may be used to
cut out the arched recess
in one piece.*

CONSTRUCTING THE GARDEN

Wherever you position it, the entire garden should ideally be built as a separate unit to be placed against the dolls' house once completed. It is easier to work on this way and can be removed later should adjustments need to be made. This garden has been designed so that it will suit many of today's dolls' houses. However, you can change the baseboard sizes and the height of the terrace to match the dimensions of any house.

Follow the garden plan for the positioning of all the elements. General materials for construction include; PVA glue, photo or display mount adhesive spray, 1/2in panel pins, masking tape, stiff card, tea bags, cling film (Siran wrap) and various paints. For general gluing, a PVA type glue can be used.

MATERIALS

MDF – 6mm

Base	12¼in x 12¼in
Terrace back	12in x 8¼in
Left garden wall	8in x 9½in
Garden wall pillar	7¾in x 1½in
Sides x 2	8in x 2⅞in

MDF – 3mm

Terrace front	8in x 12in
Steps stringer, large	7⅜in x 7⅜in
Steps stringer, small	2in x 6½in
Terrace top	12¼in x 3½in
Large flower bed base	12in x 2in

Jelutong wood

Coping stones x 13	³/₃₂in x ½in x 1½in
Small flower bed base	³/₃₂in x 5in x 2in
Flower bed sides x 2	³/₃₂in x 5³/₁₆in x ⅜in
Flower bed ends x 2	³/₃₂in x 2³/₁₆in x ⅜in
Stair treads x 7	³/₃₂in x 2¼in x 15/16in
Stair treads x 2	³/₃₂in x 2⅜in x 15/16in
Stair risers x 10	³/₃₂in x 2⅜in x ⅝in
Bottom landing	³/₃₂in x 3in x 2⅜in

Other materials

- *Bricks strips: 60in for walling (special size);
26in for flower bed*
- *Paving slabs x 25, 1½in square*
- *Perspex (plexiglass) sheet 3in square*
- *1/16in plywood 9in x 1in*
- *Oasis (floral foam)*
- *Gravel paper*

Specialist supplies
(see Suppliers page 173)
- *Hanging basket*
- *Iron basket*
- *15 small bedding plants*
- *2 water plants*
- *Large round cask tub*
- *Large, planked wooden trough*
- *Small, plain wooden trough*
- *Various clay pots, tubs and troughs*
- *Small statue*
- *Various plants to fill all the tubs,
troughs and pots*
- *Moulded fibre-glass brick sheeting*

BASEBOARD AND TERRACE
Cutting out

Prepare the baseboard from the 6mm MDF to the measurements given, ensuring that all the sides and edges are at right angles and removing any rough edges. Mark the front of this piece. In the same way, cut and prepare the two sides, back, front and top of the terrace. As MDF resists nails, pre-drill two 0.8mm holes at the base in each of the two sides and the back to take panel pins.

Mark out the position of the arched recess, or niche, on the front using a compass to ensure a perfectly rounded top. Cut out using a strong craft knife and clean up rough edges with abrasive paper. Set aside this arched section – it will be used later to form the back of the recess.

Quoin template

Quoins are key-stones, usually found at the corners of buildings, but the Georgians also used them around doors and windows. Here

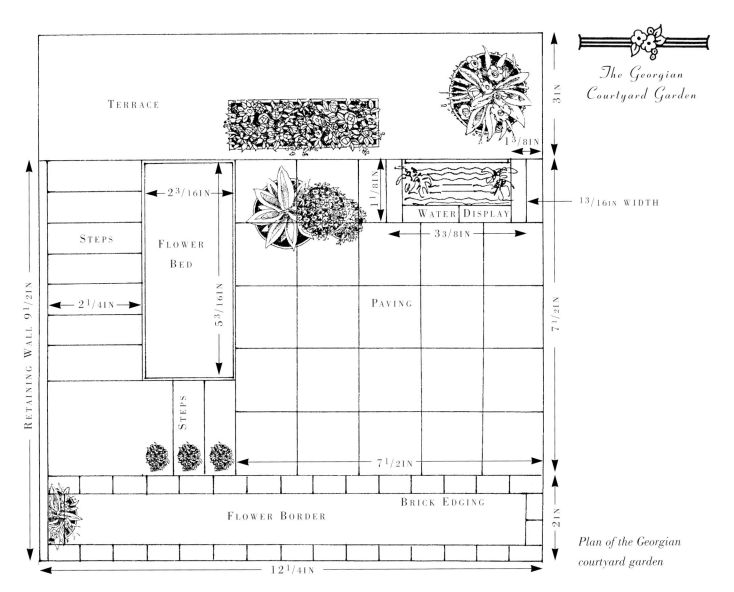

TERRACE

1 3/8IN

3IN

2 3/16IN

1 1/8IN

13/16IN WIDTH

STEPS

FLOWER
BED

5 3/16IN

3 3/8IN

2 1/4IN

WATER DISPLAY

PAVING

7 1/2IN

RETAINING WALL 9 1/2IN

STEPS

7 1/2IN

2IN

BRICK EDGING

FLOWER BORDER

12 1/4IN

*Plan of the Georgian
courtyard garden*

they have been used as a decorative feature around the arched recess on the wall of the terrace. Full instructions for making the quoins appear on page 158 but it is important to make the template before proceeding.

Lay the front wall of the terrace face down onto a piece of stiff card and trace around the recess aperture to make the quoin template. Draw a second line 1/2in outside the first. Cut out this up-turned U shape and check that it fits the recess aperture. Set to one side.

Recess

Take the arched section that will form the back of the recess and clean up any rough edges. Cut a piece of 1/8in x 3/4in jelutong the width of this section and glue it to the front, at the bottom, to form a sill.

Cut two support pieces of 1/8in x 1/4in jelutong, each 2 1/2in long, and use UHU to glue to either side of the back, flush with the edges (see fig 1). Allow the adhesive to dry thoroughly.

Measure around the outer curved edge of the recess back and cut a piece of 1/16in x 3/4in plywood to this length. Carefully bend the plywood around the recess back and check that it fits (see fig 2). When you are

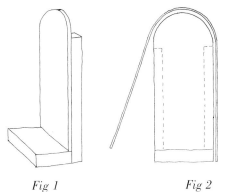

Fig 1   *Fig 2*

*The Georgian
Courtyard Garden*

TIP

When cutting out use a jig or a stop clamp in a mitre box to ensure each tread or riser is exactly the same length. You can cut the tread patterns in the stringers with a very sharp craft knife – but a razor saw will give infinitely better results.

---

sure of a good fit, glue it in place and hold with masking tape until dry.

Glue two pieces of $1/8$in x $1/4$in jelutong, each 3in long, to either side of the outer surface of the $1/16$in plywood to add extra strength.

Cut a small shelf from the $1/8$in x $3/4$in jelutong piece, making it the exact width of the recess, and glue this into place 1in from the bottom. Now glue the completed assembly into the aperture in the front of the terrace (see fig 3). Ensure that it fits perfectly into the hole allowed for it, and apply pressure until the glue has set hard.

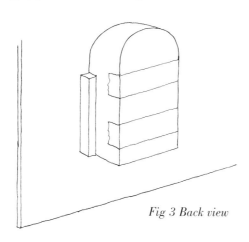

Fig 3 Back view

Assembling the terrace

Glue and pin the two short sides and back to the base, ensuring they are upright. Then glue the back and front, containing the assembled recess, onto the sides. The terrace should now resemble an open box. Pin and glue the completed retaining wall in place. Check that the top sits neatly on top of the 'box' and then glue two $2½$in square 6mm MDF offcuts to the underside to act as locating pieces, allowing it to be removed to adjust the recess if necessary. Glue the terrace top in position with the overlap to the front and to the right only. Glue on a piece of fine gravel paper to fit the terrace top.

GARDEN WALL

The large brick built wall on the left hand side of the garden divides it from that of its neighbours. Drill three

$1/32$in holes through the back $1/8$in from the base, to take panel pins. Glue the upright pillar to the outer end of the wall so that it is flush at the top, as it stands on the baseboard. Cover the front surfaces of the wall and pillar with fibre-glass brick sheet taking care to match the brick courses at each end. Set to one side.

STEPS

The staircase is produced as a separate unit that can be installed later. It is not necessary to glue this into position.

There are two step stringer-wall sections – an upper and a lower produced actual size. Using the large steps stringer template on page 157, mark out the upper steps pattern along the longest edge of the triangle, and cut twice (A and B) from 3mm MDF. Using the small steps stringer template, cut one piece to the lower right-hand steps pattern (D) and a second $2^1/6$in wider to make the left-hand steps pattern (C).

With reference to fig 4, cut the treads from a strip of $3/32$in jelutong $7/8$in wide. From this strip cut seven pieces to make the individual treads, each $2¼$in long. Cut a further two treads $2^3/8$in long.

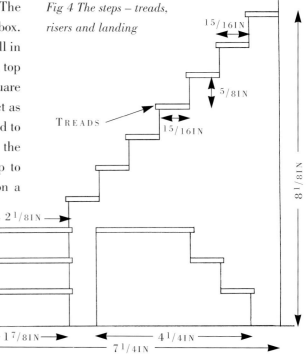

Fig 4 The steps – treads, risers and landing

$15/16$IN

$5/8$IN

TREADS

$15/16$IN

$8^1/8$IN

$2^1/8$IN

$1^7/8$IN

$4^1/4$IN

$7^1/4$IN

For the risers, cut a strip of 3/32in jelutong 5/8in wide. From this strip cut ten pieces each 2¹/8in long. For the landing, cut a piece of 3/32in jelutong 3in x 2³/8in.

Assembling the steps

Cut three pieces of 6mm (¹/4in) thick MDF exactly 1⁷/8in x 3in to use as spacers whilst building the stairs.

Glue the lower left-hand stringer C to the upper stringer A as in fig 5 ensuring that it is at right angles. Allow the adhesive to set. Glue the second upper stringer B into position using one of the spacers to maintain the 1⁷/8in gap. Glue the second lower right-hand stringer D into place, again using a spacer to keep the 1⁷/8in space between D and C.

Starting at the top, glue on each of the seven shorter steps to the top flight and leave the assembly to set. Ensure that the left side of the staircase, where it butts against the retaining wall, is flat – the stair treads only overlap toward the courtyard. Glue the three longer steps onto the bottom flight. These treads overlap on both sides of the stringers. Glue all the risers in place.

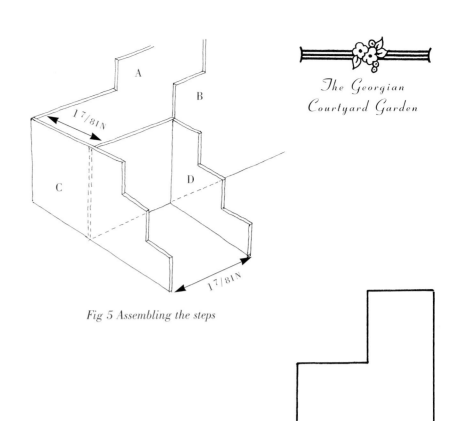

Fig 5 Assembling the steps

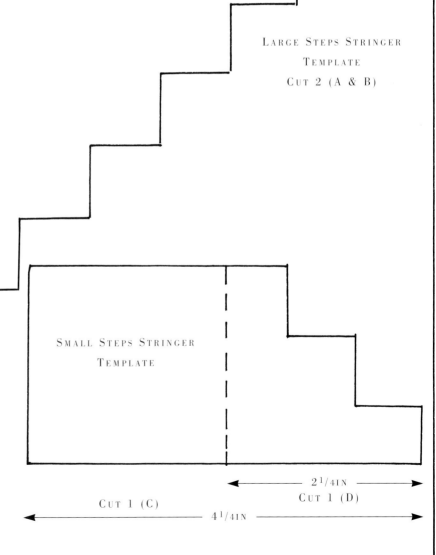

LARGE STEPS STRINGER
TEMPLATE
CUT 2 (A & B)

SMALL STEPS STRINGER
TEMPLATE

2¹/4IN

CUT 1 (C)   CUT 1 (D)

4¹/4IN

THE WATER DISPLAY

The water display comprises an arch of quoins which surround the recess in the terrace wall and a water feature contained behind a brick wall.

Quoins

The recess aperture is finished off with quoins. Using the template already made (see page 155), cut out this shape from 3mm MDF and clean up the edges with fine abrasive paper. Place against the aperture to check the fit – it should just sit on top of the little brick wall (see fig 6 right). Divide the shape into an evenly spaced number of quoins. Mark the positions of the stones and score off the jointing lines with a fine razor saw. These lines should be about half the depth. This feature is not attached until after painting.

Brick wall

The next stage is to build up the small brick wall that is positioned in front of the recess, supporting the water feature. As this is a small, decorative wall we made up some thinner bricks from wood strip, just $3/16$in thick (with the mortar joint making a total thickness of $1/4$in). See page 32 for instructions on how these bricks are made, and prepare sufficient strips to make 60in. Mark out the position of the wall on the base, using fig 6 as a guide. It is two bricks deep and four wide.

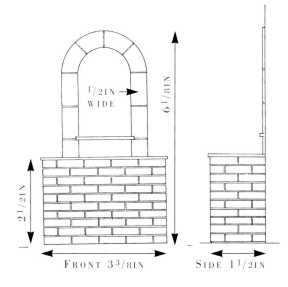

$1/2$IN
WIDE

$6^{1}/8$IN

$2^{1}/2$IN

FRONT $3^{3}/8$IN   SIDE $1^{1}/2$IN

Fig 6 The water display

In order to assemble the brick wall it will be necessary to prepare a former, around which you can assemble the brick courses. Cut a block of waste wood 3in high, $^{3}/4$in deep and $1^{7}/8$in wide. Glue this block – which will now be your former – onto a piece of blockboard and very lightly coat all the surfaces with Vaseline (petroleum jelly) to prevent the bricks sticking.

Lay the first course of bricks and assemble each row on top of the previous, gluing down as you go. These bricks form 'English stretcher' bond, where each brick joint is positioned over the centre of the brick below. Assemble the wall for ten courses, or until it is $2^{1}/2$in high. Remove the former when the wall is complete and set.

Cut four coping stones to top off the wall from 3mm MDF, each $^{1}/2$in x $1^{3}/4$in and attach these so that they overlap the tops of the bricks. Paint the inner surface of the wall and under the recess behind the wall with a dark green acrylic paint.

Cut a strip of waste wood $^{1}/8$in square and glue this all around the inside of the brick wall $^{1}/2$in from the top. This provides support for the base of the water feature. Cut a strip of waste wood $^{1}/8$in square and glue this all around the inside of the brick wall, level with the inside of the recess base. This will support the Perspex (plexiglass).

Glue the Perspex for the water into posi-

tion and insert the two water plants. Lay three small water lily leaves in the centre and glue into position, being careful not to allow any glue to show.

Water feature

Cut a piece of 3mm MDF $^{3}/4$in x $1^{7}/8$in, glue onto the base support and paint dark green. Cut a template for the Perspex (plexiglass) using a piece of card. It should fit into the recess and rest on the support glued to the inside of the brick wall and the recess. Transfer the shape to the Perspex and cut out using a razor saw. Drill two $^{1}/16$in holes through the Perspex $^{1}/4$in in from the front edge to take the plants. Place the Perspex in position when painting is finished.

LARGE FLOWER BED

Cut out the base from MDF and cut two strips of bricks to the length of the base and two short strips to fit the ends. Glue into place, ensuring that the bricks are laid correctly and that any half bricks match at either end.

Take the block of Oasis (floral foam) and, with a small hacksaw, cut it to fit snugly inside the flower border, allowing it to protrude about $^{1}/16$in above the top of the bricks. Shape the top with fine grade abrasive paper to produce a domed surface. Remove from the border, spray over the surface of the Oasis (floral foam) with photo or display mount adhesive and sprinkle tea leaves over to simulate earth. Ensure there are no bald spots and brush off any surplus. Fit the foam, now covered with 'earth', to the base and finish off.

Fit and glue the assembled flower border onto the base support so that it lies flush with the underside of the base. Fit the Oasis (floral foam) into the brick surround and fill with flowers.

Lay the completed border onto the edge of the garden as shown on pages 152-53, and draw a line for the end of the paving stones. This element will be glued in place to the baseboard when paving is finished.

> **TIP**
> *Use protective goggles and gloves when working with Perspex (plexiglass). The protective coating supplied with the Perspex should be left in place as long as possible as it will make marking out easier and protect the surface from unwanted scratches.*

SMALL FLOWER BED

This bed, placed at the bottom of the stair wall, has been constructed so that it can be made up away from the site and dropped in after the paving has been completed.

Glue the two sides to the base and add the two ends. As soon as the assembly is dry paint with two coats of white emulsion mixed with a little brown acrylic to give the appearance of weathering. Take a block of Oasis (floral foam) and, using a small hacksaw, cut and shape it to fit inside the bed as described for the flower border. Cover with 'earth' as before and fit into the base, inserting plants as required.

PAVING

At this point the garden will have both the terrace and the garden wall fixed into place, and the steps, flower bed and the border completed and ready for siting.

The paved area occupies the space between the balcony wall and the flower bed, and from the base of the steps to the right hand edge of the base. To mark out the area to be paved, place the step assembly onto the garden so that it butts against the

garden wall and the front of the terrace in the left-hand corner as the garden faces you. Fit the small flower bed against the steps and add the flower border to the edge of the baseboard. Draw a clear line around all these objects in order to show the area to be paved. Do not include the brick wall assembly that holds the water feature below the recess, as this will sit on top of the paving stones. Once all the component assemblies have been removed you will see the area that is to be paved. (Readers may wish to cut paving around the water feature wall too, in which case the height to the recess may need to be adjusted.) Find the centre of the paving area and mark this with a cross. Now extend the cross to reach the boundaries of the area. For this project we used pre-cast $1\frac{1}{2}$in square paving as it fits the area without cutting or casting special size slabs. See page 27 for casting paving. Lay the paving slabs starting from the inner corner to the outside. When you are happy with the fit, attach the paving with a small spot of PVA glue under each slab.

PAINTING

For best results you should use good quality acrylics or emulsion paints but poster paints are an alternative. Try not to use too much water in the paint mixture as this will tend to run and result in streaky finishes. Mix the paints well until the correct consistency is achieved. Cover the paving area when painting to avoid splashes of colour in the wrong place, or paint as many surfaces as possible before the final assembly.

For the recess, paint the back surface with an off-white or grey acrylic and finish the sides and shelf surfaces with white emulsion.

Colour the quoins with terracotta acrylic and use a small brush or sponge to produce a stippled effect. Avoid painting the joints if you can. Glue into position after all the painting is complete.

The back wall of the terrace is finished

with matt white vinyl emulsion, taking care not to splash paint onto other features. The terrace top is covered with gravel paper but it could be painted to resemble stone. Paint the edges of any bare wood a light grey.

For the bricks, mix up acrylic paint to make a good reddish brown brick colour, using brown ochre with a little black and red. Keep the paint fairly stiff, not too watery, and stipple onto the bricks. Allow the joints between the bricks to show by taking care not to let the paint run into them. The outer sides of terrace walls may be painted or covered in brick.

The garden retaining wall on our model features the excellent fibre-glass moulded brick sheeting which does not need further colouring, it is simply cut to size and glued in place. See page 173 for list of Suppliers. Paint any bare edges of the walls with a matching, brick coloured paint or wrap the sheet around.

The side walls and ends of the steps have been painted with off-white emulsion. This simulates a real surface and stops the project looking too bland. Mix a little brown ochre paint with some white and don't worry if some little streaks of brown show through. A realistic touch can be added by taking a very fine brush, loaded with grey paint, and running a fine line down and across the main surface to simulate a crack.

The treads and risers on the steps have been painted to simulate real stone. The surface of the treads is slightly worn and the surface is a little lighter in colour than the risers. Mix up a stone colour paint and add a small amount of grey, apply this to the risers but just use the stone colour for the treads.

FINAL 'ON SITE' ASSEMBLY

At this stage your garden will have been paved and the areas for the steps and the flower bed, border and water feature brick wall marked out. It is now time to finally position these component assemblies. Start by inserting the steps, taking care that the edges match that of the paving. Add the inner flower bed and the outer flower border. Finally add the water feature brick wall. Unless you are likely to move the garden on a regular basis none of these items need to be glued into place as the edges of the paving will keep each from moving.

Fill any gaps between paving and assemblies with a little plaster filler and cover with loose tea.

ACCESSORIES AND PLANTERS

Paint the bracket for hanging basket matt black to simulate ironwork and pin and glue to the front terrace wall 1in below the top, and 1¹/₂in away from the recess.

The statue used in this project was supplied by Gillie Hinchcliffe (see page 174) but any other suitable statuette or ornament with a Grecian theme could be used.

Finally add the planters, troughs and half cask wine butts around the garden. Using purchased or hand made flowers, fill all the beds, troughs and pots.

CUSTOMISING YOUR GARDEN

You may decide to make a garden of this type to fit your own dolls' house and modify some of the features. If this is the case, the methods used will be very similar to those given here – but you may find it useful to produce a cardboard model first. This will allow you to check all your measurements work in the way they should.

Start by deciding on the exact location of the garden. Carefully measure out the floor area and decide on the maximum height for the back wall. Deduct the thickness of the baseboard from the height to give the net dimensions of the box. If you intend to place the garden in front of the house and still want to open the doors you must include any plants in the height measurement. Finally, once you have deducted the height of the plants you will be in a position to build the terrace.

> **TIP**
> *Remember when painting the garden that solid blocks of colour look dull and uninteresting so add a few streaks of white, grey or brown to some areas to liven up the surface. Be careful not to overdo this effect.*

The Lighted Deck Garden

This is a very contemporary garden project, relying almost entirely on a geometric progression of straight lines and angles, with the inclusion of decking boards and water being an unusual feature. The owner of this garden would probably have little actual gardening to do – daily care will be a quick sweep and a feeding of the tame carp in the water, although the wooden surfaces and water would require regular maintenance. Decked gardens are particularly popular in America in those states where warm, dry weather can be relied on. The lighting brings a finishing touch and a thoroughly modern appearance to this project.

Overlaying all or part of a garden with decking or boards is particularly useful when the plot is uneven or has a marked slope as it gives an even surface on which to lounge or prepare food for the barbecue. The deck areas are often raised above the ground level allowing air to circulate freely through gaps between the boards, so bringing cooler air through from the shaded area beneath. These areas are also relatively easy to keep clean and are usually free of unwanted creepy crawlies that remain in the dark beneath!

This garden, which would be an ideal addition to a modern dolls' house or as a free standing project, combines a number of elements – decking, walls, grass, paving and a very interesting long water feature running under a part of the decking. There is also a barbecue and serving area.

CONSTRUCTING THE GARDEN

Refer to the garden plan for the positioning of all elements. You will also need to refer to the plan on page 165 showing the position of all the walls and formers and to fig 2, which shows the basic layout of the various surfaces of the garden. Give some thought too to the lighting system you want to use, planning it as early as possible.

General materials needed for construction include; PVA glue, plastic weld adhesive, spirit-based adhesive (UHU), artist's display or photo mount adhesive, panel pins, masking tape, tea bags, thick card, wood stain, white spirit and paints. For general gluing use a PVA type glue.

MATERIALS					
				F	$^7/_8$in x 10$^3/_4$in
				G	$^7/_8$in x 24in
MDF – 9mm					
Base		24in x 18in	Inner walls	M	1$^1/_4$in x 12$^1/_4$in
				N	1$^1/_4$in x 6$^3/_4$in
MDF – 6mm				O	1$^1/_4$in x 1$^1/_2$in
Outer walls	A	9$^1/_2$in x 11$^1/_4$in			
		(back right)	Formers	H–L	1$^1/_2$in x 20in total
	B	9$^1/_2$in x 11in			(see instructions)
		(back left)		P–U	$^7/_8$in x 68in total
	C	1$^7/_8$in x 13in			(see instructions)
	D	1$^5/_8$in x 7in			
	E	1$^1/_4$in x 7in	Patio support blocks, six off		6mm x 1$^1/_2$in

MDF – 2mm

Patio	10½in x 10½in
Patio paving	(see instructions)

Bases for decking and grassed area, total
20in x 20in

Jelutong wood

Decking	¹/₁₆in x ½in x 300in
Tops of walls	¹/₁₆in x ³/₈in x 90in
Pathway sides	⅛in x ¼in x 18in
Pergola	⅛in x ¾in x 26in
Formers V–Z	⅛in x ⁷/₁₆in x 50in

Note: add ¹/₁₆in to former T to allow
for the thickness of Perspex

Formers A1 and A2	⅛in x ½in x 24in

Other materials

- Fine sand
- Perspex (plexiglass) for water feature
6in x 24in x 2mm thick
- Grass matting 16in x 12in
- Oasis (floral foam)
- Plants
- Plastic sheet (plasticard) in
black and white
- White styrene plastic tubing about 6in
long x ³/₈in diameter, and a very short
length of ⅛in diameter
- Clear ballpoint pen case x 3
- Three 12v grain of wheat bulbs
- Fine rigid wire
- Twigs and charcoal pieces
- Lighting wires
- Round wire or copper tape (for lighting)
- Transformer 12v DC

Plan of the lighted
deck garden

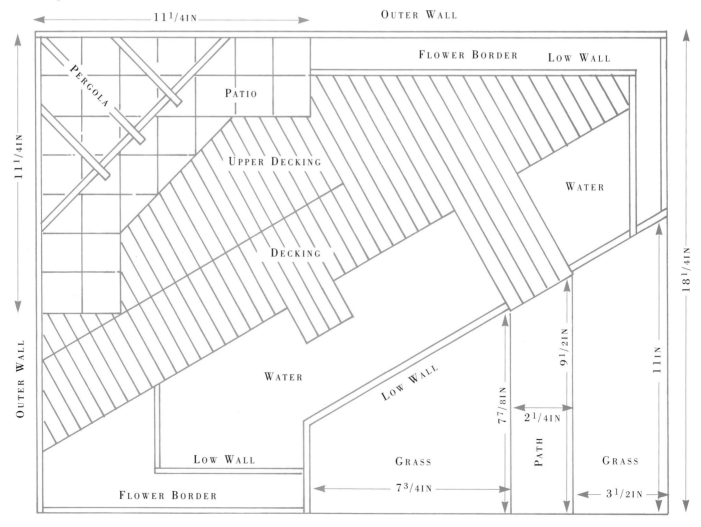

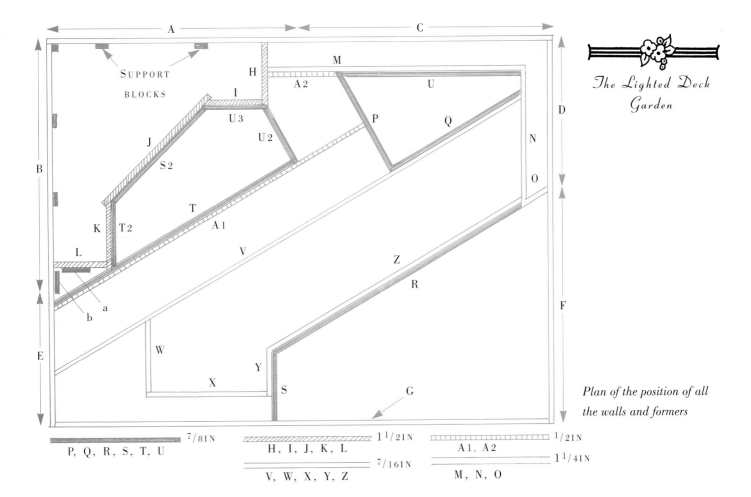

P, Q, R, S, T, U — 7/8IN

H, I, J, K, L — 1 1/2IN

V, W, X, Y, Z — 7/16IN

A1, A2 — 1/2IN

M, N, O — 1 1/4IN

*Plan of the position of all
the walls and formers*

Specialist supplies

(see Suppliers on page 173)

- *Fibre-glass sheet in Flemish red brick, for
  wall covering, 24in x 9in*
- *Fibre-glass sheet in crazy paving pattern,
  for path, 9in x 2 1/2in*
- *Black iron brackets for hanging baskets*

BASE

Prepare the base from 9mm MDF, 24in x
18in ensuring that all sides are at right
angles to each other and that the edges are
at 90 degrees. Cut small slots under the base
from the point at which the two lighting
wires appear through the base to the back or
make any special provisions for wiring.

WALLS
Outer walls

Refer to the layout of the garden plan on
page 164 and the wall and formers plan
above. Cut and prepare walls A through to G
from 6mm MDF, following the measurements on the cutting list. Check that all
surfaces are at right angles and that edges

are square. Using a soft leaded pencil, mark
each one with its identification letter in
order to avoid confusion later.

Drill three evenly spaced 1/32in-diameter
holes, 3/32in up from the bottom along the
edges of walls A, B and C to take panel
pins. Glue and pin walls A and B into position against the base following the plan,
with wall A overlapping the end by 6mm,
allowing wall B to butt against it. Glue walls
A and B together along the vertical edges
and secure with masking tape until set.

Glue and pin the low wall C into position
so that it butts against A and overlaps the
right-hand edge by 6mm, to take wall D.
Glue wall D on top of the base and butt up
against C. Glue wall E to the side of the
baseboard and butt against wall B. Note, all
of the above walls are fixed to the side of
the base, not on top of it.

Glue walls F and G on top of the baseboard, flush with the outer edge. Glue in
five patio support blocks (6mm x 1 1/2in),
6mm side down, onto the base and against
walls A and B.

165

Inner walls

Cut to shape three 1¼in wide walls, in the following lengths: M x 12¼in, N x 6¾in and O x 1½in and glue into position, 6mm side down.

Formers

Whilst care should be taken to cut and position all the formers correctly they are used only as supports for the decking and grassed areas and will not be seen when the garden is finished.

Cut to shape five 1½in formers to the following lengths: H x 2½in, I x 3⅛in, J x 6¼in, K x 3⅛in and L x 2½in. Glue all these into position as shown on the plan, 6mm side down. You will notice that the ends of all the formers butt against each other and so the ends should be cut 'on-site' to make a neat fit.

Cut eight ⅞in formers to the following lengths: P x 5½in, Q x 7½in, R x 14¼in, S x 3½in, S2 x 6in, T x 13¾in, T2 x 3¼in (optional), U x 8¼in, U2 x 3in and U3 x 3¼in (optional). Glue these into position as shown on the plan and fig 1.

Cut five ⅛in x 7/16in jelutong formers V x 25½in, W x 3¾in, x 5½in, Y x 2in and Z x 14¼in and glue as shown in fig 1a. Cut two ⅛in x ½in jelutong formers A1 x 17in and A2 x 3in, glue into position on the ⅛in edge. Glue two short pieces (a) and (b) of ⅞in x 6mm MDF as supports for formers L and T as shown on the plan.

THE WATER BED

Cover the centre of the bed with a thin layer of PVA adhesive and whilst wet sprinkle a little fine sand along the centre line and allow to dry. Mix up brown, black and green acrylic paints so that you can still see all of the colours and apply this all along the bed and up the sides. Add a little more black

and brown towards the centre to give the appearance of depth and add a few very small stones to make it more realistic.

Make a template for the surface of the water from stiff card and transfer the shape to the Perspex (plexiglass). Cut out the shape using a saw, or score with a sharp knife and snap out the shape.

Drill any small holes in the Perspex (plexiglass) for plants appearing above and below the surface and place this to one side until you have finished colouring and planting out the bed. Add fine grasses to the base. For an authentic touch you could make a few fish from self-coloured polymer clay and glue these to the base. Finally add water lilies along the length of the surface of water.

DECKING
Bases

The next step is to cut and prepare the bases for the decked and grassed areas from 2mm MDF. See fig 2 for the areas marked as 1, 2a, 2b and 2c. The decking bases are fixed into place after covering with deck boards.

Decking levels

Prepare the strips of 1/16in decking and carefully sand off any rough edges. Colour the boards with a dark oak wood stain diluted 50/50 with white spirit and allow them to dry before proceeding, keeping a

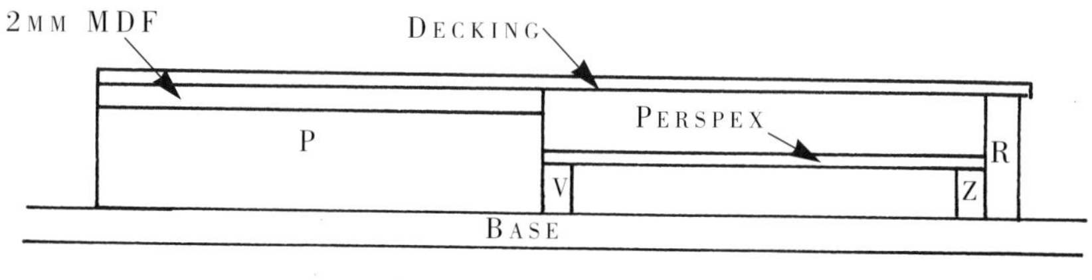

Fig 1 Positioning the formers – side view

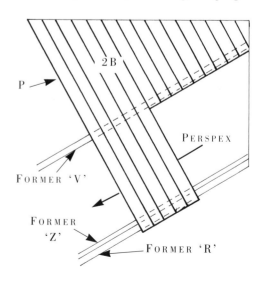

Fig 1a Positioning the formers – overhead view

little of the stain and a soft brush to touch up any cut edges as you work. You may change the colour of the stain to reflect the sort of boards you prefer.

Start with deck area 2B and lay the boards from left to right, each one flush to the back and spaced ¹/₁₆in apart. The first five strips should finish on wall R. Mark the underside of these five strips where they meet the wall. Glue on a small ³/₁₆in square offcut to act as a strengthener and to locate the boards against the wall. Continue laying boards, overlapping the formers by ¹/₈in. Cover area 2A in exactly the same manner, again overlapping the edges by ¹/₈in.

Level 1 (see fig 3 overleaf) is covered from the right-hand edge and the boards should be carefully cut to fit against levels 2A and 2B. Proceed in this way for ten

Fig 2 The layout of the various surfaces of the garden

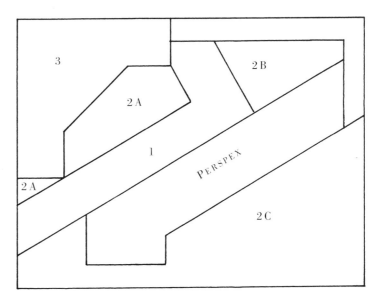

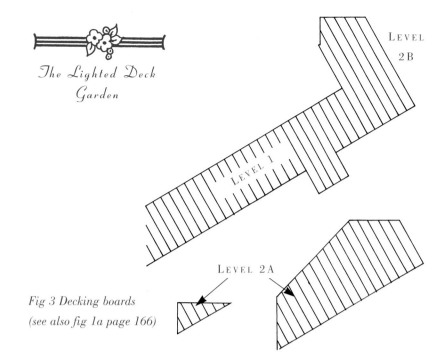

LEVEL 1

LEVEL 2B

LEVEL 2A

*Fig 3 Decking boards
(see also fig 1a page 166)*

strips and then increase the length of the next four by 1½in to form a small pier, so breaking up the straight line and allowing the pier to sit on top of the Perspex 'water'. Continue in this manner until you reach the left-hand wall.

PATIO LEVEL

This is level 3 on fig 2 and is paved not decked. Cut the sheet of 2mm MDF to obtain a good fit and mark off into 1½in squares as for normal paving. Using a steel ruler and a sharp craft knife make a 20 degree cut along each line, in both directions and remove the waste (see fig 4). Drag a sharp edge across one or two paving stones to indicate cracks and make a few small cuts in the edges of some others to indicate wear. Clean up with fine abrasive paper. Spray the whole of the area with grey primer and finish off with grey acrylic paint mixed with a little brown and white. Accentuate the joins with a slightly darker shade of paint.

BACK WALLS

Finish off both back walls by covering with moulded brick fibre-glass sheet. Measure both pieces carefully and allow 3/4in extra around the tops and sides, enough to wrap around giving a clean edge. Use either a white PVA glue, Copydex or photo mount adhesive and smooth out any air bubbles as soon as possible. Using a spirit-based adhesive such as UHU, glue the black iron brackets for hanging baskets on the outer edges of both walls 1in from the top. Prepare the hanging baskets, filling with flowers on completion of the garden.

GRASSED AREA AND PATH

Draw the area for the path onto the baseboard and measure off the amount of paving required, 2½in wide. Cut this from the crazy paving fibre-glass sheeting, and glue this down following your marks.

To finish off the path, prepare two strips of 1/8in x 1/4in jelutong, paint them a red brick colour and glue them down each side of the path. Cut two pieces of grass matting to fit into the area, as shown and glue down to the base making sure that the edges are neatly finished off.

FLOWER BEDS AND BORDERS

Paint the insides of the long 'L' shape borders in the bottom right-hand and bottom left-hand corners with a dark green/brown acrylic paint mixture and allow to dry.

Cut pieces of Oasis (floral foam) to fit both of these areas – you can do this in more than on piece and round off the corners with a sharp craft knife or abrasive paper. Spray the surface with display mount adhesive and sprinkle the contents of a tea bag over. Plant these beds up with a

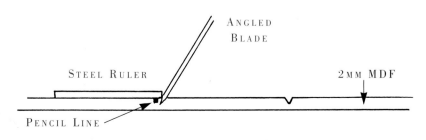

ANGLED BLADE

STEEL RULER

2 MM MDF

Fig 4 Creating a paved effect on level 3

PENCIL LINE

selection of small border plants and keep them separate until you have finished all the other work on the beds.

BRICK CAPPING ON BORDERS

Prepare a number of jelutong strips $^{1}/_{16}$in thick x $^{3}/_{8}$in to a total length of 85in and using a try square mark off brick joints every $^{3}/_{4}$in. Using a razor saw and a mitre box, make $^{1}/_{32}$in deep cuts on each mark. Using acrylics, paint the whole of the surface with a light 'mortar' colour and when this is dry paint the surface a red brick colour to match the back walls, allowing the joints to keep their colour. Cut strips to fit onto the tops of the walls shown in fig 5 and glue into position. Note, there is no capping on wall R where the decking ends.

PERGOLA SUN ROOF

Cut the fascia boards from $^{1}/_{8}$in thick x $^{3}/_{4}$in x $11^{1}/_{8}$in jelutong and cut each end across

the width at 45 degrees to enable it to fit against the back walls. Find the centre of this strip and cut a slot $^{1}/_{8}$in wide x $^{3}/_{8}$in deep. Measure in $2^{5}/_{8}$in in from each edge and cut two more slots to the same dimensions as the first (see fig 6 overleaf).

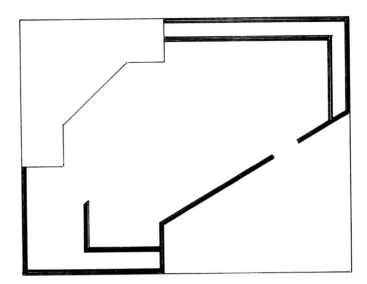

Fig 5 The position of the brick capping on the border walls

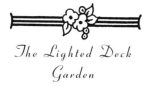

Prepare a second strip from 1/8in x 3/4in jelutong and cut three pieces, (a) and (b) both 3 3/4in long and (c) 6 1/4in long. Pieces (a) and (b) are cut at 45 degrees at one end. Piece (c) has two 45 degree cuts at one end to form a 'V'. All the lengths quoted include the angled cuts.

Mark the squared ends of pieces (a), (b) and (c) so as to leave a nose 7/8in long x 3/8in wide. Carefully remove the waste. Cut each of the noses off at 45 degrees, leaving 1/8in at the top (see fig 6a).

Lay the fascia piece with the three slots uppermost and glue each of the outer pieces into position, ensuring that the 45 degree cuts at the ends face in the correct direction, allowing the assembly to butt against the walls (see fig 6b).

Paint all the surfaces with a white silk emulsion and when dry glue the assembly into position flush with the top edge of the walls, supporting it until the adhesive has completely set.

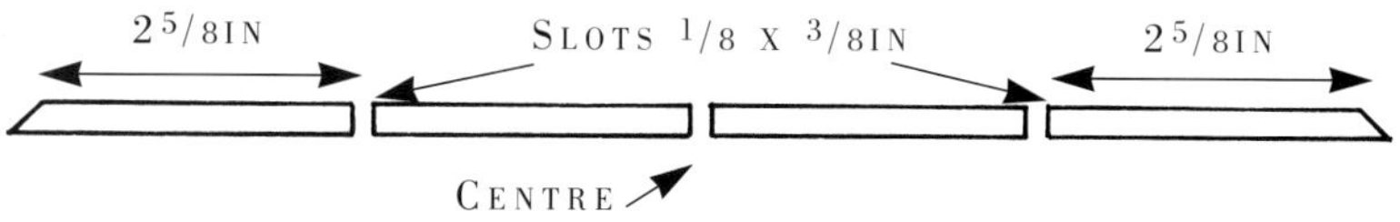

Fig 6 Preparing the front fascia board for the pergola sun roof

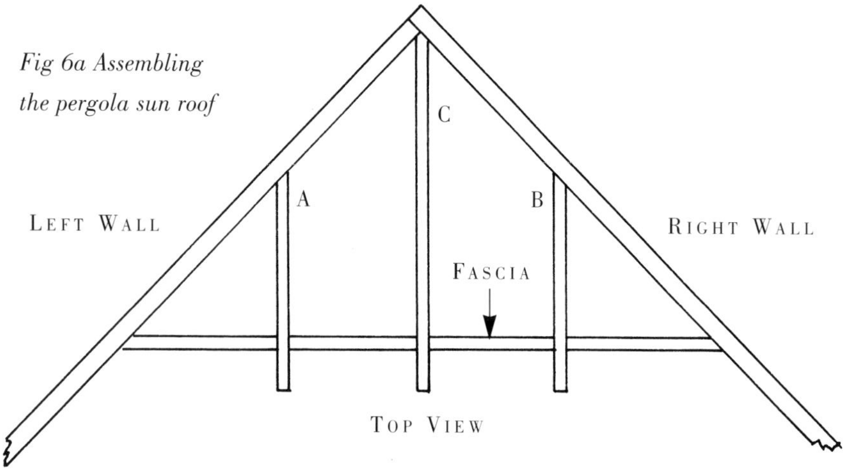

Fig 6a Assembling the pergola sun roof

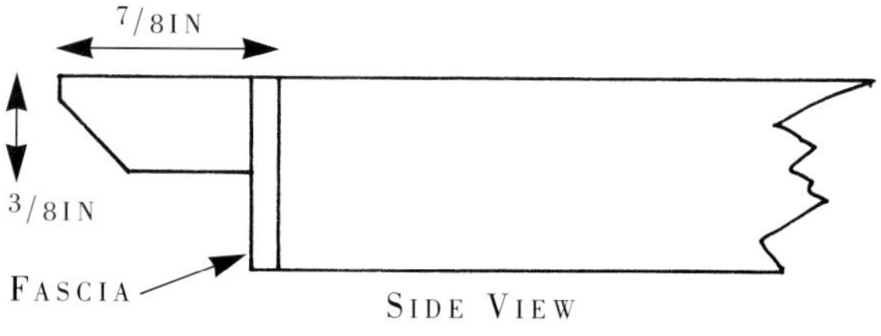

Fig 6b Assembling the pergola roof against the walls

BARBECUE

This feature has been made up from scraps of 6mm MDF (kept from making up the bases). Cut the following pieces (see figs 7 and 7a):

A, cut 2 off,	2 3/8in x 1 1/2in;
B, cut 1 off,	1 1/2in x 2 3/4in;
C, cut 1 off,	1 1/2in x 1 1/2in;
D and E, cut 2 off,	1 1/2in x 1in.

Cut piece F out of 1/6in thick jelutong or plastic card 1 9/16in x 1 9/16in (this will be glued on top of C later). Cut piece G out of black plasticard, 1 9/16in x 1 3/8in. Cut eight pieces of fine rigid wire for the grill, each 1 3/4in long.

Drill the centre of one edge of part C with eight holes, placed approximately 3/16in apart and then drill eight matching holes in part B, each 1/16in deep, to take the fine wire grill. Glue together both parts A with D and then place C on top with the fine holes on the outer right-hand edge. Stand this on one edge and glue each of the eight fine wires into position. Place the assembly the correct way up on a work surface and glue part E to the right-hand side (you will see that it does not show at the front but lies flush with the back – see figs 7 and 7a). Glue part B onto E and at the same time insert all the fine wires into their respective holes, clamp and allow the adhesives to set.

Paint the whole assembly with matt white/grey acrylic, adding some black

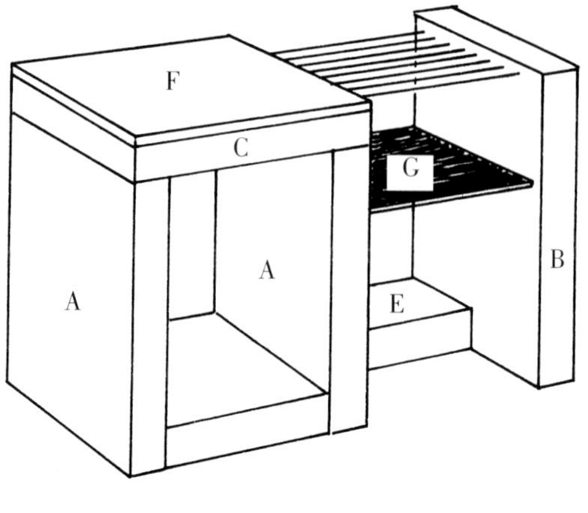

Fig 7 Assembling the barbecue

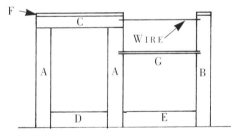

Fig 7a The barbecue – plan of the parts

streaks to make it all look used. When the paint is dry glue G into position ³/₄in below the wire grill and glue F on top of C. Finally, add a few cut twigs and some fine charcoal under the grill.

Smoke hood

Out of ¹/₁₆in thick black plasticard, cut two sides 2in high x 1in wide tapering to ⁵/₈in wide. Cut a front piece 2in high x 1¹/₂in wide and then cut a top 1¹/₁₆in x 1¹/₂in.

Lay the front face down and glue the two sides to the outer edges using plastic weld adhesive. Support the sides at right angles and glue on the top (see fig 8). Use a fine abrasive paper to obtain a smooth finish on the joints. Turn the assembly over when the adhesive has set and glue it with a spirit-based adhesive such as UHU to the back wall 1¹/₂in over the barbecue.

*Fig 8 The barbecue
smoke hood*

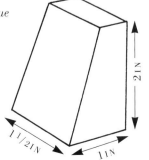

> **TIP**
>
> *Plastic weld adhesive works by dissolving the surfaces, so avoid spreading adhesive in areas that show or you may damage them.*

TIP

*When installing working
lights for your garden,
ensure that you can dis-
mantle lamps to replace
bulbs when you need to.
Simple connections
to the bulb wiring and
the main circuit beneath
the decking should
be hidden away until
required. Replaceable
screw bulb fittings
require only the removal
of the top of the lights.*

TIP

*You may find it easier to
thread the bulb wires
down through body and
then the hole in the side
of the wall lamp before
gluing on the short tube,
lens and the base.*

LIGHTING

This garden has three modern lights – two pillar lights on either side of the garden and one wall light. Use round wire or copper tape to carry power from the transformer to the lights. The following method is merely one way that wiring can be achieved and although the lights may be placed anywhere that you wish in the garden, the instructions for installation remain basically the same.

Drill two $1/16$in-diameter holes through the decking for the lighting points where you wish your lights to be (see photograph on page 162 for the positions we used) and one for the wall light through the back wall. Drill $1/16$in-diameter holes horizontally through the decking support formers and the back wall to allow connection to a suitable trans-former. Alternatively, a copper tape wiring system can be added under the base of the garden, from the back to the location of each of the lights. The wires from the bulbs can then be continued through to the base and into the slots made earlier, or the copper tape can passed up through two specially made holes.

Use white plasticard and styrene tubing throughout and glue all parts together with plastic weld adhesive, being careful not to allow this to mark the surfaces of the light pillars.

Start by cutting two lengths of $3/8$in diam-eter styrene tubing, each 2in long and one

for the wall light, $1/2$in long (see fig 9). Cut two base circles $5/8$in diameter from $1/16$in plasticard, and drill a $1/32$in-diameter hole through the centre. Cut a third circle for the wall light, $3/8$in in diameter. Use a sharp point to indent a series of 'nail heads' around the circumference on what will be the underside, The 'bumps' will show on the correct side.

Cut three caps from $1/16$in thick plasticard $7/16$in square and trim to six-sided polygons. To make the lenses, use a razor saw to cut three pieces of clear plastic tubing each $1 1/2$in in length (the shaped end of a ballpoint pen casing is ideal, just make sure it will fit inside the pillar) and insert so that $1/2$in shows above the top of the pillar. Cut a third piece $1/2$in long for the wall light, this time with $1/4$in of lens showing.

Finish off each pillar light by gluing the clear lens onto the white tubing and adding the base. Allow the adhesive to set and then thread the grain of wheat bulb through, leaving the bulb inside the lens. Add the cap to complete.

The wall light is connected to the base by a $1/2$in length of $1/8$in diameter styrene tubing. Drill a $1/16$in-diameter hole into the side of the lamp and attach the tube using plastic weld adhesive. Glue the base onto the end of the tube, then the lens and the cap in the same way as for the pillar lights. Cut a circle of $1/32$in thick card to match the diameter of the $3/8$in tube and glue this onto the base of the wall light.

Glue the complete assemblies into place and thread the wires from the bulbs through the base and connect to the wiring placed earlier. Test the circuit and connect to a suitable 12v DC transformer.

Complete your lighted deck garden by placing the flower beds and borders into their correct positions, then choose and site all the furniture and garden accessories you wish to have. Plant up the hanging baskets and tubs and find a climbing plant to trail over the pergola, such as a wisteria, clematis, rose or ivy.

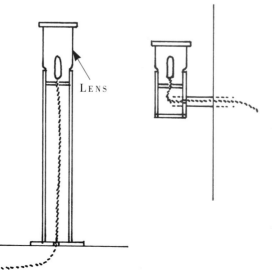

LENS

Suppliers

SPECIALIST SUPPLIES USED WITHIN
THE GARDEN PROJECTS

The Formal Georgian Garden

Reuben Barrows	Wall coverings fibre-glass sheet.
Flowers 'n Things	Fountain, lion head wall fountain, large planted urn.
Sue Cook	Classical busts, seat, pineapple ornament,decorative terracotta pots.
Sandie Sadri	Climbing rose and clematis.
The Ironworks	Railings.
Gillie Hinchcliffe	Dwarf orange and lemon trees in containers, terracotta pots.
The Mulberry Bush	Dolls.
The Singing Tree	Orange and lemon trees.

The Rustic Garden

Peter Clark	Axe in block.
Maureen Ballantyne	Blackbird, blackbird nesting in pot.
Gillie Hinchcliffe	Plants.
Sandie Sadri	Plants.
Le Petit Chou	Doves, hedging.
Terry Curran	Roof tiles.
The Mulberry Bush	Dolls.
The Singing Tree	Hollyhocks.

The Edwardian Summer House

Reuben Barrows	Wall and stone cladding fibre-glass sheet.
Sandi Sadri	Planted pots and tubs, clematis.
Gillie Hinchcliffe	Potted plants, planted trellis, metal arbour, trough.
Flowers 'n Things	Lion head fountain.
Tom Pouce Miniatures	Green metal folding chair.
John Watkins	Table.
The Mulberry Bush	Doll, dog, tea set.

The Terrace House Backyard

Reuben Barrows	Wall covering fibre-glass sheet.
Maureen Ballantyne	Magpie.
Maureen McSheehy	Runner beans.
Quality Dolls' House Miniatures	Watering can, garden fork, bucket.
Lilydale Designs	Rabbit, coils of wire, roofing felt.
Terry Curran	Scrap tiles.
The Mulberry Bush	Dustbin, doll, mangle, bath, broom, oil stove, muddy boots.

The Vegetable Garden

Terri Sutton	Vegetable plots.
Quality Dolls' House Miniatures	Garden tools and roller.
Maureen McSheehy	Runner beans.
Sussex Crafts	Round wooden tub.
Carol Mann	Pots.
Lilydale Designs	Roll of wire mesh, roll of felt, seed potatoes.
Terry Curran	Tiles.
David Lee	Barrel.
Maureen Ballantyne	Blackbird.
Le Petit Chou	Hedging.
The Mulberry Bush	Broom, pot of chrysanthemums, muddy boots, doll, cat.

Victorian Roof Garden
With Conservatory

Reuben Barrows	Gravel path fibre-glass sheet.
Sandie Sadri	Climbing rose, potted plants.
Sue Cook	Stone bench, statue.
Des Res	Wisteria, rose and trellis.
John Watkins	White metal chairs and table, green table.
Robert Longstaff Workshops	Lutyens-style bench.
Gillie Hinchcliffe	Grapes, palms, vines, potted plants.
Ann Barnard	Wicker sofa and cushions.
Le Petit Chou	Conservatory, chimney pots, doves.
Cairns Tiles	Floor tiles.
The Mulberry Bush	Tea set, chrysanthemums in pot, dog.

The Georgian Courtyard Garden

Reuben Barrows	Wall covering fibre-glass sheet.
Gillie Hinchcliffe	Plants.
John Watkins	White metal chair.

The Lighted Deck Garden

Reuben Barrows	Wall coverings and path fibre-glass sheet.
Sandie Sadri	Climbing rose, clematis.
Sue Cook	Square decorative planter.
Gillie Hinchcliffe	Plants.
Quality Dolls' House Miniatures	Garden tools.
Peter Clark	Blue tit on small planter.
Carol Mann	Clay pots.
Ann Barnard	Seed packets in trays, pansies in tray.
Jeremy Thomas	Wine bottle and glasses.
The Mulberry Bush	Chicken on tray, barbecue tools, dog, broom, frying pan, tadpole in jar, beer glasses, tray of sandwiches, cutlery.

SUPPLIER'S ADDRESSES

MAUREEN BALLANTYNE
Ashville, Bagby, Thirsk, North Yorks YO7 2PH

REUBEN BARROWS
36 Wolsey Gardens, Hainault, Ilford, Essex 1G6 25N

CAIRN TILES
6 College Green, Bideford, North Devon EX39 3JY

PETER CLARK
2 The Ridgeway, Ware, Herts 5G12 ORT

SUE COOK
Unit 5, Arundel Mews, Arundel Place, Brighton,
East Sussex BN2 1GD

TERRY CURRAN
27 Chapel Street, Mosborough, Sheffield,
South Yorks S19 5BT

DES RES (Chris and Jennie Crowley)
55 Loscoe Road, Carrington, Nottingham NG5 2AW

FLOWERS 'N THINGS (Diane Billington)
24 Goldsborough Close, Eastleaze, Swindon,
Wiltshire, SN5 7EP

GILLIE HINCHCLIFFE
La Noe, 61150 Ranes, France

THE IRONWORKS
240 Doxey, Stafford, Staffs 5T16 lEE

DAVID LEE
40 Bushwood Road, Kew, Richmond, Surrey TW9 3BQ

LILYDALE DESIGNS
10 Mill Street, Puddletown, Dorchester DT2 85H

ROBERT LONGSTAFF WORKSHOPS
Appleton Road, Longworth, Oxon OX13 SEF

CAROL MANN
1 Home Farm, Westthorpe, Southwell, Notts NG25 ONG

MAUREEN McSHEEHY MINIATURES LTD
508 Chemin d'Ostange, 71700 Tournus, France

THE MULBERRY BUSH
9 George Street, Brighton, East Sussex BN2 1RH

LE PETIT CHOU
La Poelerie, 61320 Joue-du-Bois, France

TOM POUCE MINIATURES
3 The Labyrinth, Mark Lane, Eastbourne,
East Sussex BN21 4RJ

QUALITY DOLLS' HOUSE MINIATURES
55 Celandine Avenue, Priory Park, Locks Heath,
Southampton S03 6WZ

MARGARET REID
2 Stone House, Howey, Llandrindod Wells, Powys LD1 5PL

SANDIE SADRI
Broom Cottage, 93 Eccles Old Road, Salford M6 8BH

THE SINGING TREE
69 New Kings Road, London SW6 4SQ

SUSSEX CRAFTS
Hassocks House, Comptons Brow Lane, Horsham,
West Sussex RH13 6BX

TERRI SUTTON
41c Station Road, Thorney, Peterborough PE6 0QE

JOHN WATKINS
12 Biddel Springs, Highworth, Swindon, Wilts 5N6 7BH

BIBLIOGRAPHY

BROOKES, John *John Brookes' Garden Design Book*
(Dorling Kindersley, 1991)

CONSTABLE, John *Landscapes In Miniature*
(Lutterworth Press, 1984)

CHASTY, John *An Introduction To Miniature Gardening*
(The Miniature Garden Company, 1993)

FIELD, Robert *Patterns from Tiles and Brickwork*
(Tarquin Publications 1996)

HANKE, Ruth *Miniature House Plants* (Dees Delights, 1988)

MOORE, Dot and MOORE, Candy
Basic Landscaping In Miniature (Dees Delights, 1991)

MEYER, Barbara *Meyer's Miniature Florists Shoppe*
(Dees Delights, 1983)

DODGE, Venus and DODGE, Martin
Making Miniatures in $1/12th$ Scale (David & Charles, 1989)

HENRICKS, Donna OFFO, Judy and SHAPLER, Marge
Period Floral Designs In Miniature (Dees Delights, 1984)

For a wide-ranging stock of books on dolls' houses,
miniatures, architecture and crafts, contact:
THE MULBERRY BUSH
9 George Street, Brighton BN2 1RH Tel: 01273 600471

For guidance on garden planning many large DIY outlets and
garden centres provide free leaflets and information.

MAGAZINES, DIRECTORIES AND FAIRS

In recent years the hobby has grown so rapidly that there are now more magazines and directories published in the UK than in any other country in the world. The number of fairs has grown proportionally and it impossible for us to list every person or company involved here. In order to find specialist miniaturists or fairs, new collectors would do well to purchase one or two magazines, from different publishers, until they find one to suit their interests, or refer to one of the many directories. The principal magazines, directories and fair organisers are listed below.

MAGAZINES PUBLISHED IN ENGLISH

UK
DOLLS' HOUSE & MINIATURE SCENE
EMF Publishing, EMF House, 7 Elm Park, Ferring,
West Sussex BN12 5RN

DOLLS' HOUSE WORLD
Ashdown Publishing, Avalon Court, Star Road,
Partridge Green, West Sussex RH13 8RY

INTERNATIONAL DOLLS' HOUSE NEWS
Nexus Media Ltd, Nexus House, Azalea Drive,
Swanley, Kent BR8 8HY

DOLLS' HOUSE PROJECTS
EMF Publishing, EMF House, 7 Elm Park, Ferring,
West Sussex BN12 5RN

THE DOLLS' HOUSE MAGAZINE
GMC Publications, Castle Place, High Street, Lewes,
East Sussex BN7 1TX

USA
MINIATURE COLLECTOR
Scott Publications, 30595 Eight Mile Road, Livonia,
MI 48152-1798 USA

DOLLHOUSE MINIATURES
Kalmbach Publishing Co, PO Box 1612,
Waukesha WI 53187 USA

DIRECTORIES

Those makers and craftspeople who have contributed so generously to our garden scenes are listed separately but for a full list of makers of fine miniatures in the UK there are a number of hobby directories published, and we suggest you contact one or more of the following:

Dolls' House Handbook
EMF Publishing, 7 Elm Park, Ferring,
West Sussex BN12 5RN Tel: 01903 506626

The Dolls' House Guide
Ashdown Publishing Ltd, Avalon Court, Star Road,
Partridge Green, West Sussex RH13 SRY Tel: 01403 711511

Dolls' House Hobby Directory
Nexus Media Ltd, Nexus House, Azalea Drive, Swanley, Kent
BR8 SHY Tel: 01322 660070

UK FAIR ORGANISERS

MINIATURA
41 Eastbourne Avenue, Hodge Hill, Birmingham B34 6AR

LONDON DOLLS' HOUSE FESTIVAL
25 Priory Road, Kew Green, London TW9 3DQ

THE BIG DOLLS' HOUSE AND MINIATURES SHOWS
Ashdown Publishing, Avlon Court, Star Road, Partridge Green,
Sussex RH13 8RY

ALEXANDRA PALACE DOLLS' HOUSE FAIR
EMF Publishing, EMF House, 7 Elm Park, Ferring,
West Sussex BN12 5RN

SOUTHERN DOLLS' HOUSE AND MINIATURE FAIRS
Marion Fancey, 7 Ferringham Lane, West Sussex BN12 5ND

ACKNOWLEDGEMENTS

The authors would like to thank the following people: Maureen Ballantyne, Ann Barnard, Reuben Barrows, Diane Billington, Peter Clark, Sue Cook, Terry Curran, David Lee, Robert Longstaff, Carol Mann, Maureen McSheehy, Tom Pouce, Margaret Reid, Sandie Sadri, Terri Sutton, Jeremy Thomas, John Watkins, Cairn Tiles, Des Res, Gillie Hinchcliffe, The Ironworks, Lilydale Designs, The Mulberry Bush, Le Petit Chou, Quality Dolls' House Miniatures and Sussex Crafts. And to any others we may have forgotten to name who have contributed to this book – many thanks.

Lionel Barnard would like to thank Michael whose idea this book was, Doreen Montgomery, our agent for her understanding and Linda Clements our editor for all her skill and hard work. My thanks also to Sue Hook of 'Through the Green Door', Garden Design, to Venus Dodge for listening and not least to my wife Ann for her patience when I should have been gardening for real.

Index

Entries in *italic* indicate photographs, entries in **bold** indicate diagrams